DATE DUE

FE 30			

The Environment in World Politics

For Wendy

The Environment in World Politics
Exploring the Limits

Ian Bellany
Professor of Politics, University of Lancaster, UK

Edward Elgar
Cheltenham, UK • Brookfield, US

© Ian Bellany 1997

Published by
Edward Elgar Publishing Limited
8 Lansdown Place
Cheltenham
Glos GL50 2HU
UK

Edward Elgar Publishing Company
Old Post Road
Brookfield
Vermont 05036
US

A catalogue record for this book is available from the British Library

Library of Congress Cataloguing in Publication Data

Bellany, Ian.
    The environment in world politics : exploring the limits / Ian
Bellany.
    Includes bibliographical references and index.
    1. Human ecology—Methodology. 2. Human ecology—Political
aspects. 3. System theory. 4. Environmental degradation.
5. Sustainable development. I. Title.
GF21.B45 1997   96-38307
    304.2—DC20   CIP

ISBN 1 85898 348 7
Printed and bound in Great Britain by Hartnolls Limited, Bodmin, Cornwall

Contents

Figures and Tables

Preface

All respectable projects, according to the philosopher Collingwood, are about answering questions. Since most authors are writing for their contemporaries, the questions often need not be formally stated, they are already 'in the air'. Some of the questions given answers in this work are indeed of that sort. But the author sees no need to be inexplicit about the question that determined the shape of this book.

The question was deceptively simple. What is 'sustainable development'? Is it anything more than a slogan, that is to say a ringing or even politically effective phrase but not one necessarily pregnant with meaning? Or worse, is it less than a slogan? Is it a blatant oxymoron, suggesting the falsehood that development – meaning economic growth throughout the globe – can easily be reconciled with the apparently finite limits to the global extent of agricultural land and stocks of unmined minerals, to say nothing of the finite capacity of the atmosphere and seas to accommodate the polluting side-effects of many of the activities associated with economic growth?

If it were supposed to be more than the slogan the author confesses that he originally took it for, the key to understanding what that something more might be lies in the word 'sustainable'. Sustainable implies a capacity for persisting. Anything that persists is stable.

Consider a yacht rounding a headland, with its skipper wishing to maintain a given distance from the shore in order to avoid hazardous shoals. Its course will not automatically be a stable one; wind and running seas will mean that vigilant correction from the helm will be needed. Departures from the norm (the sought after distance from the shore) will be detected by the helmsman who will make the appropriate corrections to the yacht's course. But there is more than one course round the headland. The shortest may have a strong claim to be chosen as the norm, if it were entirely up to the helmsman who can be assumed to be skilled and experienced and possessed of sturdy sea legs. But that could easily involve the yacht, its crew and its passengers in negotiating very choppy waters leading to considerable physical discomfort and perhaps sea-sickness. A longer course slightly further to the seaward might find calmer waters. This course should not only be stable as the helmsman endeavored to have the yacht's course follow the new norm, but possibly more desirable too.

So the almost casual suggestion of Murray Gell-Mann,[1] a physics Nobel Laureate, that sustainable development means development (economic growth) that is both stable (has a capacity for persisting) and desirable is seized upon. For economic growth to persist there must be the equivalent of a helmsman correcting departures from the norm. To be desirable, norms have to be set which may be different from the norms intrinsic in the economic situation (our helmsman's preferences), and this is the business of politics.

As soon as there is landlubber-talk of helmsmen, readers generally know exactly what is coming next. The science of how a network of inter-related things maintains its inter-relationships is a branch of systems analysis called cybernetics.

It is a rather unusual science. Scientists, as such, are not normally conscious of knowing anything about it at all. As Bertrand Russell says, they spend their working lives not denying the inter-relatedness of things, exactly, but making the assumption that they can study individual parts as if they did not belong to any sort of greater whole.

---

1 Murray Gell-Mann, *The Quark and the Jaguar*, (London, Little, Brown and Co., 1994), p. 347.

The author, trained as a physicist, knew virtually nothing of systems analysis or cybernetics before joining his present department at Lancaster University. There he encountered Philip Reynolds, trained as a historian, applying concepts from systems analysis to the study of International Relations.

So, in this volume, understanding sustainable development means taking a systems approach to economic activity and its polluting side-effects on a global scale. The equivalent of our grizzled sea dog of a helmsman is the market mechanism, both setting norms and correcting departures from them. Some of these norms may not be desirable, e.g. the norms set by the market for the discharge of pollutants into common spaces. Setting norms at a more desirable level and maintaining them is a job for international politics.

Abstract theorising by itself is apt to be misunderstood or not understood at all. So while the book is about a systems approach to what has come to be called international environmental questions, it also contains plenty of illustrations from the practical world of environmental norm setting.

Since the author finds Stephen Hawking's famous allegation that every equation in a book of this sort reduces potential readership by a half all too plausible, there are next to no equations employed. On the other hand, the author refuses to believe Garrett Hardin's claim that numerate or graph-rich books are automatically given unfavourable reviews.[2] Figures (in both senses) and tables are employed, but within reason.

As will probably be obvious, this book in an earlier form was the basis for a series of lectures – in this case, to third year students in the Lancaster Department of Politics and International Relations. It is to these undergraduates that the author's thanks for their forbearance and assistance must go first. They taught him what environmental questions people of their generation are most interested in the answers to – what for them are the questions in the air.

Secondly, wherever the author owes a particularly large debt to other writers on the topic, which is not a rare occurrence, he has endeavoured to make this clear in the text.

Finally, more personal thanks are due to a large number of Lancaster

---

2 Garrett Hardin, *Living Within Limits: Ecology, Economics and Population Taboos*, (New York, Oxford University Press, 1993), p. 64.

colleagues and others. It is not possible to mention them all by name, but Alastair Bellany, Steven Breuer, George Clark, Mick Dillon, Michael Faraday and David Travers all in one way or another saved the author hours of literature searches or filled in several gaping holes in the author's knowledge and understanding by giving of their time or expertise. The holes that remain are the author's own responsibility and he can only apolgise in advance to readers for any bumpiness they produce in what is intended to be, in one sense at any rate, a smooth passage.

1 Introduction

This book is about the application of a particular technique to a particular problem. The problem is the interaction of humans with their natural environment and the international regulation of that interaction. The technique is that of the 'systems approach'.

Sometimes new problems bend to the application of new techniques. Sometimes even old problems yield, eventually, to the application of an old technique. In this case a new, or relatively new problem (its appearance on the international agenda dating, it is more or less generally agreed from 1972 and the Stockholm conference on the environment of that year) is put in the ring with an old technique.

The reason for calling the technique 'old' derives from the fact that the application of the systems approach to the political sciences probably peaked not long after the publication of David Easton's *A Framework for Political Analysis* in 1965. In Britain, Geoffrey Vickers's *Freedom in a Rocking Boat* came out in 1970, and showed the power of informal systems approaches to questions of domestic government and administration. Philip Reynolds's *Introduction to International Relations*, which paid special attention to the possibilities of a systems approach to the understanding of international politics, appeared in 1971. However, the decline of social science interest in the technique since that period has been a gentle one with a number of later high points of achievement. Peter Checkland's *Systems Thinking, Systems Practice*, an influential contribution to management science, dates from 1981.[1] Checkland and Vickers form the chief inspirations for the present study.

Gell-Mann[2] describes this technique – the systems approach – as a 'crude look at the whole' and whilst professional systems analysts might reasonably object to the adjective 'crude' (although Gell-Mann does not intend it as a criticism), it is not an inaccurate description of how the technique is employed in the present volume.

Checkland's description of the technique is designedly more informative. It is 'an approach to a problem which takes a broad view, which tries to take all aspects into account, which concentrates on interactions between the different parts of the problem.'[3]

The sense in which the present work 'tries to take all aspects into account' of international environmental politics is not a literal one. Rather, it was felt to be sufficient to take a view broad enough to include not only the more obvious items on the environmental agenda, pressures on sources of food and raw materials and on the absorptive capacity of the oceans and the atmosphere to accept waste products from economic activities, but also without strain to make room for consideration of the more influential ideas and concepts thrown up by students of the subject since 1972. Thus care is taken that, to give three instances of the 'questions in the air' referred to in the Preface, discussion of 'sustainable development', or the contentious part played by natural science in helping determine political responses to environmental threats, or even the 'precautionary principle' should emerge naturally from the approach taken.

Boulding's Levels

Kenneth Boulding very usefully classifies areas for study – as systems –

---

1 David Easton, *A Framework for Political Analysis*, (Englewood Cliffs, Prentice-Hall, 1965). Peter Checkland, *Systems Thinking, Systems Practice*, (Chichester, John Wiley and Sons, 1981). P. A. Reynolds, *Introduction to International Relations*, (London, Longman, 1971). Geoffrey Vickers, *Freedom in a Rocking Boat*, (London, Allen Lane The Penguin Press, 1970).

2 Murray Gell-Mann, *The Quark and the Jaguar*, (London, Little, Brown and Co., 1994), p. xiv.

3 Checkland, *Systems Thinking, Systems Practice*, p. 5.

in an increasing order of complexity.[4]   His Level 1 system is a static structure such as a map or an organisational chart.   Level 2 is simple dynamic systems such as clocks.   Level 3 is cybernetic systems or control systems.   It is also called the 'thermostat level'.   Level 3 systems involve:[5]

> the transmission and interpretation of information.   As a rule they are systems in which [there is an] attempt to reach a desired value or norm by means of [negative] feedback.   The essential variable in such dynamic systems is the difference between observed and desired levels.   If a difference appears, the system tends to react to decrease the difference.   The best known example is the thermostat, which attempts to maintain the temperature to which it is set.

Boulding's hierarchy of systems proceeds through Level 4 which is the level of elementary life forms and eventually through Level 7 which is that of man, to Level 8 which is that of social systems.   As Kramer and Smit point out, a Level 8 system (the making of defence policy in the United Kingdom, say) can be modelled using a Level 1 system, such as an organisational chart.[6]   Naturally, using a Level 1 model in order to understand a Level 8 system – something frequently done because it is simply helpful – means omitting a great deal and therefore running risks that something significant may indeed have been omitted.   An awareness of these risks does not prevent the modelling process having its uses but inevitably affects the precision with which any conclusions drawn from it about the real world may be responsibly stated.

In the present work, the gap is narrowed and significantly less risk is run by employing a Level 3 system to model the Level 8 system that is the subject of this book – the international politics of the environment.

This has been done before.   The chief influence on the present work besides Checkland and Vickers is the string of publications coming under the heading of 'systems dynamics' or 'world dynamics'.   These began in 1971 with Forrester's quantitative and computer-based *World Dynamics*, whose content was almost immediately reflected in less technical form in

---

4   Kenneth E. Boulding, 'General Systems Theory', *Management Science*, Vol. 2, 3, April 1956, pp. 197, 208.

5   Following N. T. A. Kramer and Jacob de Smit, *Systems Thinking: Concepts and Notions*, (Leiden, Martinus Nijhoff, 1977), p. 96.

6   Ibid., p. 97.

The Limits to Growth in 1972.[7] But both the approach and the conclusions of the present work are different. The approach aspires to less precision than the world dynamics method, deliberately seeking thereby to avoid error, whilst at the same time aiming to exploit as far as possible the useful degree of realism inherent in the application of a Level 3 model to a Level 8 system. Further consideration of the world dynamics approach is given below.

Sustainability

The Gell-Mann 'whole' at which the present work takes a look in a deliberately cruder way than that taken by the world dynamics school is the world economic system and its interdependent connection with the physical environment. It is taken as given that the 'sustainability' of the whole is a matter of widespread concern in the sense that there is hardly any dissent from the proposition that what is wanted is 'sustainable [economic] development [which] meets the needs of the present without compromising the ability of future generations to meet their own needs'.[8] Furthermore, in systems terms, sustainable is taken to mean both stable (i.e. tending to persist over time) and in some sense desirable (thus, according to Gell-Mann, sustainability equals stability plus desirability).[9] By desirable is meant, following Vickers, what may be achieved by political intervention designed to regulate the interrelationships of the system at some 'level more acceptable to those concerned than the inherent logic of the situation would otherwise provide.'[10] Another name for what the inherent logic would provide is the default state.

System regulation with a view to stability is achieved through negative feedback, defined as 'a method of controlling a system by reinserting into it the results of its past performance'.[11]

---

7 Jay W. Forrester, *World Dynamics*, (Cambridge, Mass., Wright-Allen Press, 1971). Donella H. Meadows, Dennis L. Meadows, Jorgen Randers, William W. Behrens III, *The Limits to Growth*, (London, Pan Books, 1974).

8 World Commission on Environment and Development (Brundtland Report), *Our Common Future*, (Oxford, Oxford University Press, 1987), p. 8.

9 Murray Gell-Mann, *The Quark and the Jaguar*, p. 347.

10 Geoffrey Vickers, *The Art of Judgement: A Study of Policy Making*, (London, Methuen University Paperback, 1968), p. 29.

11 Norbert Wiener, *The Human Use of Human Beings: Cybernetics and Society*, (New York, Houghton Mifflin, 1954), p. 61.

Mackay's skeleton system

Donald Mackay gives an interesting account (which is followed here very closely) of how a moderately elaborate abstract system with negative feedback may work,[12] together with an opportunity to investigate what the pathologies of such a system might be.

Mackay represents the activity of the system (its output) with negative feedback symbolically as the movement of a point Y along a line F. The active agent is the effector (Mackay's term) sub-system E, which is governed by the control sub-system C. E is capable of a variety of activity, including inactivity, the function of C is to select from moment

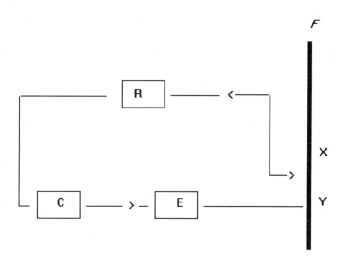

Figure 1.1 Mackay's skeleton

to moment what E will do next.

Suppose on the heavy vertical line *F* there is a point X, fixed or moving, towards which the activity of E is goal-guided, i.e. the overall pattern of

12 Donald M. Mackay, 'Towards an Information Flow model of Human Behaviour', in Walter Buckley, (ed.), *Modern Systems Research for the Behavioral Scientist*, (Chicago, Aldine Publishing, 1968), pp. 359, 368.

E's activity is designed to reduce the interval or gap between X and Y, or some time average of it, to a minimum. Equally if the interval were to be increased in some way the effector E should actively resist the increase and at the same time actively assist any agency tending to reduce the interval.

The controlling system C must be able to receive information about the interval XY. It does so through the receptor R which must be capable of detecting at least the existence of a gap between X and Y.

In the very simplest case only the existence of the interval need be signalled. C must then be designed to keep E in varied activity until the interval is reduced (to be too small to detect). Mackay compares such a system with Ashby's homeostat (Ashby's system may be represented by a cat in front of a coal fire. The fire may die down or be banked up. The cat presumably has no mental model of what the consequences of either event will be, in other words does not know what direction it should move in after the fire has been stoked, but moves towards and away from the fire until it restores its sensation of warmth to the previous level). But naturally there is altogether greater speed and efficiency when R is capable of signalling the direction and magnitude of the interval XY back to C, which it can only do if it is capable of measuring the interval.

Danger of delay

Arnold Tustin, another pioneer cyberneticist, makes a point of stressing that measurement (of the Mackay interval XY) and action by the control mechanism must be rapid enough for the job in hand.[13] Were R to be slow in the measurement of XY and/or C to be sluggish in moving E in the appropriate direction, serious failure could arise. Suppose X was moving towards Y but was still some distance away, to the north of it. R makes an accurate determination of the situation but it and possibly C too are so slow that the instruction to E to move northwards is delayed. By the time the movement is made, X is now to the south of Y and the feedback, as a result of delay, has actually worsened the situation that is, increased rather than decreased the gap between X and Y. Negative feedback, whose job it is to narrow the gap between X and Y and keep it as near to zero as possible and in other words to limit and reverse excursions from the set point, with excessive delay becomes not a force

---

13 Arnold Tustin, 'Feedback', *Scientific American*, Vol 187, No. 3, September 1952, pp. 48, 55.

for stability but a force for instability. At the same time, Mackay's reference to the possibility that the 'time average' of the gap between X and Y may be what R should be signalling is a useful reminder. There is nothing to be gained by a feedback arrangement that responded immediately to every restless twitch in the position of X. Some of these will be random, with a tendency towards a mutual cancelling out and productive of no (or very slow) net movement. So some delay in the feedback loop is desirable but excessive delay is dangerous.

The market

We can put flesh on the Mackay skeleton by taking as an example of a system with negative feedback that of a market economy.[14] We begin with the system in equilibrium: supply and demand are in balance – corresponding to no gap between X and Y. A disturbance occurs creating a gap between X and Y symbolising what we may take to be a shortage of a some commodity, say a raw material. This is reflected in higher prices, registered at the receptor R.   These in turn stimulate at C more exploration, or technical developments leading to the production of near substitutes, by entrepreneurs scenting the possibility of high profits. This produces in E a consequent increase in supply with a reduction in price once more to its equilibrium point (no gap between X and Y). Alternatively, imagine a glut of some raw material. This is signalled by a fall in its price. As a consequence the less efficient mining companies are driven out of business because they cannot make a profit at the low prices now on offer. This reduces supply of the raw material which pushes up prices again towards the equilibrium point.
  It is possible of course in the same way to think of labour as a commodity, also with an equilibrium price. An over supply of labour will drive down this price (i.e. wages). This will eventually lead to privation, which, by means of illness and premature deaths, will reduce supply. This is a classic case of a seemingly equilibrium outcome which may not pass the test of desirability. Political intervention to push the equilibrium price for labour higher than otherwise might have been set may be anticipated. There is another general point to be made here about how systems can be self-correcting but only at a very high price and there is a risk in any

14 See Garrett Hardin, 'The Cybernetics of Competition: A Biologist's View of Society', in Walter Buckley, *Modern Systems Research for the Behavioral Scientist*, pp. 449, 459.

correction that permits wide excursions of systemic collapse. In this case before starvation did its work in reducing labour supply there could be revolution and system transformation.

Political intervention in a self-regulating system (Vickers[15] with perfect justice calls the free market the greatest automatic regulator of human affairs ever devised by man) must be reasonably judicious if the self-regulating fundamentals of the system are not to be disturbed. Two tests of intervention are normally applied, one of quantity, one of quality. Intervention on a small scale, with non-market transactions within the economy making up only a small part of the whole is held to be safe. And intervention whose effect is to buttress self-regulation is similarly benign – for instance prompt publication of statistical data on supply and demand trends within the economy, funded by government, which improves the speed of the functioning of the receptor R. A similarly benign intervention is also called for to check the emergence of monopoly suppliers, as outstandingly successful competitors within the market system grow to dominate particular sectors of supply and start being able to set their own prices.

It does not follow of course that actual government intervention is always benign. Thus governments are often tempted to use subsidies to reduce the price of certain politically sensitive commodities, such as fuel or food. Real shortages of such commodities may then be disguised from the receptor R and subsequent adjustment to such shortages delayed.

The extreme *laisser faire* position of great nervousness regarding the possibility of harmonising *any* government intervention with the smooth running of the system seems questionable on two counts. One is that it seems to undervalue the resilience of the system to disturbance (in this case the disturbance of government intervention in the economy), which is the core of its attraction to the *laisser faire* school in the first place, and secondly it ignores the assumptions built into the system that property rights are respected, contracts enforceable in the courts, defence provided against external attack etc which would hardly be possible without a superstructure provided and enforced by government.

Even without these distortions booms and slumps possibly on a more minor scale seem inevitable whenever there is a rapid change in demand (through an alteration in popular tastes, for example). This can occur quickly and be detected by R through the effect on prices. But C may not

---

15 *The Art of Judgement*, p.126.

be able to cause E to respond quickly - for instance retraining a workforce or retooling a factory to meet the new demand takes time.

World dynamics

The computer model or mathematical simulation of global economic and environmental interactions, which lies at the centre of world dynamics, is an inflation to global scale of a technique first developed by Forrester at least ten years earlier to deal with exactly these problems of rapid shifts in demand when encountered by large business organisations. These were businesses which today would be called vertically integrated and consist of factories and their inventories, plus wholesalers' and retailers' inventories. Raw materials enter at the factory level and goods are supplied at the retail level in response to orders from customers. Then the technique was called industrial dynamics.

Industrial dynamics

According to Battersby:[16]

> [it] tended to concentrate on systems which are made up of chains such as factory – warehouse – distributor – retailer, in which the relevant variables are either 'levels' or 'flows' controlled by management decisions at specified points ... In one simulation ... fifteen weeks after a sudden 10% increase in an otherwise steady rate of sales, the rate of production at the factory had surged up to an increase of 45%; forty weeks later it had swung back in over-correction, and only after about seventy weeks could it be considered to have completely adjusted itself to the new rate of sales ... violent oscillations of this sort can occur in organisations with a chain structure, even though the individual links in the chain may be managed according to rational rules.

This type of unstable behaviour before reaching a new equilibrium is characteristic of a system where negative feedback – in this case information that the increase in demand had been met – is subject to excessive delays as, in this instance, the factory and other stockholding parts of the chain take their time (in this example, from 1 to 6 weeks), for bureaucratic and other reasons, to react to and absorb the changes that

---

16 Albert Battersby, *Mathematics in Management*, (Harmondsworth, Penguin Books, 1966), p. 183.

have been signalled as necessary. For a firm, overshoots and undershoots are serious matters for in the former case there is production in excess of what is demanded and unnecessary production and warehousing costs incurred thereby; in the latter case there is a failure to meet demand and a consequent loss of sales to competitors.

In world dynamics, according to Forrester:[17]

> five levels were chosen as the cornerstones on which to build the system structure: population; capital investment; natural resources; fraction of capital devoted to agriculture; and pollution.

And, according to Meadows *et al.* (of the Forrester school) these levels were linked together by flows:[18]

> Population cannot grow without food, food production is increased by the growth of capital, more capital requires more resources, discarded resources become pollution, pollution interferes with the growth both of population and food.

The world dynamics shock to the system equivalent to the industrial dynamics' sudden 10 per cent rise in demand for the firm's products is a sudden shortage in the supply of food and/or raw materials and/or natural sink capacity of the environment for the disposal of waste. This is caused, it is said, by a Malthusian collision between slow or non-existent growth in supply of any or all of these resources and exponential growth in demand (size of population and degree of economic activity).

World dynamics and Malthus

An example of this, given by the world dynamics school themselves, concerns population and food. According to their calculations, by about 1970 the world population could be fed using only a half of the available land. Since world population at that time was increasing by 2.2 per cent per annum, compounded rate, but land was not – in fact it was said to be shrinking because of human settlement on what might once have been agricultural land – all available land could be used up within 30 years or so. This is the time it would take for the population of 1970 to double in

---

17 *World Dynamics*, p. 19.
18 D. H. Meadows *et al.*, *The Limits to Growth*, p. 89.

size.[19]   This would, if true, certainly mean 'a sudden and serious shortage' of food.[20]

As in the industrial dynamics case, the outcome is the reaching of a new equilibrium but only after oscillatory overshoot, with, in this example, world population rising temporarily above the equilibrium level.   By definition this population is surplus and unsustainable and will meet with an unpleasant Malthusian end.   The reason for overshoot is again the same – lags in the responsiveness of generating processes of economic growth and population increase to negative feedback signals.   Not only is there overshoot, but the equilibrium point when eventually reached will be at a standard of life below what had been attained prior to the episode of overshoot (partly as a result of the extra pollution produced during the overshoot phase having contaminated, and therefore reduced the productivity of, agricultural land).

Self-confounding prophecy

The authors of the world dynamics exercise have often been misunderstood as predicting doom when it seems altogether more reasonable to see them as engaging in self-confounding prophecy.   Simulating what may happen in the real world produces information (at least of a kind) about the consequences of actions *before* these actions are taken.   If this information in turn leads to pre-emptive compensatory action, this is in itself a form of negative feedback and, crucially, a form of negative feedback being received early enough, possibly, to cancel out partially or wholly any lags in responsiveness in the sources of economic and population growth. Ideally, negative feedback without excessive delays to contend with will correct tendencies to overshoot and permit a smooth transition of the system to its new equilibrium.   This was surely the whole point of industrial dynamics as a management tool.   Vickers approvingly calls this process 'feed forward'.[21] Tustin refers to mankind being all the better off for being able to create 'an inner analogue or simulation of ... the external

---

19 Steady compound or exponential growth means by definition that a fixed percentage is added every year to what is growing. Anything growing this way, whether savings in a bank receiving interest or living populations with a birth rate exceeding the death rate, has a characteristic doubling time simply connected to the fixed annual percentage growth rate. Where the growth rate is steady, doubling time in years equals 69.3 divided by the percentage growth rate.

20 Donella H. Meadows *et al.*, *The Limits to Growth*, pp. 50, 51.

21 *Freedom in a Rocking Boat*, p. 96.

world [which] controls our responses, superseding mere instinct or reflex reaction'.[22]

World dynamics and international politics

This is not the place to rehearse the full range of criticisms that the world dynamics school have been subjected to: but one cannot be overlooked. Firms have objectives to meet, even national economies have objectives to meet: this book assumes that even the globe (in some sense) has an objective in the form of 'sustainable development'. But firms are more or less coherently managed in order to reach their objectives, so, usually, are national economies. Even allowing for the normal quota of rivalries and jealousies within a firm's management, the ratio of cooperation to competition within a firm is far higher that the same ratio applied to the managers of global policy, however the latter may be defined. In other words a missing dimension from the world dynamics analysis is that of international politics.

The clue lies in the school's unrepentant Malthusianism. In systems terms Malthus held that populations, with their exponential growth, would be unable to react to the running out of potential land for food quickly enough to prevent population overshooting the level that could be fed (barely so, but indefinitely). As we have seen, the world dynamics school say more or less the same thing whilst also providing dates. In subsequent editions of his book Malthus recognised the self-confounding prophecy effect and counseled moral restraint (i.e. late marriage) as a way out. Moral restraint is also the remedy preached by the world dynamics school.

One problem with Malthus, as Whitehead points out, is that he assumes that restraints upon increases in population size are secondary until they are raised to dominance by excessive population.[23] He never considers that even for persons who have never heard of him there must be other checks on population growth which are felt long before the food runs out, otherwise it becomes difficult to understand why some of the richest countries in the world in the period 1990–1995 (Germany, Italy) saw no

---

22 'Feedback', p. 54.

23 A. N. Whitehead, *Adventures of Ideas*, (Harmondsworth, Pelican Books, 1942), pp. 75, 80.

natural increase in population at all.[24] As we shall see, it is competition between states – precisely the missing ingredient from the world dynamics analysis – that gives national governments an incentive to control their population growth.

Independence and interdependence

States both pursue interdependence through their engagement in the international economic system and other ways, and independence when they pursue power and treat one another as rivals. It is a mistake to imagine that the one is wholly supportive of the international economic system and the other wholly antipathetic to it, just as it is a mistake on the part of the world dynamics school to omit power politics from their calculations.

The stability of the international economic system is capable both of being undermined and sustained by power politics, i.e. the strategic calculations of states. In the important matter of energy supplies, strategic calculations which urge states towards increasing self-sufficiency at the expense of market interdependence promote sustainability rather than undermine it. This is simply because of the very uneven geographical distribution of oil, which permits oil-producing states to use their near monopoly position for joint strategic purposes of their own.

Similarly, the tendency to national self-reliance in matters of population growth is a safeguard against excessive rises in world population. Population is also a strategic resource but unlike most such resources, it can be had in too great an abundance, as well as too little. The reason for this, as we shall see in more detail in Chapter 9, is that states with spare resources for the conduct of an active external policy will tend to prosper at the expense of those that have not. And states with the maximum population national resources can sustain will have fewer resources to put at the service of external policy than those whose population is nearer that optimum value which maximises or comes close to maximising the tax base at the disposal of government.

---

24 *World Resources 1992–93*, (New York, Oxford University Press, 1992), pp. 249, 251; *World Resources 1996–97*, (New York, Oxford University Press, 1996), pp. 190, 192.

System buffering

Vickers considers the economically unexploited parts of the earth's surface, such as the seabed and the landward part of the Antarctic continent, as useful but more or less fortuitous buffers promoting the sustainability of the international trading system. Contrived shortages of key minerals may be taken a very long way, but they cannot be taken too far without triggering exploitation of these global reserves. That such buffers exist is partly a technological accident. Until recently there was no certainty that commercial mining of the resources locked up in these areas was a practical possibility. Partly these buffers exist because states cannot agree, for strategic reasons, how their exploitation should be managed. In one case, that of the sea bed and the Law of the Sea conference (UNCLOS), there was simply failure to agree. In the other case, Antarctica, there was at least agreement to disagree.

In the case of the sea bed, UNCLOS negotiations leading towards an international exploitation arrangement collapsed in 1982 with the emergence of US hostility to the strongly non-market flavour of what was being proposed. The status of the sea bed remains in limbo. On Antarctica, in 1988 a treaty was agreed in principle between the 26 relevant states (the so-called Consultative Parties, mainly OECD[25] but also including some eastern European and less developed states, who constitute the states with a mutually acknowledged interest in the Antarctic). The treaty was called CRAMRA: the convention on the regulation of Antarctic mineral resources activities, which sought to promote orderly but prompt exploitation of the mineral resources of the continent. However, before the treaty could find its way onto the international statute book, one by one the Consultative Parties had a change of mind. Within three years CRAMRA was forgotten and the Consultative Parties had signed up instead (including, reluctantly, the USA) to a fifty year ban on all exploitation of the mineral resources of Antarctica.

It is tempting to regard strategic calculations, where they exist, and the limits they cause to be placed on international interdependence, as a

---

25 OECD member states prior to 1994 were: Australia, Austria, Belgium, Canada, Denmark, Finland, France, Germany, Greece, Iceland, Ireland, Italy, Japan, Luxembourg, Netherlands, New Zealand, Norway, Portugal, Spain, Sweden, Turkey, United Kingdom, United States. Mexico was admitted in 1994.

different sort of buffer but serving a similar sort of purpose. Too much strategic calculation, just as if too much of the world's resources were to be fenced off from exploitation, would hardly be compatible with sustainable development. But a modicum of it provides a check against monopolistic exploitation of energy supplies and excessive, that is unsustainable, increases in global population.

In systems terms, these buffers, including strategic calculation, introduce an element of slack, or as Kahn calls it 'disconnectedness' (see Chapter 9), into the system. The main virtue of slack in the system is that it promotes stability. As Boulding says, without it, 'if anything goes wrong, everything goes wrong'.[26]

With the ending of the Cold War, it seems likely that strategic calculations by states will become less important than before and greater interdependence will be countenanced. It would be premature, however, to conclude that the buffering reservoir of international rivalries is anywhere near drained.

World dynamics and precision

One final criticism of the world dynamics approach is to do with its over-confident way with numbers. Admiration here for most of the qualitative aspects of the world dynamics approach gives way to scepticism where its quantitative aspects are concerned. These turn the whole enterprise into something insufficiently crude (in the positive, Gell-Mann sense of that word) and consequently unsafe, aspiring to a degree of detail and precision of treatment not warranted by the intractability of its subject matter.

As an instance, we can return to their treatment of the population question. Malthus makes the point that he found great difficulty in knowing how to calculate the time taken for an excessive population (having overshot its equilibrium size) to return to normal. And he does not therefore venture to give a specific time. It is true that Malthus had no access to modern computers. The better situation of the world dynamics school in that regard gave them confidence to tread where Malthus did not and, moreover, to make calculations of the amount of time 'the world' had to restrict population growth before it overshot its

26 Garrett Hardin, *Living Within Limits: Ecology, Economics and Population Taboos*, (New York, Oxford University Press, 1993), p. 295.

equilibrium size. But in view of our earlier remarks on the nature of international politics and its probable impact on the population question, a Malthusian reticence would surely have been far more appropriate.

In other words, the normally laudable ambition for as much precision as possible needs to be kept on tight rein whenever a Boulding Level 3 model is applied to a Level 8 problem.

Outline of volume

The present work continues with a description of our Level 3 model of international and national trading flows. Market forces make this system self-regulating, but only to a first approximation. A closer look discloses a number of failures in the self-regulating process. There are straightforward market failures, or at any rate serious imperfections, when it comes to the international supply of energy, and oil in particular. There are more fundamental failures concerning the exploitation of resources whose ownership is held in common. And there are failures when it comes to regulating the discharge of the waste products of economic activity, not least energy production, into the common spaces of the atmosphere, seas and rivers.

Chapters 3 and 4 then deal with nuclear energy, on the face of it a near ideal solution to global problems of energy supply, since it would seem to ease the quasi-monopolistic constraints on the supply of fossil fuels whilst simultaneously adding nothing to the sorts of atmospheric pollution associated with the burning of fossil fuels. Of course, there are waste products and other problems associated with the production of nuclear energy too (not least those arising from the overlap between the technologies of nuclear power and those of nuclear weapons, which receive extensive discussion). Some of these waste products, were nuclear energy to become widely taken up, would acquire a new international significance as they added radioactive gases to the atmosphere and oceans.

Chapter 5 takes this, as yet hypothetical, problem as its starting point and discusses how an international arrangement for the benefit of all to regulate the emission of pollutants that cross international boundaries could be proofed against the insidious calculations of individual polluting states. Collective action to provide benefits which cannot be made exclusive to members of the collective in good standing is vulnerable to defections, as actual or would-be members calculate they might still get the benefit or most of it, even if they did not pay the 'entry fee', which in this case would be the cost of fitting their nuclear plant with gas traps. This question is explored formally, building outwards from the work of Mancur Olson, and connections are made and distinctions drawn between different sorts of international collective action on environmental issues.

Chapter 6 deals with what emerges as a particularly challenging problem for successful collective action – the sustainable exploitation of living resources. Whales, fish and elephants are used as examples. International arrangements setting norms for the sustainable exploitation of these things cannot be said to have had much success. This is not surprising since even when the problems of collective action in such cases have been solved another problem sometimes remains in that market signals can be perverse. An exploiter of a living resource, even when sole owner, does not necessarily have a stake in seeing to it that the resource is not exhausted. When interest rates are sufficiently high it can pay owners of natural resources to exhaust them as quickly as possible and put the income on interest-bearing deposit. From this perspective, Chapter 6 probes the emergence of preservationism, in effect a school of thought that is highly sceptical that market forces can be made compatible with the indefinite survival of living resources.

Chapter 7 deals with two arguably successful cases of collective action: the steps taken to preserve the ozone layer against the effects of CFCs and other industrial chemicals; and the range of international measures taken in Europe to cut back on the emission of acid rain-forming and other pollutants of the lower atmosphere. Success in these cases is attributed to a number of specific factors which are correlated with the theoretical predictions of Chapter 5.

Chapter 8 looks ahead without very much optimism at the unsolved problem of the threat of global warming arising as a result of the unregulated discharge into the atmosphere of carbon dioxide, coming, chiefly, from the burning of fossil fuels. One reason for pessimism is the perversity, from the perspectives of this book, of the way in which the question is currently conceptualised at the practical international negotiating level.

As already foreshadowed above, Chapter 9 returns to the theme of market failure and applies it to population. Self-regulation of world population would stabilise population at that level where there were just enough resources for the population exactly to reproduce itself. The conditions of life in such a default-state world would not be very desirable and such a population therefore would not meet our criterion for sustainability, which asks for stability and desirability. But rivalry between states automatically creates incentives for governments to keep populations below the maximum the national economy could support, in order to generate resources to be put at the service of an active foreign policy. Consequently a less than fully interdependent world is at smaller risk of over-population than a fully interdependent one. We have already seen in the present chapter how other sorts of strategic calculation can also promote what we have called system buffering.

The final chapter gives a digest of what has preceded it. In systems terms this is also a conclusion, with the book as a whole and the digest as a condensed version of it aspiring to provide in itself a Tustin simulation of the real world. Such a thing provides the possibility, at least in principle, of Vickers's feed forward, freeing corrective responses from the absolute necessity always of waiting for the actual and often unpleasant experience of error. At the same time, as pointed out in the Preface, most worthwhile projects address themselves to questions, implicit or explicit. The present work is no exception and the final chapter also contains its share of answers.

2 Systems, Science and Norms

The traditional first task of any systems approach is to define the system – what constitutes the system and what the environment within which it operates?

Defining the system

The solution adopted here is to borrow, with appropriate modifications, a plan originally mapped out by Checkland and colleagues to meet a request to throw light on the pollution control responsibilities of local authorities in England. The chief modification is an amplification from the local to the global scale.

According to Checkland:[1]

> all human activity (from the point of view of this problem) was taken to be a set of three connected systems. In one system resources are extracted from the

---
1 Peter Checkland, *Systems Thinking, Systems Practice*, (Chichester, John Wiley and Sons, 1981), pp. 199, 200.

environment and converted into material goods and energy. This system consumes some of its own products and has outputs of goods and energy for consumption, together with material and energy wastes. A second system receives goods and energy from the first system and in consuming them converts them into waste products. A third system monitors the activity of the other two and ensures that their waste does not become an intolerable burden on the environment.

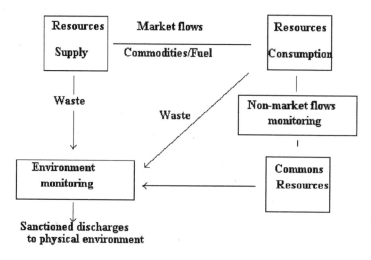

Figure 2.1 The system

Here the system definition begins with an adaptation of Checkland's first two systems. The first is now the domestic and international supply of material goods, food, fuel and services and it is connected to the second which is domestic and international demand for material goods etc. The two are regarded as subsystems together constituting the whole system of domestic and international commerce and trade essentially operating under and governed by market principles. Classically, such a system could be considered as closed in that two-way interaction with what lay outside it was almost zero. As the system has grown and technology developed, the system has become more open. This has occurred in two ways. Firstly, the effects of economic activity on the physical environment of the earth and the effects of changes induced in the physical environment on economic activity, that is pollution and the effects of pollution, are no longer ignorable. This is precisely where Checkland's third system now enters the picture: the pollution monitoring system.

At the same time, that fraction of all economic activity not governed by (nor always obviously governable by) market principles has come to loom larger than before. This is represented on the diagram by a fourth sub-system, labelled commons resources. Commons questions have come to the fore partly because, again, technology has made such activities (e.g. the mining of Antarctica or of the sea bed) possible, at least in theory. It is also because some undertakings, such as deep sea fishing, which have always been carried out without the checks due to market forces or some adequate substitute for these, have become relatively more important – in this particular example, as the development of deep sea fishing technology has transformed the world's entire oceans into virtually a single fishing ground. The system for monitoring the interaction between the supply of and demand for material goods and energy from such 'commons' sources makes up the fifth sub-system on the diagram.

If the now open economic system (made up of five subsystems) is to remain stable – which is defined here as possessing the ability to persist – it needs to be regulated as a whole. Regulation means the setting of the norm and the detection of departure from the desired norm followed by appropriate action to restore the situation.

I

The market's central position

A core assumption of the present work is that the impressive if imperfect self-regulating powers of the market system set a standard which regulation elsewhere in the total system should seek to emulate and to build upon. There are three reasons for saying this.

Market and prosperity

One is the success of the market system of international trade as set in motion particularly in the years since 1950 in promoting economic growth within the participating states. According to Drucker in 1994:[2]

> Since 1950 there has been a close correlation between a country's domestic economic performance and its participation in the world economy. The two major countries whose economies have grown the fastest in the world economy, Japan and South Korea, are also the two countries whose domestic economies have grown the fastest. The same correlation applies to the two European countries that have done best in the world economy ... West Germany and Sweden. The countries that have retreated from the world economy (most notably the United Kingdom) have consistently done worse domestically.

It is assumed here that regulation elsewhere in the total system that was antipathetic to the functioning of the international trading system or poorly attuned to it would risk slowing or preventing this growth process altogether. Without growth, it is hard to see how the aspirations of poorer sections of the world could be fulfilled. To quote Hirsch:[3]

> The growth process has the statistical property that a relatively short period of compounding would raise the consumption of the mass of lower income groups to levels higher than would result from redistribution ...

He adds that harmony in the economic system is sustained by the promise of growth that through time all benefit.[4] If there cannot be unimpeded growth or 'social limits' get in the way, then the basis for harmony dissolves – redistributional arguments are heard again.

Whilst Hirsch is not talking about international trade particularly, and pollution is only one of a number of the 'social limits' his book is concerned with, it is entirely reasonable to extrapolate the warning it contains. Denying the world's mass of low income groups the promise of growth would insert a further element of friction into international relations. Domestic political stability is widely thought to be put at risk not by poverty but by a failure to sustain a promise of better economic conditions: it would seem to be a gamble to assume that international political stability is immune from similar problems.

---

2 Peter F. Drucker, 'Trade Lessons from the World Economy', in Charles W. Kegley and Eugene R. Wittkopf, (eds), *The Global Agenda: Issues and Perspectives*, (New York, McGraw-Hill, 1995), p. 273.

3 Fred Hirsch, *Social Limits to Growth*, (London and Henley, Routledge and Kegan Paul, 1978), p.107.

4 Ibid., p. 175.

Market and self-regulation

The second reason for deferring to the market where possible is simply the obvious benefits of taking advantage wherever possible of its self-regulating powers.

So, to give an example from the regulation of pollution of the atmosphere, one way of decreasing the emission of noxious gases is to set a legal limit, requiring each emitter, say, to reduce emissions perhaps by stages to some lower historic level. Polluting emissions can equally be decreased by simply taxing them. This has the advantage over the other scheme of giving polluters an incentive to reduce emissions indefinitely and at the same time enhancing the market prospects for low polluters over large polluters since the latter have to carry larger costs.

Sometimes, however, the taxation method will not be suitable, as when it is necessary to achieve a specific reduction in pollution in order, say, to meet an international obligation. Without an accumulation of relevant experience, setting the appropriate level of taxation in order to reach the target figure for reduction in pollution will be a hit and miss affair. More assurance of hitting the target but without resorting to the crude and market-insensitive method of statutory limits is obtainable through the issuing of pollution permits. Polluters can be issued with permits to pollute to within a given total value (per year, usually) which will represent a significant cut on the existing amount. These permits can then be traded amongst polluters, ensuring that pollution will be cut first and furthest where it is cheapest to do so.

Whilst the above looks at how best to make the polluter pay for the damage it is causing, it does not follow that requiring the polluter to do the paying should be elevated into an unvarying principle. Coase is usually credited with first drawing attention to the possibility that discouraging pollution in this way, even through the apparently sensible method of taxation, can have consequences not usually associated with the smooth working of the market.[5] Taxing pollution means an increase in the price of the good whose production is accompanied by the pollution in question. In the round, the loss in welfare on the part of those who now buy less of the good than formerly may or may not be compensated by the gain in

---

5 See, for example, Ronald Coase, 'The Problem of Social Cost' in Robert Dorfman and Nancy S. Dorfman (eds), *Economics of the Environment*, (New York, W.W. Norton and Company, 1972), pp. 142, 171.

welfare obtained by those now facing smaller amounts of pollution. In addition Coase makes the point that it is a matter of indifference to the smooth running of the market whether a polluter compensates those affected or those affected pay the polluter to desist.

OECD countries on the geographical perimeter of the transitional economies of central Europe and the former Soviet Union, have a natural interest in minimising the exposure of their populations to routine and accidental releases of radioactivity from nuclear power sources. The most cost-effective step in this regard available to them could be to subsidise the attempts of their central European neighbours to rid themselves of poorly built and maintained nuclear power stations. More than most forms of development aid it is plainly beneficial both to giver and recipient.

Market and system coherence

The third reason for looking to harmonise regulation with market principles is a simple one. Since the aim is to create, at a minimum, stability as a property of the whole system, the risk that there may be mutually destructive interference between the different regulating arrangements of each of the five sub-systems will be reduced if the principles behind these regulating arrangements had a property in common. Market principles become that property in common. That this risk is real can be seen from the potential friction between an economic system which extols competition between companies (which is indeed inherent in its self-regulation) and the two other systems, the exploitation of commons and the discharge of waste, whose regulation requires cooperation (albeit, in this case, more often between governments). Hirsch, although writing more with a domestic situation in mind, puts it more elegantly when he says that the continuation of growth (if it is not to run into social limits, including pollution effects) needs collective responses that its own success has weakened through its individualistic (market) ethos.[6] Governments encouraging an individualistic ethos internally and internationally as a means of promoting domestic economic prosperity may find it difficult to change gear, so to say, when collective responses are required to head off the growth-limiting effects of pollution or exhaustion of a common pool of resources.

---

6 Hirsch, *Social Limits*, p. 175.

Equilibrium without political intervention: default states

Strictly speaking, without political intervention in the form of sub-systems to regulate pollution and the exploitation of commons, an equilibrium point could still be reached but it could scarcely be described as desirable. As we have seen, even the market sub-system apart from tendencies to father monopolies would set the equilibrium price for labour at too low a point. Commons supply left unregulated would set the equilibrium rate of extraction of fish from the ocean commons at a very low level consistent with a situation where all or almost all fish had been extracted. The environmental monitoring sub-system, left to itself, might also reach equilibrium, perhaps of the kind referred to by Lovelock.

Gaia

Lovelock theorises that life on earth and its inanimate surroundings form a Boulding Level 3 system because of a number of naturally operating negative feedback loops. His theory, originally associated with the use of the word 'Gaia' to describe an earth that possesses this property, is best explained via a description of a computer model which he calls 'Daisyworld'.

As Lovelock says, this is a cybernetic model.[7] In its simplest version the earth is home only to a number of white daisies, that thrive best when the mean temperature is at some optimum value. Too far above or too far below that temperature they wither and die. The crucial innovation in the model is that it assumes also that the mean temperature is not a 'given' but something within the control, up to a point, of the daisies. So if the temperature rises for some exogenous reason, such as a warming of the sun, and the existing temperature is somewhat below the optimum for daisy growth, the daisies will flourish and multiply. As they do so, because they are white, they increase the earth's albedo, i.e. the power of the earth to reflect back into space the light and heat from the sun, thus reducing the mean temperature once more back very near to its original value. Conversely, if the temperature of the sun were to decrease, more daisies will die. This will reduce the amount of heat from the sun reflected back into space and allow the earth to warm up again. (Any type

---

7   James Lovelock, *The Ages of Gaia: A Biography of Our Living Earth*, 2nd Edition (Oxford, Oxford University Press, 1995), p. 58.

of white daisy growing when the temperature of the earth was above the optimum for growth would not persist long in this state. If the sun warmed, more daisies would die. This would reduce albedo, making the earth warmer still, killing off more of the daisies, and so on. If the sun cooled instead, more daisies would grow. This would lead to further cooling and more daisies. Eventually equilibrium would be reached at a temperature somewhat below the daisy optimum.)

Lovelock and his supporters claim that more elaborate and realistic computer models which allow for the existence of competing species in addition to the white daisies of the ultra-simple version of the model, still point to the same conclusion.

It is a short step to regard the warming of the earth thought to be caused by man-made (anthropogenic) emission of carbon dioxide into the atmosphere as just the sort of exogenous disturbance to the system envisaged by Lovelock. The real world, which is just a complex version of Daisyworld and therefore possessing this same tendency to self-correction, should be able to shrug this off. It is true that it seems to be difficult to pinpoint the real world equivalent of the white daisies and while there certainly are mechanisms whereby carbon dioxide can be more or less permanently captured back from the atmosphere, there is disagreement as to the comparative importance of plant and animal life to this process, relative to inanimate chemical reactions.

Even if this dispute were to be settled in Lovelock's favour, there would seem to be two other, distinct problems with Gaia. The first is that Lovelock's theoretical contention that the stability exhibited by a simple Daisyworld is also a property of a world containing numerous species, faces serious challenges from other theorists. Lovelock does not seem to have a definitive answer to the mathematician May, whose own models show that the more species that are present and the more interdependent they are, the less stable the system they comprise.[8] Secondly, even if Lovelock and his supporters are right here too, the time required for Daisyworld negative feedback to effect its correction to temperature excursions may still be exceedingly long. How long, may be gleaned from references Lovelock himself makes to the possibility that the norm point for the average temperature of the earth is much lower than today's and indeed comparable with that enjoyed (or endured) during the latest

---

8 Robert M. May, 'Patterns in Multi-Species Communities', in Robert H. May (ed.), *Theoretical Ecology: Principles and Applications*, (Oxford, Blackwell Scientific, 1981), p. 222.

glaciation 10,000 years ago.[9] Ten thousand years may be very little in the age of the planet but it is a long time in politics.

II

Science and norm setting

Science and the precautionary principle

But, returning to politically significant timescales, wherever system regulation involves significant political intervention there is a considerable risk that delay will become embedded in the regulatory process. This is for a number of reasons. As Vickers says,[10] the regulating or monitoring body's job is to compare the actual with the norm which is rather difficult when the regulator's information about the current situation is scarcely ever up to date but more often refers to some past state of affairs. This is notoriously true about statistical data available to national governments and even more the case where international statistical data are concerned. As an instance of the latter, the semi-official biennial publication of global economic and environmental data, *World Resources* (produced in collaboration with the UN Environment Programme and the UN Development Programme and, more recently, the World Bank), whilst extraordinarily useful,[11] is rarely able to cite data less than three years old.

Moreover, there is likely to be conflict between the regulating authorities and those involved in activities to be regulated. In other words, as Vickers has it, time will inevitably be necessary to arrive at a sufficiently agreed view of the situation. In addition, perhaps especially in the international sphere, time will be required for the remit of the regulating body to be adequately acknowledged.[12]

---

9 Lovelock, *The Ages of Gaia*, pp. 220, 223.

10 Geoffrey Vickers, *The Art of Judgement: A Study of Policy Making*, (London, Methuen University Paperback, 1968), p.107

11 Two issues have been employed in the present volume: *World Resources 1992-93* (New York, Oxford University Press, 1992) and *World Resources 1996-97* (New York, Oxford University Press, 1996).

12 See Geoffrey Vickers, *Freedom in a Rocking Boat*, (London, Allen Lane The Penguin Press, 1970), p. 83 and pp. 133, 137.

These delays can all be made worse by technical factors. Reducing the emission of certain gaseous wastes into the atmosphere today may only start to have a measurable effect at the surface of the planet twenty years into the future. For the latter sort of reason and conceivably out of some tacit recognition of the former sort, lip service at least has been paid in international environmental politics to the 'precautionary principle'.[13] The Rio Declaration of 1992, Principle 15, states (in admittedly watered down language):

> In order to protect the environment, the precautionary approach shall be widely applied by States according to their capabilities. Where there are threats of serious or irreversible damage, lack of full scientific certainty shall not be used as a reason for postponing cost-effective measures to prevent environmental degradation.

As noted in the previous chapter, it is because of the dangers delay presents to a system regulated by negative feedback that Vickers praises the merits of 'feed forward' and Tustin commends 'an inner analogue or simulation of ... the external world'. Armed with a simulation or model of the real world, it is possible to act less sluggishly than otherwise would be the case. A good model of the physical or biological worlds, which is another name for the natural sciences, should give early warning of when actions need to be regulated, buying time for the naturally slow political process. The reference above to the interval between the release of certain waste gases into the atmosphere and the time when they begin to have polluting effects is precisely a case in point. The interval is establishable, at least in principle, by scientific experimentation and/or theory well ahead of what would be provided by experience alone.

Science and critical loads

Science is also helpful in buying time through determining where environmental priorities lie, both qualitatively and quantitatively, in setting limits. For instance, virtually all energy produced for whatever purpose finishes up in the form of waste or 'low grade' heat discharged into the environment. In this sense almost all energy produced is eventually wasted and discharged into the physical environment in the form of heat.

---

13 See Ian H. Rowlands, *The Politics of Global Atmospheric Change*, (Manchester, Manchester University Press, 1995), p. 260.

Equally, all carboniferous fuel (coal, oil, natural gas, wood) burnt produces carbon dioxide gas, much of which ends up as an addition to carbon dioxide naturally present in the atmosphere. Scientists would almost instinctively ask in each case as a first crude question what proportion of the natural flows of energy and carbon dioxide respectively is anthropogenic (caused by human economic and social activity). In the case of energy, flows from commercial production of energy as a proportion of the total flux of energy from the sun reaching the earth in any one year is extremely (perhaps surprisingly) small (less than 0.2 per cent in 1989,[14] with a doubling rate of about 50 years): in the case of carbon dioxide, anthropogenic waste as a proportion of natural flows (respiration and decay, weathering of rock) is significantly larger, at about 4 per cent.[15] *Prima facie* therefore, as between the two, there would seem to be a greater onus on the dischargers of carbon dioxide to show that no harm was being done, than on the users of energy. In its very aggregated way, this is a simple example of what is called the critical loads approach to pollution.

It might with more precision be described as a crude scientific model applicable to a range of pollution and related issues (but not all) whose guiding principle comes from 'order of magnitude' calculation. Thus, a human intervention that amounted to more than 100 per cent of natural flows would almost certainly be unsustainable. An intervention amounting to between 10 and 100 per cent would probably be unsustainable; between 1 and 10 per cent possibly sustainable; and intervening to less than 1 per cent almost certainly sustainable. We use this crude model in our study of pollution connected with the production of nuclear power, referred to below but dealt with in more detail in Chapter 4.

As with all scientific models there are uncertainties. One example arises from a case already discussed. Dismissing anthropogenic releases of heat into the environment on the grounds that they form in total an extremely small proportion of the natural rate at which heat is received by the earth overlooks possible regional factors. Some parts of the world where consumption of energy is very high could easily be releasing into the regional environment a much higher proportion of the heat that region itself receives from the sun. And climate, after all, is a regional matter.

---

14 See Appendix to current chapter.

15 John Houghton, *Global Warming: The Complete Briefing*, (Oxford, Lion Publishing, 1994), p. 30.

In 1993 Britain discharged heat into the environment at roughly 7 per cent of the rate at which it received heat from the sun. Or, natural flows are all very well, but it is not always apparent which flow is appropriate. Routine public exposure to nuclear radiation from a nuclear power programme could be compared to exposure to natural sources of radiation, or the calculated death rate from cancer due to routine (and very small) leaks of radiation from a nuclear power programme could be compared to the 'natural' death rate from all cancer. The latter calculation flatters the safety of nuclear power more than the former.

At the same time these very uncertainties are fruitful and encourage the asking of searching questions and trigger further scientific enquiry.

Where there are literally no natural flows against which to compare the flow of the pollutant, as would be the case where a completely synthetic chemical compound was involved, the order of magnitude model would ring alarm bells extremely loudly since however small the releases in question were, they would form an unmeasurably large percentage of the natural flow. It would be harder to find a better support for the precautionary principle.

Science versus precautionary principle?

A more precise definition of critical loads is found in Levy – 'a quantitative estimate of an exposure to one or more pollutants below which significantly harmful effects on specified sensitive elements of the environment do not occur according to present knowledge'.[16] Levy also notes that:[17]

> There is some opposition to basing future protocols [formal international environmental protection agreements] on critical loads .... The chief alternative – what is sometimes called the German approach - would be to base future protocols on applications of 'best available technology' (BAT) ... justification for BAT rests on the precautionary principle, which entails a *prima facie* commitment to reduce emissions as far as is economically feasible, even if there is not full knowledge of environmental benefits.

---

16 Marc A. Levy, 'European Acid Rain: The Power of Tote-Board Diplomacy', in Peter M. Haas, Robert O. Keohane and Marc A. Levy, (eds), *Institutions for the Earth: Sources of Effective International Environmental Protection*, (Cambridge, Mass., MIT Press, 1994), pp. 100, 102.

17 Ibid., p. 103.

Other serious observers such as Albert Weale have also concluded that science stands in some sort of opposition to the precautionary principle. He may have been influenced by the fact that in European environmental politics prior to 1990 at any rate it was Britain – the dirty man of Europe – that asked for 'a scientific understanding of cause-and-effect relationships in natural systems as a necessary condition for ... [environmental] policy making'[18] (in other words a critical loads approach), whilst the Germans, with a rapidly growing reputation for taking a responsible attitude to the environment, supported the precautionary principle. But in fact, as we have seen in the contribution of science to 'feed forward', it is at bottom integral to the precautionary principle.

Science and norms

Political intervention to set regulatory norms in order to be most effective or in other words to be least hampered by its own tendencies to incur delay should go with, rather than against, the grain of Tustin's 'simulations of the external world'. This of course leaves considerable scope still. Political intervention within the liberal democracies to set the norms of the domestic economic system covers a wide spectrum usually bracketed by parties representing on one hand the interests of capital and on the other those of labour. Liberal democracies may be defined as states whose governments of whatever party are interested in setting economic norms that go with the grain of the market. Parties and governments that have been influenced by Marxist ideas will normally have less confidence in the market system since it was seen by Marx as merely a link in a dialectic process and hence by definition not possessing a tendency to persist.[19]

The international economic system since 1950 has been governed by liberal democracies and regulated along market principles. The chief role in holding the ring of maintaining market-derived norms and deterring national departures from them has been accepted by the United States, through its leadership of GATT. It has done so because acting unselfishly is not in this case incompatible with acting selfishly. The US economy benefited from the growth of international trade at a time when the rival superpower, the USSR, strongly influenced by Marxist ideas, scarcely

---

18 Albert Weale, *The New Politics of Pollution*, (Manchester, Manchester University Press, 1992), p. 81.

19 See Oskar Lange, *Introduction to Economic Cybernetics*, (Oxford, Pergamon Press, 1970), p. 1.

participated in the international trading system at all.

Setting and maintaining the regulatory norms for environmental pollution or extraction of living resources from international commons is also a political process. Here, the equivalent of the market principles which broadly inform the regulation of the international economic system is scientific principles.

The parallels are quite striking.

Internationally, the getting of agreements for the regulation of international trade and implementing them – in other words the setting up of regimes – would have been impossible without a prior agreement, in the background and which did not itself have to be negotiated, on market principles. Without the latter, agreement is simply much more difficult and in the Cold War years the world trading system did not contain those states that professed Marxist principles. Naturally, disagreement on important detail remained, not least on the question of setting norms, even when going with the grain of the market. For instance, in an analogy with the equilibrium price of labour being normally unacceptably low in a purely market-determined national economy, something similar could be argued concerning the equilibrium trading position of poor countries in a purely market determined international economic system. Tariffs for the 'infant industries' of newly developing countries to develop behind might not be inconsistent with market-orientated norms. Intervention in the form of aid from richer countries to poorer has been practiced in order to make the latter's equilibrium position more desirable than it might otherwise have been. Or as Geoffrey Vickers puts it, Western moves towards the redistribution of global income during the Cold War years were stimulated by the same three forces that have operated domestically – moral obligation, political expediency and a 'lively interest in keeping up the volume of trade'.[20]

Epistemic communities

Similarly, the getting of agreements for the regulation of environmental pollution or exploitation of international commons is lubricated by a prior consensus on scientific principles. In the environmental literature the term commonly given for the global collectivity of scientists and scientific advisers to governments with expertise in these areas is an 'epistemic

---

20 Vickers, *Freedom in a Rocking Boat*, p.176.

community'. According to List and Rittberger, 'shared knowledge is ... a necessary condition of [environmental] regime formation, and transnational scientific contacts may help bring this about'.[21] But the existence of an environmental epistemic community of global dimensions (the community is regarded in the present volume as representing something more than shared knowledge, more of a shared basis for knowledge) can be no more taken for granted than the existence of a parallel epistemic community on the principles of international trade. Peterson, writing about the setting up of international regimes to control commons fishing speaks of the usefulness within such regimes of a *multinational* scientific staff, since developing countries 'are often reluctant to take the word of foreign (particularly industrial country) experts'.[22]

Science and Green politics

Whilst Vickers is probably correct to say that Western science is an increasingly internationally accepted view of the natural order (as market principles, after the Cold War, are becoming – no doubt temporarily – an increasingly accepted view of the economic order) his lurid warning that science and technology are often associated in non-Western minds with 'mass slaughter ... and world pollution' does not in some ways go far enough.[23] Even Western minds are capable of taking a jaundiced view of science and technology.

Robinson says of the change of name of the British Ecology Party to Green Party in 1985 that 'the decision [to change the name of the party] was welcomed by many members who no longer wished to be associated with a scientifically orientated ecology'.[24] In his study of the politics of the disposal of radioactive waste, Kemp refers to what we have called the setting of norms as the problem of 'how to synthesize the two cultures of

---

21 Martin List and Volker Rittberger, 'Regime Theory', in Andrew Hurrell and Benedict Kingsbury, (eds), *The International Politics of the Environment*, (Oxford, Clarendon Press, 1992), p. 103.

22 M. J. Peterson, 'International Fisheries Management', in Peter M. Haas *et al*, *Institutions for the Earth*, p. 273.

23 Vickers, *Freedom in a Rocking Boat*, p. 177.

24 M. Robinson, *The Greening of British Party Politics*, (Manchester, Manchester University Press, 1992), p. 50.

technical and practical rationality'[25] in the context of the disparity seen in Britain and elsewhere between scientifically assessed and popularly perceived levels of risk associated with the production, processing and disposal of radioactive waste. We look at this and related questions more closely in Chapters 3 and 4. It is enough to note for the present that in Britain and elsewhere, substantial numbers of the electorate apparently view the risks associated with a nuclear power programme as too large to be acceptable and considerable difficulty and delay have been encountered in setting this particular norm. So much so, in fact, that the future of nuclear fission power in Britain and a number of other states is doubtful.

Analogous difficulties with setting norms can arise with the exploitation of commons resources, at least where these are living resources. The collision in this case is between what Passmore helpfully (on balance) tags as conservationism and preservationism. Conservationism would seek to perpetuate exploitation of a particular living resource indefinitely, such as whales (for food) or elephants (for ivory) by maintaining a proportion between the rates at which these animals are killed and their rates of reproduction. Knowledge of the latter is science-based although not necessarily simple to acquire or operationalise – for instance the age and sex of killed animals are as important as their numbers if reproductive potential is not to be reduced. Preservationists, on the other hand, regard any non-zero rate of exploitation as excessive. As a result, setting international norms has proved difficult. In the case of whaling, the majority of states who once had an economic stake in whaling have become preservationist, with a minority enjoying pariah status as whalers, pursuing a kill policy which may or may not follow conservationist principles. This entire matter is considered at greater length in Chapter 6.

Domestic and international norm setting

The setting of norms, whether domestic or international, is the business of politics. Science on its own is no more appropriate to the setting of environmental norms than liberal economic theory pure and simple is to the setting of economic norms. As Grove-White points out, the attention of governments domestically and internationally has very often been drawn to the necessity of setting environmental norms not by scientists but by

---

25 Ray Kemp, *The Politics of Radioactive Waste Disposal*, (Manchester, Manchester University Press, 1992), p. 76.

Green activists.[26] Green politics and the setting of environmental norms is the parallel of labour politics and the setting of economic norms. It is not unusual for the parallel to be taken even further. Kemp sees the unsatisfactory nature of the environmental norms set by science alone as an example of the thesis of the neo-Marxist thinker Habermas that the drive of modern technology is running counter to democratic ideals.[27] Majone (amongst others) describes the setting of environmental norms as a 'trans-scientific' activity and agrees with Grove-White, claiming that 'technological expertise cannot be relied upon to discover the characteristic risks and social implications of new technologies'.[28]

That there is a demand for trans-scientific norm setting can be seen simply in the rise of Green activism.   Meeting this demand is a job for government. How this is best done within states is unclear. Majone calls for an adversarial quasi-courtroom procedure that involves both scientific experts and generalists which he correctly says often succeeds in 'bringing out unstated assumptions' and illuminating the risks involved in new public projects as well as simply educating the broad public.[29] Indeed, within Western market economies one variant or another of this seems to have become almost settled procedure.   In the USA groups of the public wishing to see a different pollution or commons-exploitation norm from those tacitly or explicitly set by government are apt to take either the polluter or the government to law. In Germany, assisted by constitutional arrangements that encourage the proliferation of political parties, the Green Party carries the adversarial procedure into parliamentary debates.   In Britain, Majone's recommendations are followed almost literally with the public enquiries into, for instance, the construction of new nuclear power stations. But the *ad hoc* nature of the British public enquiry and their marked tendency to be very time-consuming strongly suggest that they are not a full answer. A further reason for concern with the British approach and its *ad hoc* nature will be seen in Chapter 4. There it is shown that in setting norms for the disposal of nuclear waste, British policy has been quite irrational.

---

26 Robin Grove-White, 'Environmentalism: A New Moral Discourse for Technological Society' in Kay Milton, (ed.), *Environmentalism: The View from Anthropology*, (London, Routledge, 1993), p. 20.

27 Kemp, *The Politics of Radioactive Waste Disposal*, p. 76.

28 Giandomenico Majone, *Evidence, Argument and Persuasion in the Policy Process*, (New Haven, Yale University Press, 1989), p. 5.

29 Majone, *Evidence, Argument and Persuasion in the Policy Process*, pp. 5, 7.

Internationally, norm setting is also political and is also trans-scientific. It is also influenced by Green activists who perform the same service internationally as they do domestically in helping to bring out Majone's 'unstated scientific assumptions'. Green non-governmental organisations often are granted at least observer status at international environmental protection conferences. But in this case science must also contend with the inequalities of power distribution amongst the relevant international actors. A scientific treatment from the epistemic community concerning a particular environmental threat will be welcomed or challenged partly according to how states concerned saw themselves relatively strengthened or weakened by the argument's acquiring credibility. States with large reserves of fossil fuel, for instance, will ensure that international discussion of global warming (caused, it is thought, mainly by the commercial combustion of fossil fuels) is not conducted purely according to a scientific agenda.

Green activism itself may be manipulated and used as an instrument of state power. Benedick, a former US Foreign Service official involved in international negotiations over the protection of the ozone layer, tells of the period when tactical, at least, differences had grown up between the United States and its allies on the one hand and the European Community countries on the other over the form of international controls on the production of chemicals implicated in the destruction of the ozone layer. The British government, sensitive to what it saw as manipulation of the British publishing and broadcast media by US Green activists, sent an official diplomatic note of protest to Washington in April 1987.[30]

Regimes to set and maintain international environmental norms may be science-based just as international economic regimes may be market-based, but will themselves not be stable unless they also reflect the wishes of the most powerful states.

However striking and important the parallels between science-based norms and market-based norms may be, it remains to be said that the correspondence is not perfect. Modern science and liberal economic theory may both be social constructions but they are social constructions of a different kind. Martell summarises the situation: 'our knowledge of nature is, in sum, partly a social construction but is also dependent on

---

30 R. E. Benedick, *Ozone Diplomacy: New Directions in Safeguarding the Planet*, (Cambridge, Mass., Harvard University Press, 1991), p. 39.

objective properties of nature itself.'[31] Science is simply the more definite and less arbitrary of the two and further from politics. Science is non-reflexive: theorising about the natural order does not alter it. Theorising about the economic order can provoke changes. The upward surges in oil price coordinated by the oil producing countries in the 1970s may have been partly occasioned by the publications of the world dynamics school.

III

Regulating the system

Three instruments of regulation are specifiable.

The market

First, the details of the interrelationship between the sub-systems of supply and demand are assumed to be regulated by the market. Up to a point this is a homeostatic system. That is to say that equilibrium is maintained through negative feedback working automatically in the market place. Under this arrangement shortages of a particular raw material (energy source or hard mineral) are reflected in higher prices which encourage frugality in further consumption, further exploration of the natural environment for additional but presumably more inaccessible sources of the same, and scientific exploration of the possibilities of a substitute, some or all of which then act to remove the shortage and restore the original equilibrium. On the other hand surpluses of some commodity are reflected in lower prices which reduce the rewards to producers. The least efficient of these then go out of business, reducing supply of this commodity and correspondingly restoring the original equilibrium.   For this desirable homeostatic state of affairs to be maintained it is only necessary that the rules of the market be observed and enforced. These rules are derived from liberal economic theory and do not need much enforcement since virtually all that is required for stability to reign is that individual economic actors making up the system should pursue their own selfish ends.

But some rules are in need of enforcement. Economic competition could

---

31 Luke Martell, *Ecology and Society: An Introduction*, (Cambridge, Polity Press, 1994), p. 175.

lead to the survival of only a few very efficient suppliers who, once free of competitive constraints, could choose to create artificial shortages. Such large winners in the economic competition may aim to influence domestic government to defend their monopoly or near monopoly position by having tariffs erected against overseas competitors. A no-tariff rule prevents this provided it is supported by domestic legislation curbing monopolistic tendencies in the market within the national frontiers of, at any rate, the largest domestic economies (smaller domestic economies can normally discipline their own domestic near-monopolies by exposing them to international competition). Setting these rules and maintaining them is a political matter through international agreements on trade.

Common sources

The second interrelationship to be regulated is that between sources of supply that are in the nature of commons – that is to say sources without recognised owners – and demand. Here there is no tendency towards automatic equilibrium at a flow of supply greater than zero. Rather, in the absence of explicitly created and enforced rules for restraining access, the tendency is for such sources to be rapidly exhausted. These rules both have to be devised and enforced politically. Rationing rules require scientific input, since to ration extraction of fish from seas intelligently it is necessary to know how rapidly fish stocks breed relative to extraction rates and what rate and manner of extraction may be compatible with indefinite exploitation of this particular resource.

Common sinks

The third interrelationship to be regulated is that between the two systems of supply and demand and the physical environment which receives waste matter and energy from the operation of the other two systems. Here too there is no tendency to automatic equilibrium within politically significant timescales.

Establishing the rules for how much waste may be discharged into the physical environment on a sustainable basis is a political and scientific matter. Politics determines what degree of environmental damage is undesirable. Science provides the links between cause and environmental effects. Implementing these rules is a political matter.

Energy

Figure 2.1 is drawn with the assumption that in the enlarged system only one sub-system – the international market economy – has automatic tendencies towards persistence (no additional sub-system is specified for its regulation although such exist – GATT and its WTO successor). The market economy has the valuable property that it signals its own failures, where they exist. Thus if the price of some raw material were to show a persistent rise this would indicate *prima facie* a mismatch between supply and demand that had proved incapable of correction via the usual market remedies, either through further exploration, development of substitutes, or economies in use. As can be seen from Figures 2.2 and 2.3, no raw materials fit this description. Accordingly, the undifferentiated alarm of the world dynamics school over the supposedly excessive consumption of raw materials (the rapidly closing gap between their finite amounts and the exponentially increasing demand represented by exponentially increasing economic growth) is not shared. Because raw material and food prices do not show long run tendencies to increase, market forces are taken to be working successfully and therefore the topic as such has no claim on our attention.

Oil

But there is one important caveat. Whilst the price of oil has not increased either in the long term, there have been previous sudden interruptions in its supply and consequent dramatic if temporary price rises engineered in the past by the OPEC group of oil-exporting states.[32] The first such rise came in 1973 on the heels of the Middle East Yom Kippur War, although producing governments had three years earlier begun to wrest control of oil production within their borders away from the multinational companies and global production had begun to reach the then limits of capacity (these limits correspond to either all working oil fields pumping oil to the maximum rate of which they are capable, or tanker fleets and pipelines similarly working to capacity, or both). Measured in constant 1982 US$, the 1973 'shock' increased oil prices from about $3 in 1970 to $19 a barrel by 1979 when the Iranian revolution precipitated a further increase to $40

---

32 These are Algeria, Ecuador, Gabon, Indonesia, Iran, Iraq, Kuwait, Libya, Nigeria, Qatar, Saudi Arabia, United Arab Emirates and Venezuela.

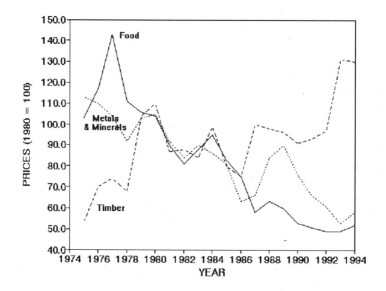

Figure 2.2 Commodity price trends A (World Resources 1992–93,
p. 242 and *World Resources 1996–97*, p. 170.)

a barrel (by 1981). The OPEC producers were able virtually to sustain
their quasi-monopolistic hold on prices for a further five years.[33]

That OPEC producers may be able almost at any time to repeat the
exercise is due to the twin facts that these countries between them supply
40 per cent of the global demand for oil but command 75 per cent of
known world reserves[34] and that by the mid-1990s the producers of oil
were again working at over 90 per cent of capacity.[35]

Shortages

The particular problem with oil, in systems terms, is the classic one

33 Joseph Stanislaw and Daniel Yergin, 'Oil: Reopening the Door', in Kegley and Wittkopf, *The
    Global Agenda: Issues and Perspectives*, p. 324: Ronald Mitchell, 'Intentional Oil Pollution of
    the Oceans', in Peter M. Haas *et al.*, *Institutions for the Earth*, p. 188.

34 *The Economist*, October 7th 1995, p. 28.

35 Stanislaw and Yergin, 'Oil', p. 329.

referred to originally by Forrester's industrial dynamics model. The previous oil shocks were reacted to by oil-consuming states through a policy mixture comprising economies in use, a substitution by near alternatives, including nuclear fission, a technical search for substitutes and the exploitation of oil reserves previously disregarded because of high extraction costs. Inevitably, such responses, although exactly what market economics would predict, were slow in comparison with the suddenness of the price increases and the consequence was a period of depression and inflationary instability in the international economy.

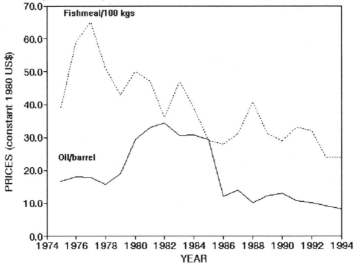

Figure 2.3 Commodity price trends B (*World Resources 1992–93*, p. 242 and *World Resources 1996–97*, p. 170.)

Response would have been slow and half-hearted in any event for the central reason that investment in alternatives to any commodity whose high price may be a result of monopoly rather than a real shortage is shrunk from because of the risk that the price of the commodity in question could drop at any moment, rendering the investment defunct and losing the investors almost everything. Monopoly means that trust can no longer be put in the market to signal emerging real shortages through price increases which then encourage the exploration of substitutes.

Contrived shortages virtually restrict the range of practicable responses to alternatives already researched and developed and more or less ready for use (although the actual construction of a large nuclear power station is a major engineering undertaking and can take five years). The risk to the investment represented virtually rules out the exploration of alternative sources of energy such as solar power or new sources of propulsion such as lightweight electricity storage cells (batteries). The nuclear option was available after the oil shocks only because the investment costs had been already carried under the heading of the defence budgets of the major powers (as we shall see in the following chapter, there is considerable overlap between the technology for the manufacture of nuclear weapons and that for the production of nuclear power).

But what compounded the slowness of response was a growth in an awareness of the environmental impacts of the energy alternatives available. A widespread if not universal concern with the environmental acceptability of the nuclear fuel cycle restricted the nuclear fission option, and at a minimum slowed its availability significantly. To a lesser extent the same is true of hydroelectric power schemes (including tidal barrages) – in any case, the geographical opportunities for water power are limited. And nuclear power could no more than other less proven options such as solar or wind or sea power fill the role of oil as a propulsive fuel for motor vehicles.

It is true that oil, natural gas (methane) or even hydrogen can be manufactured quite easily, if not particularly efficiently, with further inputs of energy (from burning coal if needs be), starting with coal as raw material. Coal itself is far more widely available, globally, than oil (when the world oil price doubled in real terms between 1979 and 1981, that of coal actually fell by about 10 per cent). But the environmental impact of burning coal whether measured in the relatively localized pollutants, sulphur dioxide and oxides of nitrogen, or in global terms with the production of carbon dioxide, joule for joule of energy produced, exceeds that of oil (although oil can be extremely sulphurous) and greatly exceeds that of natural gas.

Strategic commodities

We saw in the previous chapter that states pursue both interdependence and national independence. Commodities that are perceived as crucial to the assertion of national independence are usually described as strategic: these typically include energy sources and particularly oil. Strategic does not only refer to commodities seen by the same governments as essential to the operation of their armed forces (militarily strategic) but in some sense also critical to the working of national economies (economically strategic).

One convenient if simplified measure of the sensitivity of national economies to the availability of energy is their so-called energy intensity. This is simply the ratio of the commercial energy consumed within an economy in any one year, to the gross national product of the country in question. If the energy consumed is calculated in the same units and the gross national product expressed in terms of some standard (using for instance the currency equivalent in US dollars, corrected for inflation) rough comparisons can be made internationally and over time.

Energy intensities

For the year 1993, on a scale from 5 to 100 (in million joules per constant 1987 $US of GNP), world energy intensities fell into two classes separated by more than half an order of magnitude: the 10s and the 50s (see Appendix for a brief description of energy units). The OECD countries are the 10s; more precisely, their energy intensities fall within the range 5 to 20. The USA and Canada are at the upper end of this range (USA, 16: Canada, 21) and Japan is at the lower end (6), with European Community countries in between. The transitional economies of Central Europe and the former member states of the Soviet Union, together with the developing world are the 50s. Their energy intensities fall mostly between 20 and 100 (Hungary is 47, China 69, India 27, South Africa 42).[36]

Where commodities fall into the militarily or economically strategic category there is a reluctance by government to allow market forces the determining hand in questions of price and supply. Fear that supplies of such commodities from overseas could be disrupted in the event of major war leads them to stockpile the commodity or develop and protect alternative domestic sources of supply at above market prices. It can also lead them from an equal awareness of the sensitivity of their economies to

---

36 *World Resources 1996–97*, pp. 286, 287. The developing world is defined as that part of the world which belongs neither to the OECD nor to what is sometimes called the transitional group of economies of Central Europe and the successor states to the former Soviet Union. OECD states plus the transitional states make up the developed world.

energy availability and cost to protect users from high energy costs (as a result of artificial or real constraints on supply) by simply subsidising the cost to consumers through general taxation.

The former approach of actually buttressing energy supplies against the day when supply may fall short, because it is working with the grain of market forces (in effect diluting the potential monopoly status of the OPEC group) is prudent. In the Cold War period when the risk of major international war was high, examples included France's extensive civil nuclear power programme and the US emergency stockpile of oil.

If the danger of the OPEC oil producers repeating their coups of the 1970s is as high as claimed above, anything designed along these lines to insulate consumers of energy from a disruption to supplies whether in war or peace by increasing availability or by having arrangements in place to do so is quite consistent with stabilising the international energy economy. The small fly in the ointment is that with the danger of great power war now considerably reduced, the militarily strategic argument for such buffers is also weakened.

Naturally, the reduction in the danger of great power war is generally a welcome development from the perspective of the stability of the international trading system as a whole, in that the military strategic argument for any interference with market forces will be weakened. In particular arguments from this direction for giving protection to domestic agriculture will be heard less often with possibly beneficial effects not only on the cost of food to consumers in the developed world but also to the income of food producers in the developing world. But energy is an exception, basically because international trade is distorted by the potential monopoly position of the OPEC group.

Half of all global commercial energy consumption is within the OECD countries. Within the developed world, or the OECD part of it where domestic economic policy is strongly conditioned by market economics, there is very little tendency to protect consumers of energy against world price increases by subsidising energy costs out of general taxation. The incentive to do so in any case is reduced further by the relatively low energy intensity of such economies (one consequence of which is a comparative insensitivity of the level of economic activity domestically to increases in energy prices). This is not to imply that an application of taxes to encourage energy conservation is something that governments anywhere are prepared to do lightly. They may be deterred from doing so either by politically influential domestic producers of energy who fear for their profits, or even by large domestic consumers of energy who might threaten to relocate their business elsewhere in the globe where energy costs were lower. Inside the OECD, European countries have been more willing traditionally than the United States to countenance energy taxes. It is probably significant in this respect to note that while OECD Europe and Japan have energy intensities of 10 or below, the USA stands at 15.

Outside the OECD group the situation is different. Firstly, energy intensities are higher, so the temptation to subsidise energy costs (and the disinclination to tax energy consumption) is also stronger. In 1995 developing countries – which account for about one quarter of all commercial energy consumption, with energy intensities, as we have seen, around 50 – were estimated to subsidise electricity prices (from economically strategic motives) to the extent of $120 billion annually.[37] Secondly, the influence of liberal economics theorising is also weaker in such countries and political straining to work with the grain of market forces is correspondingly less evident.

The trend, however, in energy intensities is downward in eastern European states and the former Soviet Union (together accounting for about a quarter of commercial energy consumption) as market forces are starting to be felt. It is also downwards on average, slightly, in the developing world (upwards in Africa and Latin America, but downwards elsewhere), for the same reason.

Against this, as global economic growth continues, overall commercial energy consumption remains on a rising trend. As a result of faster economic growth outside the OECD countries than within, extrapolation of these trends shows that the share of consumption in the hands of the OECD states will decline. OECD economies are expected to grow, but small and declining energy intensities as these economies become increasingly service-based, will mean small or no increase in energy demand. Correspondingly the share of consumption in the developing world is expected to increase as it experiences economic growth at a stage in development when growth is almost synonymous with progressive industrialisation.

Stability in the international energy market then requires of developing countries buffers against contrived shortages at least comparable to those already in place in the developed world. In 1993, one such buffer, nuclear

---

37 *The Economist*, October 7, 1995, p. 17.

power, was almost exclusively – more than 95 per cent – installed outside the developing world (other less proven alternatives to fossil fuel for electricity production, such as wind power were even more concentrated in the developed world). At the same time, only further shifts towards market economics will discourage energy subsidies and their damaging side effects of discouraging efficient use. Equally, setting and enforcing norms for controlling pollution arising from the burning of fossil fuels will require the full participation of the developing world.

Setting commons norms

The sub-system representing exploitation of commons resources, also signals its own failure and departure from equilibrium. The signal in the case of marine fishing is a drop in the total catch (marine fishing means fishing in the seas as distinct from freshwater fishing and fish-farming and accounts for about 80 per cent of the total global catch of fish, with freshwater fishing and fish-farming making up about 10 per cent each).

Fish

Of course this signal typically comes rather late. Moreover, in practice, it is somewhat unreliable, in that fluctuations in population of particular species of fish occur naturally as a result of fluctuations in their food supply and/or in the population of their natural predators. It is customary to look for drops in catches over a run of years before concluding that it is not natural forces that are at work. Obviously this adds to delay if overfishing is indeed the cause. Added to which, in a world where there is already some awareness of the dangers of overfishing and consequently some political measures, however inadequate, in place to restrict fishing, drops in catches can be the result of deliberate policy.

A more prompt, and in principle more reliable, warning that catches of a particular species of fish were set to exceed what was sustainable would come from a correct scientific understanding of its life cycle, vulnerability to pollutants, and pattern of interaction with other species. With this knowledge, the size and composition of catches that could be sustained indefinitely could be predicted.

As a matter of fact, the world catch of marine fish dropped in 1990. Between 1950 and 1989 the catch of fish from the sea had risen nearly five times, to reach a peak of 86 million tonnes in 1989. By 1993 the total had dropped back to 84 million tonnes.[38] That this was consistent with over-fishing can be seen from a comparison between actual catch sizes and the approximate sustainable catch predicted at the present level of scientific understanding.

Table 2.1 Fish catches, million tonnes (World Resources 1992-93, p. 339.)

Region (Ocean/Sea)	Average Annual Catch 1977-79	Average Annual Catch 1987-89	Estimated sustainable catch range	Mean sustainable catch
Atlantic	22.3	21.5	28–37	33
Pacific	31	48.4	34–49	42
Indian	3.4	5.4	5–8	7
Med/Black Sea	1.2	1.6	1.2–1.5	1.4
Antarctic	0.45	0.48	-	-
Arctic	0	0	-	-
WORLD	58.3	77.5	69–77	73

Were the fish owned, indications that their stock in trade was running out would cause the owners who were interested in maintaining an indefinite flow of income from this source naturally to be concerned. They would in all probability react by rationing access of fishers to their fishing grounds by, for instance, increasing the price of licenses to fish. This would in turn push the least efficient fishers out of the business and reduce the amount of fish extracted. At some point equilibrium would be restored.

It might be thought that even without ownership, that is, where fishing grounds represented a commons being exploited by fishers, the fishers

---

38 *World Resources 1996-97*, p. 296.

themselves should be able to form a cooperative to ration their own fishing activities when faced with evidence of overfishing, when they themselves have a stake in prolonging indefinitely their own flow of income.

The logic, collectively, of fishers behaving in this way (provided – not a small proviso necessarily – the valuation attached to future incomes is not too heavily discounted compared to present incomes) is impeccable. The problem is that such a cooperative, if formed, will normally have no tendency to persist, because individual fishers will have every incentive (in the form of profits to be made) to cheat on the arrangement. Fishers will want to take advantage of the relatively high prices created by the cooperative decision to restrict supplies of fish to the market by exceeding their quota. If one fisher reasons this way, so can others and the cooperative will collapse. Political action to enforce the collective interest becomes essential when collective interest does not coincide with selfish interest.

Common sinks

The third subsystem involves the flow of waste material and energy into the physical environment as a result of the operation of the other three subsystems. Left to itself this flow will reach equilibrium. In this steady state any increase in pollution of the atmosphere or oceans or land surface would so further blight the lives of the population that premature deaths and the consequent reduction of industrial and agricultural activity would reduce the pollution back to its equilibrium value. Naturally the equilibrium value would not be reached smoothly but only after a series of oscillations of population above and below the equilibrium state, given the lags between the appearance of privation and a fall in population, and between the emission of waste and when its polluting effects would be felt. Of course this is a classic case where a stable outcome fails to meet the test of desirability. A sustainable level of waste discharge – the sanctioned discharge of Figure 2.1 – would normally set tighter limits on discharges than this default level. Science would help determine where priorities lay, both qualitatively and quantitatively, in setting limits.

As with the case of fishing, there is a tension between collective and individual rationality. Collectively, polluters have no rational interest in permitting pollution to occur whose damaging effects exceed in value the cost of preventing the waste discharges from occurring in the first place, even after allowing for the probability that the bill for the damage caused may be delayed in presentation for a number of years. But where there are a large number of states involved, say, in discharging waste into the atmosphere or a sea common to all, individual states have little incentive to desist.

How the tension between national and international rationality in the cases of pollution of a common sink or extraction from a common source may be resolved and desirable norms set for polluting or extraction rates is a large question.

Before we attempt to answer it, something else needs to be considered first. We have mentioned nuclear power in passing a number of times in the present chapter, sometimes as if it was a promising substitute for fossil fuel and therefore a possible solution to problems of contrived shortages of oil that was moreover innocent of most of the pollutants associated with the burning of fossil fuel. Sometimes, on the other hand, we have mentioned it as if it were more of a problem rather than a solution, especially when it came to setting norms for permissible discharges of its own particular waste products. So before we move on it is important first to try and resolve the issue.

Appendix: Energy and Power Units

The joule (named after the 19th Century Manchester physicist) is the scientific standard unit of energy, although it is a little small for industrial usage (even the calorific, or heat, content of individual helpings of foods is shown on the labelling in thousands of joules). The scientific unit of power, which is the rate at which energy may be produced or lost, is the watt (named after the earlier Scottish inventor); also rather on the small side for use outside the laboratory. A modern nuclear power station may typically be rated at 1 gigawatt of electrical power. This is a power of 1000 million watts, or 1000 Megawatts. Run for a nominal year (300 days) it would produce 26 petajoules (26 million billion joules) of electrical energy. The amount of energy extracted from the nuclear fission process to produce this much electrical energy would be much greater, twice that amount, or more. This is because all processes for converting energy from one form to another incur losses: modern power stations tend to be more thermally efficient than their predecessors, but 100 per cent efficiency is not obtainable.

One petajoule is equivalent to the energy obtainable from the burning of 163,400 'UN standard' barrels of oil, or 34,140 'UN standard' tonnes of coal (since both oil and especially coal can contain different amounts of energy according to type, the UN standard is adopted for accounting purposes).[39]

A coal-fired power station of 1 Gigawatt electrical output and 50 per cent efficient (a nuclear station would not reach such high thermal efficiencies) would need, therefore, about 34,000 tonnes of coal supplied every week to keep it running.

To illustrate, 1996 figures for world commercial energy consumption, which relate to the year 1993, put the total at 325 thousand petajoules.[40] In that same year, world installed nuclear capacity was 331 Gw(e).[41] To produce this latter amount of electricity by burning fossil fuel in a 50 per cent efficient plant would involve burning fuel sufficient to produce $331 \times 2 \times 26$ petajoules. So in 1993, nuclear could be said to account for

---

39 *World Resources 1992–93*, pp. 143, 148 and p. 315.

40 *World Resources 1996–97*, p. 286. This normally reliable publication calculates the nuclear proportion at 7 per cent by erroneously (it would seem) assigning fossil fuelled electricity generating plant the same low efficiencies as nuclear.

41 *IAEA Bulletin*, Vol. 35, No 4, 1993, p. 60.

about 5 per cent of world energy production.

Another illustration starts small. The so-called solar constant is the figure for the maximum amount of energy one square centimetre of the earth's surface can receive from the sun every minute. It is measured to be 0.48 joules.[42] In one year, over the entire surface of the earth, this heat adds up to 310 million petajoules. How does this compare to the amount of heat released anthropogenically from human burning of fossil fuel and other energy uses? Commercial energy consumption plus burning of traditional fuels amounted in 1993 to 345 thousand petajoules.[43] So the latter is less than 0.2 per cent of the former.

---

42 S. Glasstone, *Sourcebook on the Space Sciences*, (Princeton, Van Nostrand, 1965), p. 305.
43 *World Resources 1996-97*, p. 286.

3 Nuclear Origins, Nuclear Spread

Introduction

The burning of fossil fuel may not be a sustainable procedure, on two counts. First, as we saw in Chapter 1, supplies of oil are uncertain, partly by virtue of the near monopoly held by OPEC producer states. Secondly, the consumption of fossil fuel leads to atmospheric pollution at both regional and global levels which is beginning to have noticeable effects on habitability and has provoked international political responses both at regional and global levels.

If a fictitious inventor were to announce the existence of a proven additive to fossil fuel that would allow combustion to continue to grow at current rates for the next twenty years, but which would freeze emissions of carbon dioxide and sulphur dioxide and reduce the rate of increase in nitrogen oxides and methane emissions globally and add only a few percent to costs, the proverbial path would surely be beaten to the inventor's door. Twenty years would be a worthwhile breathing space and allow time not only for a clearer scientific understanding of global warming to be obtained but also for the manufacturing of appropriate international political responses for the longer term and, not least, for research into fusion power.

Nuclear fission power is the equivalent of that additive. It is a proven technology, which means that no delays in the rate with which it can be taken up need be anticipated from technical uncertainties, as such. In addition it is affordable at least in the sense that two modern states not known for the uncompetitiveness of their economies, France and Japan, have made large and ongoing investments in nuclear power. The emerging economies of the Far East, often held up as a model of modern capitalism in action, seem poised to expand their own investment in the technology.

Nuclear power emits virtually no greenhouse gases nor any of the regional level pollutants associated with burning fossil fuel. It is not subject to the geographical or climatic constraints that restrict the availability of certain alternatives, such as hydropower, or the less proven tidal, wind or solar power. Connectedly, it is marketable internationally and can be made available in units of size reasonably appropriate to local conditions of demand. Certainly, apart from a very restricted role in the propulsion of ships (mainly warships), like virtually all other mooted substitutes for fossil fuel, it cannot substitute directly for the part played by oil as fuel for transport. However, like any source of electrical power, it could be used, at a cost, to produce oil, petrol, natural gas or even hydrogen, at whatever degree of purity desired, from coal.[1] Of all fossil fuels, coal, as we saw in Chapter 1, is the most free of constraints on supply.

As a matter of fact, in some respects nuclear fission power is better than the inventor's imaginary additive which would do nothing, of course, to reduce dependence on the oil-producing states. At present, any corrective or deterrent effect nuclear power may have on the oil producing states' market dominance can be only slight. Installed nuclear capacity on a world-wide basis met in 1993 only about 5 per cent of commercial energy demand, compared to about 27 per cent for coal and 40 per cent for oil.[2]

---

1 The technology for transforming one fossil fuel into another, or in the case of hydrogen into a non-fossil fuel, is proven (combustion of hydrogen, which is a gas at normal temperatures and pressures, yields only water – hydrogen can also be manufactured more directly, by applying an electric current to water).

2 *World Resources 1996–97*, (New York, Oxford University Press, 1996), pp. 275, 285. The 5 per cent figure for nuclear needs to be interpreted. It corresponds approximately to the increase in fossil fuel consumption that would be needed to replace the electricity currently generated by nuclear. See Appendix to Chapter 2.

But a ten-fold increase in nuclear capacity over the next twenty years, the expansion necessary to absorb all estimated extra demand for energy over that period (see below), would bring the proportion up to about 30 per cent of the total.

Of course in practice nuclear fission power is not a new invention: rather, as will be obvious, it is something that comes already encumbered with a formidable amount of political baggage.

There are two particular items of that baggage that require further examination. One is how far something approaching a ten-fold expansion in installed nuclear capacity is consistent with the strategy of limiting the spread (proliferation) of national ownership of nuclear weapons: an objective which currently enjoys almost unanimous international support. The other question is more domestic. One important reason why the International Atomic Energy Agency (IAEA) was so far mistaken in its 1979 projection of the future growth in nuclear power – it estimated 500 gigawatts of electrical power $(Gw(e))^3$ as the likely figure for 1995 as opposed to the actual figure of 340 Gw(e), an overestimate by 47 per cent – was environmental concerns. The IAEA failed to forsee the growth in popular resistance within OECD countries to an expansion of national nuclear energy programmes. A number of OECD governments experienced difficulty, in other words, in the setting of norms for the environmental impact of nuclear installations at the national level. At a minimum this slowed down installation of nuclear capacity whilst public concerns about environmental impacts were addressed. It also added to costs through expenditure perceived as necessary to enable nuclear facilities to meet the tightening of norms.

The present chapter concentrates on simply describing what nuclear power is, saying something about its military origins, and goes on to consider how far an expansion of nuclear power would be compatible with restricting the international spread of nuclear weapons. It is followed by a sister chapter that looks directly at the environmental impact of nuclear

---

3 In order to pre-empt confusion, the distinction between electrical power and thermal power ratings should be explained. Nuclear reactors run for the production of power are always rated in terms of their electrical power, i.e. the useful power produced. Thus 1 Gw(e). Non-power reactors, such as research reactors are normally rated in terms of their thermal power. Thus, 10 Mw(th). The thermal power of a reactor is its total power production. The electrical power rating refers to the proportion of this total power that can be converted to the production of electricity. Even modern nuclear power plants convert less than half their total power to electricity. See Appendix to chapter 2.

power.

Origins

The origins of nuclear power lie in the development of nuclear weapons. The earliest (by a margin of weeks) nuclear weapon to be developed was the simplest and used uranium highly enriched in the isotope U-235 (^{235}U). The second design to be developed used instead plutonium in the form of the isotope Pu-239 (^{239}Pu).

The operating principle of nuclear weapons is the release of energy obtainable when either of the above nuclei can be induced to split or fission. This can be prompted by arranging for the nuclei to be bombarded by sub-nuclear particles called neutrons. Since a splitting nucleus of U-235 or Pu-239 not only releases energy but also releases neutrons (on average, more than one), a sufficiently large lump of either substance can be made to release a large amount of energy in a short space of time as each neutron released goes on to cause other nuclei to fission and produce further neutrons and so forth, in the well known chain reaction.

Nuclear reactors

The technical link with nuclear energy is simply that a tamed and controllable version of the same process is possible, with the energy produced continuously drawn off by a coolant and used to raise steam to drive turbines to produce electrical power. With careful design it is even possible to use natural uranium as fuel (U-235 is present in natural uranium at a concentration of 7 parts in one thousand). The earliest nuclear reactors were indeed designed this way. The latest designs of nuclear reactor, by contrast, do not get their energy from uranium at all but use plutonium as their working fuel. However, plutonium-fuelled reactors, so-called fast reactors, are not much beyond the prototype stage and are under development only in France and Japan.

Not yet even in the prototype stage and certainly unproven is the nuclear fusion reactor. The starting point here is the same mechanism that lies behind the hydrogen or thermonuclear bomb. Just as certain heavy nuclei like plutonium-239 and uranium-235 are unstable and can be prompted to release energy when induced to split, or fission, certain light nuclei, usually isotopes of hydrogen, are also unstable and can be prompted to release energy by making them combine, which is to say fuse together. Compressing light nuclei into a small volume and arranging for them to collide with each other sufficiently frequently and energetically eventually creates so many instances of fusion that the energy released exceeds the energy required to hatch the process. In the hydrogen bomb, the compressing and heating of light nuclei is done using a nuclear fission bomb as the trigger. In a fusion reactor it is naturally necessary to use a more controllable and continuous method for igniting the self-sustaining fusion process, as well as to devise a mechanism for drawing off the energy surplus as useful heat. In spite of more than 40 years of research as yet no prototype version of such a reactor has been shown to run successfully.

Added to these technical links between nuclear energy and nuclear weapons there are also practical links. In order to obtain plutonium-239 for bomb purposes (or any other purpose) it is necessary first to construct a nuclear reactor. As we have seen, this may be fuelled with natural uranium. In the reactor controlled fission takes place and heat is generated. But some of the neutrons created in the fission process do not go on to cause further fissions but are captured and absorbed by a nucleus of uranium-238, the isotope that makes up 99.3 per cent of the natural metal. The end result is that one element, uranium, is transmuted into another, plutonium. Uranium-238 becomes plutonium-239.

Plutonium

Thus by extracting the containers of fuel (usually know as fuel elements) from the reactor periodically and emptying them, a relatively simple chemical process using a combination of inorganic and organic solvents (Purex process) can be used to extract the plutonium. The plutonium can then be used as raw material in bombs. This became the preferred route to the acquisition of nuclear weapons for Britain partly because of the overall efficiencies promised. Not only was the alternative material, U-235, considered rather difficult and expensive to extract from natural uranium, but there was an obvious possibility of putting nuclear reactors to dual use. They could be simultaneously used for producing power and for the production of Pu-239 for bombs.

Whilst the British bomb programme derived its first plutonium from the so-called Windscale piles which were indeed natural uranium nuclear reactors, the piles were purely used for plutonium production and the heat generated simply discarded into the atmosphere. The piles proved problematic. One caught fire in 1957 and released radioactivity into the surrounding countryside: attendant publicity was kept to a minimum. The piles were soon supplanted by the Calder Hall reactors, built on the same site, which were dual use. These began operating in 1956 and one was still running in 1995. The Calder reactors were the world's first commercial-scale nuclear power station, producing enough electricity for a town of 100,000 persons. Their nearest rival, a US reactor in Pennsylvania, came on stream more than a year later. Interestingly, although the US reactor was not dual-purpose, it too had a military link. Its design was wholly different from the Calder type, using slightly enriched uranium as fuel, and was virtually a scaled-up version of a design of reactor used for propulsion in warships.

Uranium supply and demand

Nuclear power could hardly be a substitute for fossil fuel if it offered no more long term reliability of supply than that presented by oil and natural gas. All nuclear power relies directly or indirectly on natural uranium as fuel (strictly speaking this is true, but a little misleading in that it omits mention of thorium-232, which can substitute in reactors not for uranium, quite, but for the U-238 isotope). Uranium is of course a fuel of a quite different sort from fossil fuels. Amongst other things, it possesses (assuming full recycling) an extremely high energy density. For every million sea voyages by an oil tanker supplying oil to oil-fired power stations, one voyage by a bulk carrier of the same tonnage over the same distance would be all that was needed to supply uranium fuel to the same number of nuclear power stations of the same size for the same length of time.

As with oil, the long term trend in the market price of uranium since the end of the 1970s has been downwards: in the case of uranium, even without allowing for inflation, from $116 a kilogramme in 1978 to $20 a kilogramme in 1992 (these are so-called 'spot prices' whereas most uranium is actually purchased under long term contracts at prices which may well be different from the prevailing spot rate).[4] Unfortunately long

---

4 D. H. Underhill and E. Muller-Kahle, 'World Uranium Supply and Demand: The Changing Market', *IAEA Bulletin*, Vol. 35, No 3, 1993, p.11.

run trends in the price of uranium are no more of a guide to whether market forces are operating efficiently than is the case with oil.

The parallels between the history of the two markets are quite striking. In the early post-War period, in both markets suppliers were dominated by the consuming states. Oil prices were kept artificially low by the dominance of American and British oil companies until their grip was broken by the OPEC states in 1973. Similarly, up until 1963, the uranium market was dominated by the power of a single purchasing body representing the interests of two states, the USA and Britain, through their Combined Development Agency (CDA).[5] This was a Cold War organisation with the objective of pre-empting efforts by the Soviet Union and its allies to secure uranium supplies beyond what was obtainable from their domestic sources. Although this bilateral organisation had among its stated aims the encouragement of exploration for uranium reserves, it is difficult to see how it could have achieved this. A market dominated by what was in effect a single purchaser could hardly have encouraged entrepreneurs to make the extensive investments necessary to open up and develop new uranium mines. That this was not simply a theoretical risk was shown only 5 years after the CDA was wound up, when, in 1968, the US government introduced a ban which was to last for 10 years on the import of uranium into the country.

Power shift in uranium market

But just as power in the oil market has come to lie with the supplying states, so too has power in the uranium market shifted towards suppliers. The two turning points were related. The large oil price rises in the 1970s stimulated renewed interest internationally in nuclear power as a substitute. But this rang alarm bells in the USA, for strategic reasons. Without further international controls on nuclear technology transfer and uranium transfers (further to those already internationally agreed within the Nuclear Non Proliferation Treaty which entered into force in 1970), in the estimation of the US government the capability to manufacture nuclear weapons was threatening to become almost universal. The US government sought and obtained domestic legislation to restrict domestic nuclear exports, including fuel, and encouraged allies to take similar steps.

---

5   A. W. Hills, 'Uranium Supply', in W. Marshall (ed.), *Nuclear Power Technology, Volume 2: Fuel Cycle*, (Oxford, Clarendon Press, 1983), p. 80.

Australia and Canada adopted similarly restrictive policies, requiring assurances that the end-use of fuel exported is unconnected with nuclear weapons.

Uranium reserves

According to Hills, eight states – the USA, Canada, South Africa, Australia, Sweden, Niger, Namibia and France, in order of size of total national deposits – are thought to possess between them over three-quarters of the world's supply of uranium in the form of so-called 'reasonably assured resources' and 'estimated additional resources'.[6] The former are essentially known to be present, the latter are probable additional deposits, all marketable at $130 per kilogramme of uranium (equivalent to $50 per lb uranium oxide) or less. The total of the two categories is about 5 million tonnes of uranium. The important sub-category of 'reasonably assured resources', refers to uranium available at $80 per kilogramme or less. 1979 data put this at 1.85 million tonnes of uranium. 1993 data report this figure as essentially unchanged.[7] On the other hand the significant Swedish deposits (300,000 tonnes at the more expensive – $130 – end of the 'reasonably assured' category) are less to be counted on because of the probable environmental dislocation involved in their extraction and the Swedish decision to abandon nuclear power for themselves. Against this, none of the above figures takes account of possible reserves in the transitional states of Central Europe and the former Soviet Union, or China. Hills separately estimates these to amount to half as much again as those of the big eight.

At least until the effect of the political and economic changes consequent on the collapse of the USSR on the uranium market becomes clearer, the small number of suppliers is reminiscent of the situation with respect to oil. But from the perspective of economics alone the virtual absence of overlap between oil exporting and uranium exporting states means that in principle competitive forces can work and that engineered shortages of either cannot be taken too far without prompting importers to turn to the alternative fuel.

---

6 'Uranium Supply', p. 90.

7 B. A. Semenov and N. Oi, 'Nuclear Fuel Cycles: Adjusting to New Realities', *IAEA Bulletin*, Vol. 35, No 3, 1993, pp. 4, 5.

Nuclear cost structure

Peculiarities in the cost structure of nuclear power require that this statement be qualified. The capital cost of the nuclear reactor is the dominant feature in the cost of electricity from this source. Construction times are also long. The latter means that self-correcting responses to shortages in fossil fuel may be dangerously slow. In addition, without some assurance that there will be demand for nuclear power, owners of capital will be reluctant to commit it to such ventures. On the other hand, market forces can be assisted by the nuclear cost structure.

High capital cost means that the raw material cost of uranium accounts for less than 20 per cent of the cost of electricity produced (enrichment services and fuel element fabrication naturally add to this). For fossil-fuel power stations, fuel costs form 75 per cent of the cost of electricity. Interest rates are accordingly very important for the competitiveness of nuclear power. When interest rates are low, investment in nuclear power is encouraged because funds for capital projects can be borrowed cheaply. But these are precisely the circumstances where, in the quasi-monopolistic world of oil supply, oil producers will be otherwise least inclined to put their product on the market. It is only when interest rates are high that a monopolistic or quasi-monopolistic producer of a raw material will be keen to turn its assets into cash for it is only then that the flow of income will be higher as a return on cash put into government stocks, say, than what can be obtained by a more conservationist attitude to the raw material.

The market position with respect to uranium supply is better balanced than so far indicated in two distinct respects but which jointly help redress matters in favour of the importing states.

Uranium enrichment

The first of these is the flexibility users of uranium reactor fuel have over enrichment policy.

It is true that Britain sought to base its first nuclear weapon on plutonium derived from natural uranium-fuelled reactors because of the promise of cost savings. But it has become apparent that where reactors are designed explicitly for power production and hence without any dual-use compromises, greater efficiency is obtainable in the use of uranium. The British Magnox nuclear power stations use almost twice the amount of uranium per unit of electricity produced than does the latest British reactor, the Sizewell B PWR (pressurised water reactor). The PWR, like most modern reactors, is a lineal descendant not of Calder Hall but of Calder's original American rival and uses not natural uranium as fuel but uranium slightly enriched (about 3 per cent) in the uranium-235 isotope. Further improvements in the design of this family of reactors are likely to lead to further, although less dramatic, savings in fuel.

Of course, designing new reactors to be more efficient in their use of uranium is not the sort of response to uranium shortages that can be turned on and off like a tap. A more flexible response to fuel shortages whether real or contrived comes from the uranium enrichment process itself.

Enriching uranium is an activity that shows very strong economies of scale. It is an extremely energy intensive process. Enriching small amounts, measured in kilograms per annum, is not especially difficult, although in terms of cost per kilogram, it is expensive. But enriching even on an industrial scale where tonnes per annum may be involved remains expensive unless the scale can be made very large indeed, when cost savings in running costs begin to appear. The first British uranium enrichment plant, using the gas diffusion method that had been developed jointly by Britain and the USA during the war, was built to service the British nuclear weapons programme which had been forced into unexpected self-sufficiency by political decisions made in the United States early in the early Cold War period. The plant, which was built in Capenhurst in Cheshire, was operated for military purposes between 1956 and 1960. Work was subsequently done on the plant to convert it to the production of slightly enriched uranium as reactor fuel, but this approach was soon abandoned, in 1968, on cost grounds. Capenhurst was simply too small and too energy intensive to be competitive. On a scale of 0 to 10 (in millions of separative work units per annum – MSWU/year) its capacity stood at about 0.4 MSWU/year.[8] It was replaced by new purpose-built plant using the centrifuge principle with a capacity of about 0.8 MSWU/year. This method allows economies of scale to show up in undertakings of relatively modest size, although Britain still sought international collaborators to help spread the costs. The tripartite Almelo agreement with Holland and West Germany on sharing centrifuge technology was signed in 1970.

---

8 A. Wohlstetter, T. A. Brown, G. S. Jones *et al.*, *Swords from Plowshares: The Military Potential of Civilian Nuclear Energy* (Chicago, University of Chicago Press, 1979), p. 213, provides a useful table of world enrichment plant.

The very much larger gas diffusion plants in the USA and Russia (the USA has three with total capacity of about 28 MSWU/year) seem to have presented no difficulties when turned over to civilian work.   France built its original small Pierrelatte gas diffusion plant for military use but sited it in the Drome department to take advantage of the cheap hydro-electric power available on the door step.   Its much larger civil plants were built later not far away at Tricastin, for the same reason.   The two Tricastin plants are each of capacity 10 MSWU/year.

In rough terms, every 10 Gw(e) of PWR or similar reactor installed (which roughly corresponds to 10 reactors of the very commonplace 1 Gw(e) capacity) needs fuel services to the extent of 1 MSWU performed each year.[9]

In all enrichment plants the natural uranium feed is turned into two streams.   Unless there is a military requirement for highly enriched uranium for bombs or propulsion reactors, one stream is enriched to about 3 per cent in U-235 as fuel for PWR and similar reactors.   The other, larger stream, known as the tails, still contains a small amount of U-235, and the calculation in the preceding paragraph makes the normal assumption that the tails contain 0.2 per cent of U-235.   But in practice, enrichment procedures can be tailored to adapt to changing circumstances in the uranium market.

'Storing' electricity

To illustrate, we may assume that sensible uranium purchasing policy will include building up stockpiles or reserves when uranium prices are low. The high energy density of uranium fuel means that extra transport and warehousing costs for uranium stocks are a negligible consideration. This step already redresses somewhat the market imbalance back in favour of the importer. But the importer can do more to help itself than this, provided it has access to enrichment facilities.   When energy is comparatively expensive, reactor fuel is best made by subjecting comparatively large amounts of natural uranium feed (from stocks) to comparatively little separative work, leaving possibly half of the original amount of uranium-235 unseparated. Alternatively, when energy is cheap, a much smaller - about half as much - amount of natural uranium can be

---

9   J. H. Tait, 'Uranium Enrichment', in W. Marshall (ed.), *Nuclear Power Technology, Volume 2: Fuel Cycle*, pp. 149, 150.

subjected to intensive separative work, leaving virtually no uranium-235 unseparated. Thus, during periods when electricity costs are comparatively low (which should also coincide with periods when uranium is relatively cheap), prudent policy would economise on uranium consumption by going in for intensive separative work and stockpiling the surplus uranium purchases. When market conditions are reversed, low intensity separative work would make sense, running down some of the uranium stocks. Another way of looking at the policy is as a long term means of storing electricity, when it is cheap, for use when it becomes dear.

Fuel reprocessing

The second thing that uranium importers can do to lessen their exposure to the risk of shortage of supply is to take advantage of a unique property of uranium. Alone among proven fuels, it is capable of what can almost be described as recycling. Essentially this means that suppliers of uranium are themselves in competition with at least some of their customers who can respond to real or contrived shortages by recycling reactor fuel that has already been 'once-through'.

The principle of recycling reactor fuel is not very complicated. Like the Calder Hall original, all commercial nuclear reactors produce plutonium as a by-product, even if not at the same high rate nor of the same detailed isotopic composition that was characteristic of the Calder design (later closely replicated in the obsolescent British Magnox series of civil nuclear power stations). In addition, all reactors are really rather inefficient users of their original charges of fuel, in that exhausted fuel elements contain a potential power source in the form of plutonium (and some unused uranium, still containing in most cases useful amounts of U-235). By extracting this plutonium, recycling or 'reprocessing' spent reactor fuel is tantamount to allowing supplies of uranium to be used not once but as much as fifty times (the logic is that 'once through' makes use only of the U-235 isotope, which is 0.7 per cent or 1 part in 140 of all uranium, whereas recycling uses plutonium derived from the abundant isotope U-238. With perfect efficiencies plutonium recycling would stretch uranium supplies by a factor of 140: in practice only a factor of 50 is reached).[10]

---

10 A. A. Farmer, 'Recycling of Fuel' in W. Marshall, (ed.) *Nuclear Power Technology Volume 2: Fuel Cycle*, p. 4.

Breeder reactor

To achieve even this sort of efficiency a substantially different design of reactor is required as part of the nuclear programme. This uses as fuel plutonium in a rich mixture with uranium-238, obtainable from the tails of an enrichment plant. Just like the more conventional fuel which is a mixture of U-235 and U-238, when this reactor is used to produce power, plutonium is also produced. In this case, however, in the so-called fast reactor or fast breeder reactor, more plutonium is produced than is used up. It is this factor which produces the enormous gain in fuel efficiency. It cannot be said that this technology has been fully proven. As already noted, large fast breeder reactors at the prototype stage have been constructed so far only in France and Japan. As an intermediate step, it is possible to refuel conventional reactors using plutonium instead of or in addition to U-235. The maximum gains in fuel efficiency from this elementary recycling process only amount to a factor of two.

Naturally, states with nuclear power programmes but lacking the assurance of secure long term supplies of uranium possessed by states with large domestic reserves, have taken a strong commercial interest in fuel reprocessing. This means virtually every state with a nuclear power programme, except the USA, Sweden and Canada.

Britain and France (the latter's national supplies of uranium are far from excessive in comparison with its degree of domestic reliance on nuclear power for electricity production) not only reprocess their own fuel but also offer international reprocessing services. The United States, which has twice as much nuclear power installed as France but twenty times the uranium reserves, has not only abandoned domestic reprocessing but has also used its political weight to discourage fuel reprocessing elsewhere. In 1976 US President Carter, giving as his reasons that the same plutonium produced in nuclear reactors can be used to make nuclear weapons, announced that the USA would abandon reprocessing for the foreseeable future.[11]

The US position is of course quite consistent with its restrictive attitude to the supply of uranium generally. Britain and France, and most other states with nuclear power installed but without domestic supplies of uranium to match, find themselves in broad alliance with the USA in the political aim of restricting the proliferation of nuclear weapons, but see

---

11 Wohlstetter *et al.*, *Swords from Plowshares*, p. 78.

themselves threatened economically by the tactics adopted by the Americans.

Accordingly, debate on reprocessing has become thoroughly politicised and with it debate on the true likely extent of global supplies of uranium, upon which the sustainability of the nuclear power option rests, at least in part.

Transatlantic differences

The US view on nuclear proliferation is, as we have seen, that reprocessing and the implicit 'plutonium economy' is a direct encouragement to the production of nuclear weapons. Without it, the reasoning goes, plutonium, the raw material for one type of nuclear bomb, remains locked up in spent fuel elements (containers) extremely difficult to access because the elements also contain so-called fission products. These substances, in their chemistry a long way from uranium and literally products of transmutation, often themselves unstable, are formed of the fragments of the fissioned uranium-235 nuclei. Where they are unstable, they decay radioactively into more stable daughter products. This property of radioactivity, which means in the case of fission products spontaneous emissions of gamma rays and sub-nuclear particles in quantities and at energies dangerous to life, defends the plutonium from all but most determined would-be bomb makers.

The view on the eastern shore of the Atlantic is the opposite of this. Plutonium will be even better safeguarded, it is said, if it is extracted from spent fuel elements and incorporated into the reactor fuel economy where its normal physical location will be securely inside an operating reactor rather than sitting in a warehouse full of spent fuel elements whose radioactivity in any case declines rapidly with the passage of time.

The politicisation of the reprocessing debate also makes it difficult to assess the true position regarding the global supply of uranium. In the absence of a perfect market, estimates of the rate of consumption of a raw material set against the size of known reserves, are an indicator, albeit crude, of the sustainability of the existing pattern of, and trends in, use. Estimates of global reserves of uranium given currency in Britain can naturally be anticipated to lie on the low side, since this justifies Britain's position as a keen supporter of reprocessing. (Global thorium reserves, which could in theory be used to eke out uranium reserves to a limited extent are not considered here first because their contribution could only be small since, apparently, they amount only to a third of uranium reserves and secondly, because thorium has only so far been used in the nuclear fuel cycle in prototype reactor designs.)

Hills foresaw the complete consumption of known and probable uranium reserves before the year 2015 with no reprocessing and world installed nuclear capacity at that date of around 1500 Gw(e) (supply and demand in China and the transitional economies of Europe taken to be in balance). As we have seen, Hills put known and probable reserves at 5 million tonnes of natural uranium. Hills put the total world reserves of uranium, lumping known and probable reserves together with speculative reserves, at around 20 million tonnes. These would be obtainable, if at all, only at greater costs, although this need not be a disqualification when it is recalled that the cost of electricity from nuclear reactors is only weakly dependent on the cost of fuel.

Hills's 1500 Gw(e) installed capacity was at the bottom end of an earlier International Atomic Energy Agency (IAEA) projection made in 1979 (the upper limit was 3000 Gw(e)).[12] A much more recent estimate of the likely situation in 2015, also coming from the IAEA, tells a remarkably different story. The new lower estimate for installed nuclear capacity by that year, now including China and the transitional economies, stands at 370 Gw(e), with the upper estimate 520 Gw(e).[13] Actual installed capacity in 1995 was 340 Gw(e), which included 46 Gw(e) from China and the transitional economies, and 275 Gw(e) in the OECD states.[14] If these projections are accurate, obviously shortages of natural uranium are not going to be a constraining factor on the nuclear option over the next twenty years or so.

But this is scarcely a pertinent observation in the context of the present chapter. Rather, the issue concerns possible supply constraints in the event of the 1995 IEAE projection being grossly on the low side, as would be the case if nuclear power was taken up as a substitute for fossil fuel on a large enough scale to have a significant influence on global warming. Inevitably, projections of how large a share of global energy production this would allocate to nuclear power must have a certain arbitrary quality. As a sort of practicable upper limit we may extrapolate from the case of France.

---

12 Hills, 'Uranium Supply', p. 94.

13 *IAEA Bulletin*, Vol. 37, No. 2, 1995, p. 45.

14 Ibid., p. 53.

Expanding nuclear power

In 1996 France, with about 2 per cent of the world's 'known plus probable' reserves of uranium, had the world's largest national take-up of nuclear power, with nuclear generation accounting for 75 per cent of all electricity produced (strictly speaking, Lithuania derives an even larger share of its electricity from nuclear, 76 per cent, but has only 2.4 Gw(e) of nuclear installed). French installed nuclear power (1995) amounts to 58.5 Gw(e). If global nuclear capacity were to be in the same ratio to global uranium reserves as that of France is to French uranium reserves, global capacity would be 50×58.5 Gw(e), or 3000 Gw(e), in round figures. As we have seen, in 1995 world total installed capacity was 340 Gw(e).

There are two further sorts of validation for the 3000 Gw(e) figure. One comes from the fact that it corresponds to the 1979 IAEA upper projection for global installed nuclear capacity by 2015, which reinforces the suggestion that it may not imply an unbearable strain on uranium reserves. Another comes from the record of the nuclear construction industry during the 1970s and 1980s. In 1993 global installed nuclear capacity was thirteen times what it was in 1973.[15] If this same *rate* of growth could be achieved in the period 1995–2015, a further increase in installed capacity by ten times would be comfortably reachable. So even the considerably telescoped timescale now being proposed compared to the IAEA's original 1979 projection may not put an unbearable load on the nuclear construction industry.

Effect on CO$_2$ emissions

Supposing such an expansion were to occur, what would its impact be on carbon dioxide emissions? This can only be answered through making a further series of assumptions.

The first thing to be noted is that total energy consumption globally has been rising at about 1.8 per cent per annum since 1973. Unsurprisingly, since this expansion has been almost exclusively in the form of increases in the output of coal, oil and natural gas, this has been matched by an equivalent rise in carbon dioxide emissions. If commercial energy production were to continue to grow between 1995 and 2015 at the same

---

15 *World Resources 1996–97*, p. 284.

rate (in response to a parallel growth in demand), the growth in nuclear capacity to 3000 Gw(e) projected above could meet virtually the whole of that increase in demand. Or, in other words, an expansion of nuclear power (admittedly at the upper limits of what is probably feasible since it would ask that the world's main users of energy adopted nuclear power if not quite to the same proportionate extent as 1996 France, then to that of contemporary Spain) could permit fossil fuel combustion and hence carbon dioxide emissions to be frozen at the 1995 value for twenty years. Since commercial energy consumption in the OECD and transitional economies has virtually stopped rising, a high proportion of the mooted take up of the nuclear option might be expected to occur in the LDCs, where energy consumption continues to rise rapidly. Of course this would not rule out developed countries replacing older fossil-fuelled electricity generating capacity with nuclear, on a one for one basis. This would permit developed countries actually to reduce their carbon dioxide emissions.

Given, then, a projected high take up of nuclear energy in precisely those parts of the world where there are at present no (or very few) nuclear weapons, along with the clear links between nuclear energy and nuclear weapons, may this not be a case of getting out of the frying pan only to enter the fire?

Nuclear proliferation

The centrepiece of international anti-nuclear proliferation strategy is the nuclear non-proliferation treaty (NPT) which came into force in 1970. By 1995 and its Review Conference in New York the treaty had been endorsed by 178 states. The treaty, which had been originally given a probationary period of 25 years, was granted an indefinite extension of life by the Review Conference.

The treaty is a network of reciprocal bargains. International access to nuclear energy (equipment, fuel, technology) on the part of states not belonging to the class of acknowledged nuclear weapon states, is exchanged for promises to use nuclear facilities for peaceful purposes only. These promises are verified by periodic inspections of the nuclear installations of parties to the treaty by specialists employed by the IAEA. Treaty parties who already possessed nuclear weapons at the treaty's original coming into force (1970) complete the bargain by a promise to reduce their weapon stockpiles, or at any rate to restrain their growth. In

New York, a new commitment was accepted by the acknowledged nuclear weapon states (China less enthusiastic than the others) to aim to halt all nuclear weapon tests by 1996.

It is the first of these bargains that is our main concern here (the ending of the Cold War has removed most of the obstacles in the way of the fulfillment of the second bargain). It has proved difficult to restrict nuclear exports exclusively to signatories of the NPT. Not all potential exporters have always been 100 per cent supporters of the NPT. France and China did not sign it until 1992. Even when exporters have been thoroughly pro-NPT they have sometimes been willing to settle for *ad hoc* IAEA inspections of the nuclear facility or nuclear fuel delivery in question, without having the whole of the importer's declared nuclear facilities placed under safeguards, as would be the case were it a treaty party. Difficulty has also arisen when treaty parties and nonparties have claimed to have an inspection procedure already in place, possibly organised on a regional basis, and resisted the application of IAEA inspections for that reason. US pressure on fellow nuclear suppliers to bias their export policies in a restrictive direction (finding expression in particular, but not solely, in its hostility to the provision of reprocessing technology and reprocessing services) can reasonably be seen as an attempt to compensate for these perceived shortcomings of the treaty in practice.

US policy

However, US policy has never been as disinterested as that suggests, which in turn naturally encourages states with nuclear export industries to see behind official US policies the fell hand of US commercial interests. There has no doubt been a tendency, first made evident during the Cold War but still present, for US restrictive nuclear export policies to be quite selective. During the Afghanistan war, Pakistan's somewhat delinquent reputation in matters of nuclear proliferation was overlooked by the US government whose main concern was to build regional support for anti-Soviet forces. Israel's equal lack of dedication to the principles of non proliferation has never been allowed by Washington to stand in the way of warm bilateral relations. Iran, a signatory of the NPT in good standing, but a *bête noire* of US foreign policy, faced problems in 1995 in ordering nuclear reactors from Russia as a result of US objections on broad political grounds.

A basis for progress in meeting these difficulties was achieved in 1992 at the Warsaw meeting of the group of nuclear exporting states, a body with no standing with regard to the NPT itself and set up in 1974 as the London Suppliers' Group (with France as a member). The Warsaw meeting saw suppliers agree, amongst other things, to confine nuclear exports to states that were either parties to the NPT, or, if non-parties, to supply only on condition that the importing state accepted IAEA safeguards on all its nuclear installations.[16] Reaching such an agreement with international demand for nuclear energy in the doldrums is one thing. Whether it will be allowed to stand in the event of a new surge in orders for nuclear energy is another matter. It was the rise in orders in the wake of the 1970s oil crises that first brought the USA into sharp conflict with its co-exporters of nuclear equipment and materials. What reasons are there to think that a future expansion of demand for nuclear energy will be restrained only by the very reasonable Warsaw guidelines?

Proliferation and nuclear expansion

The ending of the Cold War indirectly provides one reason. Not only will Britain and France be as keen as ever to see exports of nuclear materials and services minimally restrained, but they will also be joined by Russia, looking to secure hard currency in exchange for products in which its industrial sector still possesses a comparative advantage. In addition, US confidence that Britain or even France would not in the Cold War period have wished to push any quarrel with Washington too far, cannot be what it was. Furthermore, the 1995 Review Conference of the NPT ratified a tendency for states that were historically hesitant about NPT membership either to accede to the NPT, or at least to accept IAEA safeguards. This tendency was reinforced by another, with regional non-proliferation arrangements in Latin America and Africa making their peace with the IAEA and aligning their safeguards procedures with those of the IAEA.[17]

A fourth reason derives from the passage of time since the last surge in demand for nuclear energy. During this period there has been further convergence of the opinion of good judges as to the design of nuclear reactor most appropriate to the efficient generation of electricity. This is

---

16 John Simpson, 'Nuclear arms control and an extended non-proliferation regime' in Stockholm International Peace Research Institute, *SIPRI Yearbook 1994*, (Oxford, Oxford University Press, 1994), p. 615.

17 Hans Blix, 'The IAEA, United Nations, and the new global nuclear agenda', *IAEA Bulletin*, Vol. 37, No 3, 1995, pp. 4, 5.

widely seen to be the advanced or improved pressurised water reactor, such as the British (but essentially US-designed) reactor Sizewell B, on stream in 1995, which is a long way from the dual-use (plutonium for bombs, electricity for power) British Calder design which became the model for the British Magnox stations.

Proliferation-proof reactors?

Some simple calculations bear this out. First, to produce the same amount of electricity, the APWR requires only half as much uranium feed as the Magnox type, although the APWR fuel requires slight enrichment in U-235.[18] Secondly, on producing electricity, to the extent of 1 Gw(e) over one complete year (which would be typical for a modern reactor), the APWR design produces about 300 kgs of plutonium. By comparison, a Magnox reactor of the same size would produce 1600 kgs of plutonium.[19] Lastly, not all plutonium is equally useful for military purposes. The most convenient is plutonium rich in the isotope Pu-239, of which about 6 kilogrammes are necessary for one bomb. The plutonium from a Magnox reactor is typically 80 per cent Pu-239. Plutonium from an APWR is 56 per cent Pu-239.[20]

None of these calculations imply that it is impossible for a state bent on acquiring plutonium for weapons purposes to do so via the purchase of an APWR. Rather it suggests that the most efficient power generating reactors available in the mid-1990s defend themselves against being diverted to military purposes a good deal more effectively than did the most efficient power generating reactors of a generation ago. Evidence that this view has currency even within the US government came in 1994. As part of an arrangement to secure the standing of North Korea as a state party to the NPT, the US arranged for the existing nuclear energy programme in that country, which was based on reactors with a family resemblance to the Magnox type, to be abandoned and for a new programme based on pressurised water reactors (or similar) to be put in its place. It is true that in addition the US successfully insisted that construction in North Korea of a fuel reprocessing plant should also be

18 Hills, 'Uranium supply', p. 83.

19 A. A. Farmer, 'Recycling of fuel', in W. Marshall, (ed.), *Nuclear Power Technology, Volume 2: Fuel Cycle*, p. 16.

20 Ibid., p. 17.

abandoned.[21]

Plutonium bomb route unfashionable

The final reason to expect fewer obstacles from non-proliferation considerations to a future upswing in demand for nuclear energy comes from increasing evidence that states wishing clandestinely to acquire nuclear weapons may prefer to avoid the plutonium route altogether in favour of enriched uranium. The two countries known beyond all doubt to have pursued a nuclear weapons programme in secrecy in recent years, Iraq, whilst a party to the NPT, and South Africa, whilst outside the treaty, both gave priority to uranium enrichment. In each case, the advantage of the uranium route seems to have been a greater inherent concealability than is offered by the alternative, which at a minimum requires a nuclear reactor of some sort and a means of reprocessing fuel. The technical difficulty of enriching uranium is eased considerably in practice when the quantities sought are very small, say 10 kilogrammes of highly enriched U-235 annually, and when the efficiency of the process is a secondary consideration.

South Africa seems to have employed a centrifuge technique but in a variant that has not found favour in the commercial enrichment field, presumably because of its inefficiencies.[22] South Africa, according to the statement of March 1993 by State President De Kleerk, had assembled six nuclear weapons out of a planned seven over the period 1974-1989.[23] Seven uranium bombs would require about 150 kilogrammes of highly enriched uranium.

The Iraqi programme was not originally owned up to. It was uncovered and indeed disrupted by the Gulf War of 1990/91. Once more the focus was on enriched uranium. But on this occasion there was no aspiration to the technical ingenuity shown by the South Africans. Instead Iraqi scientists merely replicated the extremely simple calutron (electromagnetic) technique first used for uranium enrichment during the Second World War in the USA. The simplicity of this method had never before been enough

---

21 Stockholm International Peace Research Institute, *SIPRI Yearbook 1994* (Oxford, Oxford University Press, 1994), p. 655.

22 South Africa probably employed a variant on the jet nozzle process originally developed at Oxford during the Second World War. See J. H. Tait, 'Uranium Enrichment', in W. Marshall (ed.), *Nuclear Power Technology, Volume 2: Fuel Cycle*, pp. 132, 136.

23 Speech transcript, *SIPRI Yearbook 1994*, pp. 631, 634.

to prevent its being seen as strictly something for the laboratory, within which its unsuitability for operations on even a semi-industrial scale had imprisoned it, or so it had been thought, as early as the 1940s.[24]

What the South African and Iraqi programmes also had in common was a lack of interest in diverting nuclear materials from the nuclear energy fuel cycle. This leaves open at least the possibility that the theoretical vulnerability of the nuclear fuel cycle and the plutonium economy to diversion, especially when reprocessing is involved, may have been overstated historically.

It is reasonable, taking all the above together, to anticipate that non-proliferation concerns may prove a negotiable obstacle to the sort of new spurt in nuclear energy that would be entailed in its substituting for fossil fuel globally to the same extent that it currently does in a small number of west European countries.

---

24 Tait, 'Uranium Enrichment', pp. 105, 106, gives a brief description under the title of 'the electromagnetic process'.

4 Nuclear Power and the Environment

However, the proliferation of nuclear weapons is not the only obstacle to the expansion of nuclear power.

If there has been a growth in the compatibility of nuclear energy and nuclear non-proliferation since the previous international surge in interest in nuclear energy on the heels of the oil crises of the 1970s, the apparent compatibility between nuclear energy and environmental protection has decreased. The lower boundary for the 1995 IAEA estimate for global installed nuclear capacity by the year 2015, as we have seen, stands at 370 Gigawatts (electrical) (Gw(e)). Actual installed capacity in 1995 was 340 Gw(e), with a further 39 Gw(e), according to the IAEA, under construction.[1] A simple sum shows immediately that the IAEA envisages the possibility that more nuclear reactors will be decommissioned than will be built in the period to 2015. With 109 nuclear reactors already on stream, the USA has only one on order. Britain, with 35 on stream (counting Sizewell B), has none on order. Sweden, with 12 on stream meeting more than 50 per cent of its electricity needs, has decided to phase

---

1 *IAEA Bulletin*, Vol. 37, No 3, 1995, p. 53.

out nuclear power entirely. Italy, which once had ten reactors at the official planning stage and beyond, now no longer generates any nuclear power at all (in spite of being almost entirely without domestic reserves of fossil fuels).

Part of the explanation for the pessimism of the IAEA projection certainly derives from an appreciation that the tendency within the OECD countries for economic growth to occur without an accompanying rise in commercial energy consumption may well continue indefinitely. In other words, decreasing energy intensity may have become a permanent feature of these economies. With no growth or even a fall in energy demand in the OECD countries, new nuclear capacity will be ordered only as existing electricity generating plant become obsolete. But another part of the explanation is an awareness that because of difficulties in setting norms nationally for environmentally acceptable levels of nuclear power, what replacement plant is built in place of existing fossil or nuclear fuelled plant that have reached the end of their working lives may be fossil fuelled rather than nuclear. It is extremely difficult to see the model global target of the previous chapter of freezing fossil fuel consumption at the 1995 level by 2015 being reached if it has to contend with, for example, the USA progressively replacing its 109 nuclear reactors with fossil fuelled plants. Not only would this affect the arithmetic (of how or where this new growth in fossil fuel dependence could be offset), but it would also prejudice the chances of nuclear power being taken seriously elsewhere.

Environmental impact of nuclear power

Nuclear power, like any other commercial power source, has an environmental impact at three points: the mining or extraction of the fuel, and its transport; the consumption of the fuel at the site of the power station; and the disposal of the waste products associated with the consumption of the fuel. But before any sensible comparative assessment may be made between the environmental impact of nuclear and that of fossil fuels, it is essential first to return to the idea of radioactivity.

Nuclear power, as we have seen, relies on the fact that one isotope of uranium, uranium-235, is unstable. It can fission spontaneously and fissions very readily when struck by neutrons. It is unstable in another way besides. It and the more abundant naturally occurring isotope U-238 are both subject to radioactive decay. They are only slightly unstable in this respect (otherwise uranium would all have decayed before mankind had the opportunity to notice its existence), but unstable enough during the lifetime of the Earth to have given rise to a number of daughter (and granddaughter etc.) products which are found in the ground, normally, close to uranium deposits.   These are generations of new unstable elements, progressively less heavy than the generation before from which they have been given birth by radioactive decay – in this case essentially the emission of a particularly heavy sub-nuclear particle called an alpha particle (on a scale where the hydrogen nucleus weighs in at 1 and the uranium-238 nucleus, by definition, 238, the alpha particle stands at 4). Eventually, eight generations of alpha particle emitting descendants later, uranium-238 is transmuted into a stable element, lead-206. It is because uranium-238 itself is only very slightly unstable, taking 4.5 billion years for half of any given amount to have emitted an alpha particle and to begin the sequence of begetting daughter products, whilst the daughter products themselves are significantly more unstable, that uranium-238 and its radioactive descendants are found together in nature.

Natural radioactivity

Uranium and its daughter products, together with a closely similar element thorium-232 (the similarity, as noted above, is close enough to allow it to be substituted for uranium-238 in nuclear reactors) and its daughter products, form the single largest source of natural radioactivity to which the inhabitants of Britain are exposed.   Natural radiation from other sources, including cosmic rays, total about 90 millirems a year (see appendix to this chapter for a brief discussion of units of radiation): uranium and thorium plus their daughter products add a further 100 millirems. Of this added amount 80 millirems comes from one particular radioactive daughter product, radon, which is a gas and capable of escaping from rock formations. In confined spaces it is easily breathed into the lungs.[2]

Leaving radon out of the picture, because it is not unavoidable, the average exposure to natural radioactivity in Britain is 110 millirems per annum.   In Aberdeen, inhabitants meet with higher exposures, at 130

---

2 Reliance for radiation data, particularly for Britain, is placed in P. A. H. Saunders & B. O. Wade, 'Radiation and its Control', in W. Marshall (ed.), *Nuclear Power Technology Volume 3: Nuclear Radiation*, (Oxford, Clarendon Press, 1983), pp. 1, 49.

millirems per annum; in London, lower, at 90 millirems. The difference is entirely due to the fact that Aberdeen buildings are frequently constructed of the local stone – granite – which has a relatively high concentration of uranium and thorium.

As we have seen, in spite of Aberdonian granite, Britain has no commercially worthwhile deposits of uranium or thorium, unlike a number of other parts of the world (original small Cornish deposits have long since been worked out to provide uranium for the Victorian decorative glass industry). In parts of the world where such exploitable deposits of uranium or thorium do exist, local inhabitants are exposed to comparatively high natural levels of radioactivity. Again omitting radon, whilst the US average exposure is 100 millirems per annum, exposures in Colorado, a uranium-rich area, are as high as 250 millirems per annum.

These levels of exposure are natural in the sense that humans have been exposed to them throughout history. But this does not imply that they are unalterable. Radon exposure is a natural hazard of living in draught-free houses built in parts of the country where the bedrock contains some uranium. Minor structural modifications in such cases can virtually eliminate radon build-up. As we have seen, an allowance for radon exposure brings British average exposure levels up from 110 mrem per annum to 190 mrem per annum. If every house at risk were fitted with anti-radon devices, average exposure would obviously drop, and exposures for persons actually living in houses with radon build-up would drop even more. Such devices do exist and can be fitted cheaply but public interest in them is very low.

Radon exposure is natural but largely avoidable. In addition to natural radiation, the British public (not untypical of the population of any developed country) accepts on average a further exposure every year to about 50 mrem of radiation arising chiefly from medical and dental X-rays and radiotherapeutic treatment.

Low level radiation and health

Because some radiation exposure is natural it does not follow that it is safe. After some original hesitation within the epistemic community (comprised of what would today be called health physicists), when there seemed to be a possibility that very low levels of radiation (i.e. comparable to natural levels) were completely harmless, there has been convergence since the 1950s on the more conservative view that even low doses of radiation carry two sorts of risks to human health. The first is the risk to the person exposed of a fatal cancer induced (often after a delay of tens of years) by the radiation. The second is a risk of damage to the exposed person's genetic material, expressing itself in the form of inherited disease or disability to subsequent offspring of the exposed person. It is usually assumed that protection from the first risk automatically ensures protection from the second.

The size of the cancer risk is estimated at 125 fatal cancers for every 'million person rem' of accumulated dose over a lifetime.[3] So, taking the British average exposure as 110 mrems per annum, over a lifetime of 70 years, each inhabitant will accumulate 7.7 rems.   Over the whole population of 58 millions, this comes to 447 million person rems, which will give rise to $447 \times 125 = 56,000$ (approximately) fatal cancers. Since about one fifth of the British population die of cancer of some kind anyway, the radiation induced cancer total has to be compared with deaths from cancer of all kinds at 11.5 million, approximately.

We can recast the figures of the preceding paragraph. In Britain 58,000 persons die in an average month (British crude death rate is 12 per thousand per year). Of those, 11,500 die from cancer. Of the cancer deaths, 56 are attributable to natural radiation (assuming average exposure is 110 mrems per annum). If we took a rough and ready critical loads approach to the assessment of what additional levels of radiation might constitute a substantial change to the natural level as a few per cent, a five per cent increase in exposure to radiation would produce an additional exposure over the lifetime of an average person of less than half a rem and would lead to an additional number of 3 cancer deaths per month. A ten per cent increase would lead to an extra 6 cancer deaths per month.

But because 58,000 Britons die every month only on average and one fifth of the deaths are from cancer only on average, in reality there is considerable fluctuation in monthly figures. The fluctuation is not so great that the lives saved by the disappearance of all natural radiation (could that be conjured up) would not be noticed. But it is great enough to render statistically invisible the effect of small reductions or increases in the radiation background. A ten per cent increase in the radiation background with 6 extra cancer deaths a month would be on the threshold of statistical invisibility. A five per cent increase (or decrease) would be invisible in its effects. So the argument from critical loads would take the form of an

---

3 Saunders and Wade, 'Radiation and its control', p. 12.

uncertainty principle.   Reducing the contribution to the radiation background coming from nuclear energy much below ten per cent would be irrational since the returns on the expenditure involved would be too small to measure.

ICRP norms for radiation exposure

Norms for acceptable levels of exposure to radiation from and within the nuclear power industry and other undertakings where employed personnel or the general public may be exposed to radiation have been discussed internationally since 1934.   It is interesting to note that the first occupational limit was set at ten per cent of the dose that produced visible effects (skin burns) from an X-ray machine. This corresponded more or less to a permitted occupational exposure of about 50,000 mrem a year. In 1934 the International Commission on Radiological Protection (ICRP), representing the epistemic community, set the occupational limit at 70,000 mrem a year. This limit was in force until 1950, when the ICRP reduced it to 15,000 mrem a year. In 1953 the ICRP set limits for the exposure of the general public to radiation at 10 per cent of the permitted occupational exposure. In 1956 new, lower limits were set, at 5000 mrem a year for employees and, hence, 500 mrem a year for the general public. 1990 saw lower limits still, at 2000 mrem for occupational exposure and, with the old ten per cent rule now changed into a five per cent rule, 100 mrem a year for the general public.[4]   Earlier, in 1977, the ICRP had added qualitative recommendations to the effect that 'radiation doses should be as low as reasonably achievable (ALARA), economic and social factors being taken into consideration'.[5]

British practice and that in other countries with substantial nuclear power programmes has been to accept the ICRP guidelines.

What are we to make of these? First, the setting of higher permissible levels of exposure to radiation for workers in jobs where some radiation exposure is to be anticipated (including the nuclear industry) than for the general public seems simple common sense. Workers in such jobs have presumably accepted the associated risks voluntarily and this may indeed be reflected in the going rate for the job (workers are recompensed for the

---

4 Abel J. Gonzalez, 'Radiation Safety: New International Standards', *IAEA Bulletin*, Vol. 36, No 2, 1994, pp. 2, 11.

5 Saunders and Wade, 'Radiation and its Control', p. 18.

risk, in other words). However, the reasoning behind the set exposure levels for the general public seems to be no more than that it should be an 'order of magnitude' less. Secondly, the ICRP has constantly adjusted its safe levels of exposure downwards, albeit at a declining rate. Whilst this in one sense simply shows that the epistemic community is capable of learning from experience, it also shows that the record of the ICRP has invariably been to underestimate the dangers of radiation, casting doubt on the efficacy of its theoretical models of the interconnection between illness and radiation exposure. Thirdly, the 1990 figure for permissible levels of exposure for the general public is very high compared to our own 'order of magnitude' model, that anticipates environmental problems whenever waste flows exceed about 10 per cent of the natural level.

Against this, actual practice in the British nuclear industry has been to limit occupational and general public exposures to levels well within ICRP recommendations. Of course pure chance plays as much part in this as virtue, since Britain does not mine any uranium. Uranium mining is relatively hazardous by dint particularly of exposure of miners to radon. Transport of uranium once mined, by contrast, has very little environmental impact by comparison with fossil fuel chiefly because the very high energy density of uranium means that relatively little transportation occurs. However, only France can be said to have a complete 'cradle to grave' nuclear programme, from mining at one end to fuel reprocessing at the other.

Categories of radiation exposure

Occupational and general public exposure to radiation from the nuclear industry can best be understood if it is first broken down into categories. The first cleavage is between exposures arising from normal day to day running of the nuclear plant in question, and those arising from an accident of some kind. The second cleavage is between nuclear plant in the form of nuclear power reactors and ancillary nuclear plant involved in the preparation and reprocessing of fuel for the reactors.

To a good approximation, the risks of radiation exposure consequent on an accident are very low in the case of ancillary plant but higher in the case of reactors. By contrast, radiation exposures arising from routine day to day operation are high in the case of ancillary plant, particularly reprocessing plant, but low in the case of nuclear reactors. Indeed, average public airborne exposure to radiation resulting from the routine operation of a modern nuclear reactor is so small (less than one twentieth of a millirem per year) that it is probably less than the radiation received by the public from the normal operation of a coal-fired power station (as a result of trace amounts of radium-226, a uranium and thorium daughter product, in coal).[6] But radiation has other pathways, especially water. The Magnox nuclear reactor at Trawsfynydd in North Wales (which would not be classed as a modern design and was closed down in 1991) exposed some of the local population to radiation doses amounting to 15 mrem per year. These doses were experienced by persons who customarily ate fish caught in the eponymous lake from which the reactor also drew cooling water.

This difference between average public exposure to radiation and maximum exposures that may be experienced in the immediate locality of a nuclear power station is echoed, but raised an octave, when we consider reprocessing plants. Average public exposure to radiation in Britain arising from the operation of nuclear fuel reprocessing plants (especially the plant in Cumbria at the former Windscale, now Sellafield) is only one quarter of a mrem per year. But maximum exposures can be very much greater. Cumbrian residents eating fish and shellfish caught in coastal waters experienced doses in 1975 and 1976 as high as 220 mrem a year.[7] This was over 40 per cent of the ICRP limit in force at the time and over 100 per cent of the natural background. Since then the Sellafield plant has changed its procedures and reduced its discharges of 'low level' radioactive waste into the sea to about one third of this level. If this is translated into a new maximum dose of 70 mrem a year it is now 70 per cent of the new 1990 ICRP limit.

'Not in my backyard' explained

This difference (by about a factor of 500, typically) between average exposures to radiation from the normal operation of nuclear plant and maximum exposures – the latter almost invariably experienced in the immediate locality of the plant – by itself does much to explain the so-called 'not in my backyard' (NIMBY) syndrome. It may be thoroughly

---

6   T. F. Johns, 'Environmental Pathways of Radioactivity to Man' in W. Marshall, (ed.), *Nuclear Power Technology Volume 3: Nuclear Radiation*, p. 209.

7   Ibid., p. 190.

rational for the British public both to conclude that nuclear power is safe and environmentally benign and to object to any nuclear plant being built in their locality.

The arithmetic also explains something else, namely the reputation for adverse environmental impact enjoyed by nuclear reprocessing plants. Compared to nuclear reactors, in the British experience, both maximum (local) radiation exposures and average exposures arising from nuclear reprocessing plant are higher by about a factor of ten. The argument that nuclear fuel should be reprocessed coming from considerations of possible restrictions on the supply of uranium contends with an argument against reprocessing coming from adverse environmental impact.

Nuclear waste

Of course, only plutonium and uranium are actually reprocessed. Irradiated fuel elements (containers), as we have seen, also contain highly radioactive fission products. These constitute radioactive waste. The mechanical and chemical processes of extracting plutonium and uranium from spent fuel elements also create wastes, usually of lower radioactivity.

The waste produced is normally scheduled for indefinite storage, after suitable packaging, provided sites sufficiently isolated from the environment can be identified. The total volume of waste arising from the reprocessing of the fuel associated with the production of 1 Gw(e) for one year (the power produced by a typical modern nuclear power station) is about 1800 cubic metres (about the volume of two semi-detached 3 bedroom houses).

In Britain it has been customary to classify wastes after reprocessing under four headings, arranged by how 'hotly' radioactive they are. The categories are high level waste; two categories (one made up of long-lived radioactive materials, the other of shorter-lived) of intermediate level waste; and the final category of low level waste.

High level waste

High level waste exists in very small quantities. If total annual waste from 1 Gw(e) occupies two houses, the high level waste, after packaging, could almost be fitted into the householders' baths. However, high level waste is extremely radioactive: so much so that it is literally hot. It is packaged by dissolving it within glass which in turn is poured into tall (3 metres by about 50 centimetres) stainless steel bottles, where it solidifies. These bottles then are stored in concrete racks, around which air is circulated. The concrete protects the surroundings from radioactive emissions and the circulating air draws away the considerable heat that the radioactive decay processes continue to generate inside the bottles. Each bottle generates heat to the equivalent of 10 single bar electric fires, although radioactive decay reduces this by a factor of ten after about 75 years. Obviously this type of supervised waste disposal is better thought of as storage.

At some point, when they have cooled sufficiently, unsupervised storage (i.e. disposal) of these bottles can be contemplated. An underground geologically stable repository, highly impermeable to water is normally thought to be called for.

Interestingly, there is very little practical difference between the storage of high level waste after reprocessing and the indefinite storage of spent reactor fuel elements without reprocessing, except that in the latter case there would be a larger volume to contend with. Whilst storage techniques would not need to be quite as elaborate, watch would need to be kept for damaged fuel elements, from which radioactive leaks could occur.

The difference between a once through use of uranium and reprocessing in terms of environmental impact does not, then, lie with high level waste. It does arise when we come to deal with the other two headings of waste. Technically, even here it is a matter of degree. The same categories of waste would arise, on a smaller scale, even in the complete absence of reprocessing. But reprocessing, as we shall see, leads to a great increase in the volume generated.

Low level waste

It is convenient to consider first low level waste in its solid, liquid and gaseous forms.

The solid part of this waste is created in considerable bulk and arises from the day to day operation of a nuclear power programme. It consists of such things as 'miscellaneous trash from laboratories, reprocessing plant and reactor operating areas, consisting of clothing, paper, equipment, scrap metal, tools ... often only suspect or slightly contaminated with radioactivity.'[8] Even when this waste is mechanically compressed into small volumes (an oil drum as full of contaminated clothing as human packing would permit can be sealed and mechanically compressed to less than one tenth of its original volume), there is no question of its radioactivity giving rise to heat.

If disposal of this category of waste has to be arranged in principle even where there is no reprocessing, it is safe to assume that where reprocessing occurs it is responsible for a large fraction of the low level waste arising from a nuclear programme. Indeed, Keen gives figures for the liquid and gaseous low level wastes which show the ratio to be about 10 to 1 between the annual waste flows from a reprocessing plant and those of the reactor which is the source of the spent fuel (this ratio makes sense as a guide only when British reprocessing plant is serving British reactors only, it will rise whenever Britain reprocesses fuel for overseas customers).[9] It is the direct emission, after treatment, of some or all of these gaseous and liquid low level wastes into the atmosphere or lakes or coastal waters that give rise to the average and localised exposures to radioactivity from the British nuclear power programme.

Safe disposal of solid low level waste is thought to be achievable through burial in shallow (1 metre deep) trenches, provided there is no pathway for any water present to enter human drinking supplies. This is not necessarily a trivial matter to arrange, and until stopped eventually by international pressure (other states party to the London Dumping Convention had agreed in 1983 to an informal ban on dumping radioactive waste at sea, although this was not to lead to an actual amendment to the Convention until 1994) the British practice was to dump some of this class of waste at sea.

Intermediate level waste

For every cubic metre of high level waste, 30 or 40 cubic metres are created of each of two sub-categories of intermediate waste. These categories are both different from high level waste in that they are not literally hot and therefore more easily stored and disposed of, at least in

---

8 N. J. Keen, 'The Management of Radioactive Waste from Civil Nuclear Power Generation', in W. Marshall (ed.) *Nuclear Power Technology Volume 2: Fuel Cycle*, (Oxford, Clarendon Press, 1983), p. 297.

9 Ibid., p. 297.

principle. They are distinguished from each other by the fact that one contains elements (actinides, which include traces of plutonium) which will remain radioactive for an extremely long time (more than 1000 years), whereas the other will lose its radioactivity much more quickly. Again, it seems probable that having reprocessing as part of a nuclear programme increases the volume of intermediate level waste arising by about a factor of ten.

The differences between the two types of intermediate waste are reflected in the options for disposal. The long-lived variety might most naturally be disposed of alongside high level waste, once the latter has cooled. The short-lived variety would obviously need less elaborate arrangements, although something more than those considered appropriate for solid low level waste.

Setting norms for nuclear waste disposal in Britain

In Britain, setting the norms for the disposal of radioactive wastes in the low level and intermediate categories has proved extremely problematic. The trans-scientific problem of selecting appropriate storage sites whilst winning the support or acquiescence of the local populations of the areas chosen cannot be said as of 1996 to be solved.

The problem essentially acquired political visibility at the end of the 1970s after the OPEC-engineered rises in oil price. It was anticipated that there would be further growth in the size of the British nuclear programme, including the probable construction of a 'commercial demonstration fast reactor' to enter service in the 1990s. Conventional nuclear reactors were officially expected to expand from providing 7.4 Gw(e) in 1980 to 19.7 Gw(e) by 1995.[10] In the upshot, by 1995, the fast breeder had been reduced to a transnational research programme and conventional reactors were generating only 12.9 Gw(e).

The expected growth in capacity raised at first simply practical concerns over the disposal of low level and intermediate level nuclear wastes. Being more bulky than high level wastes, storing the wastes indefinitely on or near the reprocessing plant (on site) seemed less sensible than catering explicitly and immediately for their disposal. Rather than having to build (eventually) two sets of safe means of storage/disposal, it would be more economic (and safer, environmentally) to build only one, for

---

10 Hills, 'Uranium Supply', p. 93.

disposal only. In addition there was thought to be something of a hurry since existing on site storage facilities would soon be full up. Very curiously, as a result of a report on nuclear power from the Royal Commission on Environmental Pollution (Flowers Report) in 1976[11] which broadly cautioned against going ahead with nuclear expansion before a method existed for securing indefinitely the self-containment of *high* level wastes, the government began by exploring high level disposal options, including the investigation of possible sites around the country.

High level waste and the puzzle of Flowers

Given the scientific representation on Flowers's committee, this was puzzling advice, based on a carelessly drawn up model for the long term handling of nuclear waste which would not survive its first contact with the real world. There was not really the hurry over high level waste that there was over other waste categories. High level waste, as we have seen, requires supervised storage on site for about 30 years before disposal can even be considered.[12] A sophisticated on site storage system is inescapably required and the relatively small volume of high level waste means that keeping it on site even for more than 30 years if necessary could do very little harm to the nuclear economy. The real priority was for the safe disposal of low level and intermediate level wastes.

By 1981 the search for a suitable high level waste disposal site was abandoned. It is hard to say whether this was simply because the good sense of the above paragraph had already made itself felt or the good sense itself came about as a result of a rethink forced by unexpected public opposition to consideration being given to placing such a site in Scotland.[13]

A new body, Nirex, owned jointly by the three bodies then responsible for running nuclear reactors and fuel reprocessing plant respectively (the Central Electricity Generating Board, the South of Scotland Electricity Generating Board and British Nuclear Fuels (BNFL)), plus the UK Atomic

---

11 Royal Commission on Environmental Pollution 6th Report (Sir Brian Flowers, Chairman) 'Nuclear Power and the Environment', (Flowers Report), Cmnd 6618, (London, HMSO, 1975-76).

12 Keen, 'The Management of Radioactive Waste from Civil Nuclear Power Generation', p. 320.

13 Ray Kemp, *The Politics of Radioactive Waste Disposal*, (Manchester, Manchester University Press, 1992), p. 39. Kemp's book is a useful guide to the dizzying swings in government policy over the disposal of radioactive waste.

Energy Authority, was set up in 1982 with the explicit remit to explore possible sites for the long term disposal of intermediate and low level waste. In 1983 it announced that it had secured a deep site in Billingham (near Stockton-on-Tees) for storage of long-lived intermediate waste and a (shallow) site at Elstow (Bedfordshire) for low level waste and short-lived intermediate waste. Local public protest led the owner of the Billingham site, ICI (its Billingham division a long term private sector pillar of the British nuclear programme but now Brutus to the government's Caesar), to withdraw their offer. This and the decision in 1984 by the National Union of Seamen to 'black' the disposal of nuclear waste (low level mainly) at sea forced another shift in policy.

The government decided in 1985 to abandon consideration of the disposal of long-lived intermediate waste for the time being and to concentrate on finding alternative shallow sites for short-lived intermediate and low level wastes. Nirex identified three such sites in addition to Elstow, which also meant three new local protest movements.

In 1986 the government announced that all intermediate level waste would now be disposed of in deep sites but failed to pacify local protests in the areas identified for shallow sites (now to contain only low level waste). In 1987 the government retreated and decided to treat all intermediate and some at least low level waste alike and to dispose of it together in a deep site not qualitatively very different from the sort of site that would eventually be needed for high level waste.

By 1995 the search for the combined deep site had narrowed to a region near Sellafield (between Sellafield and Gosforth in west Cumbria). This will take all intermediate level waste plus some low level waste: the rest of the low level waste will go for shallow disposal at Drigg, also near Sellafield.[14]

Unsustainable solution

This is not a sustainable solution. Low level waste and short-lived intermediate level waste by definition need less elaborate and costly insulation from the environment than is needed by long-lived intermediate waste. But British policy is now to lavish the same high degree of containment facilities on all three categories of non-high level waste, apart

---

14 Nigel Monckton, 'Ready for the UK Rock Lab', *Atom*, No 436, September/October 1994, pp. 22, 27.

from the portion of the low level category assigned to Drigg. The cost of elaborate underground disposal for long-lived intermediate level waste is unavoidable. But extending the same facilities to the additional volumes of short-lived intermediate and most especially low level wastes (when costs of buildings, even when 700 metres underground as proposed by Nirex, are proportional to volume) is not consistent with an economically competitive nuclear programme. The British waste disposal plan is echoed only in Sweden, where some low level waste and short-lived intermediate level wastes are both accorded elaborate deep disposal 50 metres below the Baltic seabed. But in 1980 the Swedes decided after a referendum that they would abandon nuclear power by 2010. France, by contrast, limits deep disposal to the long-lived category of intermediate level waste (apart from the small volumes of high level waste). The Billingham problem is unknown in France. According to a Nirex spokesman,[15] 'four potential locations [for deep disposal of long-lived intermediate level waste in France] have been announced drawn from *volunteer* regions with adequate geology' (emphasis added).

Nuclear accidents

The Swedes voted to abandon nuclear power in the aftermath of the notorious accident to the US PWR reactor at Three Mile Island near Harrisburg in Pennsylvania.

In March 1979 one of the units at this two reactor station accidentally lost some of the cooling water that normally circulates around the fuel elements and conveys the heat produced within the elements to the steam generating plant.[16] This exposed the tops of some of the fuel elements and at the high temperatures prevailing, the metal cladding of the fuel elements (a zirconium alloy) chemically reacted with steam. This naturally dissolved the fuel cladding, allowing volatile (meaning compounds usually solid or liquid but easily capable of becoming gaseous) and gaseous radioactive fission products normally contained within the fuel elements to escape. The most dangerous of these fission products is the volatile solid iodine-131, which is a reactive element readily taken up by the human

---

15 Ibid., p. 26.

16 J. G. Collier, 'Light Water Reactors', in W. Marshall (ed.), *Nuclear Power Technology Volume 1: Reactor Technology*, (Oxford, Clarendon Press, 1983), pp. 274, 275.

body where it concentrates (alongside natural iodine) in the thyroid gland. It is in fact customary to measure the size of a nuclear reactor accident by the amount of iodine-131 released into the locality. The amount of iodine-131 released at Three Mile Island seems to have been about 10 curies (see Appendix).[17]

In April 1986 an even more serious accident occurred at Chernobyl in the Ukraine (then part of the Soviet Union) when one unit of a four reactor nuclear power station caught fire and burned for 10 days.[18] Fission products were released into the atmosphere and deposited downwind, to the north and west, as radioactive fallout. Iodine-131 in particular was released in large quantities – 10 million curies, approximately. This may be compared with the Windscale fire of 1957, when 20,000 curies of iodine were released (as with the very much smaller Windscale pile, graphite was implicated in the fire at Chernobyl). Exposure in the Chernobyl case was again chiefly a matter for the immediately nearby population, some of whom were evacuated, but some escaping radioactivity crossed international boundaries. Ten years later the consequences of iodine began to show up as an increased incidence of thyroid cancers among the surrounding population, particularly in children. There are indications that this incidence (and likely subsequent deaths) may both be more widespread (reaching into Belarus and Russia) and showing up sooner than current scientific understanding would seem to predict.[19]

A perfectly safe nuclear reactor is unlikely ever to be built.[20] Real reactors present a risk of accidental death to near by populations (and a smaller risk to populations further afield). If this risk to the locality can be made small enough to be acceptable (which on grounds of consistency we postulate as 5 or 10 per cent at most of the natural background risk) it will be even smaller to the population at large.

---

17 Hans. A. Bethe, *The Road from Los Alamos*, (New York, American Institute of Physics, 1991), p. 216, implies rather than states that about 10 curies of iodine-131 were released, but states that no caesium-137 was released at all.

18 L. A. Ilyin and O. A. Pavlovskij, 'Radiological consequences of the Chernobyl accident in the Soviet Union and measures taken to mitigate their impact', *IAEA Bulletin*, Vol. 29, No 4, 1987, p. 17.

19 F-N. Flakus, 'Radiation in Perspective: Improving Comprehension of Risks', *IAEA Bulletin*, Vol. 37, No 2, 1995, p. 11.

20 The discussion of risk in this section owes a great deal to G. H. Kinchin, 'Risk assessment' in W. Marshall (ed.), *Nuclear Power Technology, Volume 3: Nuclear Radiation*, pp. 217, 235.

Setting norms for acceptable risk

What is the background risk? It is taken here to be the risk of premature death arising outwith the control of the individual. Obviously this includes things like being killed by lightning, but the risk of this is extremely low (one chance in 5 million in a year). Other risks of accidental death should obviously be included. The total risk of accidental death for a British citizen is about 1 in 3000 in a year and is largely independent of the age of the individual.[21]   Some of these risks are run in the course of an occupation or lie in some other way more or less within the individual's control, so ought not to form part of the background risk.

The chief cause of accidental death in Britain and the USA is death on the roads (US roads are twice as dangerous). Of these deaths about one half are passive, i.e. pedestrians killed by the actions of others as a side effect of their using the roads for motor transport. If we estimate that half of all accidental deaths are similarly passively run, this puts the background risk of accidental death at 1 in 6000 in a year. Five per cent of this is 1 in 120,000 or 8 chances in one million.

The Farmer criterion for reactor safety

In Britain the benchmark for reactor safety is the Farmer criterion which seeks to set design limits for the accidental release of iodine-131. A reactor that lost most of its coolant would soon see its fuel elements ruptured which would allow gaseous and volatile fission products to escape. The worst accident conceived of by the Farmer criterion involves the escape of 10 per cent of all the iodine-131 in the reactor fuel elements into the surrounding environment (the Chernobyl accident involved at least this much;[22] recent estimates, in fact, put the release at 50 per cent and deaths from thyroid cancer at 4000, eventually). For a 1 Gw(e) reactor this would amount to 10 million curies of radioactive iodine. The Farmer target for reactor design would limit the probability of this very large and alarming sort of accident happening to one reactor to 1 year in 10 million, on average. Smaller accidental releases become more likely the smaller they are but at a progressively diminishing rate, so that a release of 10

---

21 Kinchin, 'Risk assessment', p. 220. The Flowers Report, p. 77, gives a higher figure (1 in 2000).

22 *The Economist*, March 9, 1996, p. 119.

curies of iodine-131 is judged to be an event that may occur once in one hundred years in a reactor designed to Farmer standards. Roughly translated this means that by the Farmer criterion a Three Mile Island accident or its equivalent might occur in the United States about once a year (in 1995, the USA had 109 commercial reactor units in operation). In fact the safety standards of US reactors at the time seem to have been more lax than the Farmer criterion, with small accidents (Three Mile Island and smaller) anticipated to occur slightly more frequently and larger accidents perhaps ten times more frequently.[23] Since then, however, US reactors have been re-engineered to higher safety standards.

Kinchin calculates that the Farmer criterion translates into a probability of delayed death (from thyroid cancer) in any one year due to iodine-131 uptake of about 3 in 100,000 for persons living in the semi-urban neighbourhood of a typical British commercial reactor (neighbourhood translates as a radius of 15 miles or 24 kilometres either side of the reactor complex: US usage has neighbourhood extending to 20 miles).

Reactors designed to meet the Farmer criterion more or less also meet ICRP standards for reactor safety.[24]

Risks presented by a reactor safe by Farmer/ICRP criteria

A risk of death of 3 in 100,000 or 30 parts in a million is 10 to 15 per cent of the passive background risk as derived above and by a crude order of magnitude critical loads approach probably only on the margin of acceptability. Pessimism about its acceptability may be justified by a further calculation. The risk in Britain of being killed in a road accident as a pedestrian (1990 figures) is 30 chances in a million. Asking people to accept a nuclear reactor in their locality is equivalent to asking that they accept, in their role as pedestrians, roads half as safe as those in the rest of the country (or a turning back of the road safety clock for pedestrians by about 30 years). Anyone with the slightest experience of local politics in semi-urban parts of Britain will know that agitation for improvements in the safety of roads for pedestrians is almost a daily fact of life, indicating that the apparently small risk involved is perceived as

---

23 The 1975 Rasmussen report is taken as a guide to the safety of US reactors at the time, although this in turn was criticised for excessive optimism. For the comparison with Farmer, see Saunders and Wade, 'Radiation and its control', p. 46.

24 G. H. Kinchin, 'Risk assessment', p. 231.

significant.

It may be objected that while the background risk (including being run over by a bus) is the risk of more or less immediate death from an accident, deaths arising from releases of iodine-131 (and other volatile fission products such as caesium-137) are delayed deaths, by ten years or more. It could be claimed that such deaths, like debts falling due some time in the future, are more tolerable by reason of the delay, but it is hard to see how to put a figure on this. Even if this were possible, an offset in the opposite direction might be deemed right because of the tendency for radiation-induced deaths to strike disproportionately at the younger section of the population, as the Chernobyl experience seems to be bearing out.

Without any 'discounting' for the delay, then, it does seem clear that persons living in the vicinity of a nuclear reactor designed to be safe by the Farmer criterion run a new passive risk to life clearly smaller than those they already run, but not so much smaller as to be comfortably below the threshold of concern. Persons living away from the immediate vicinity are also exposed to risks, but these are smaller and have been calculated by US specialists for the US case.[25] For persons living outside the immediate neighbourhood of the reactor, in a zone out to a radius of 800 kilometres (500 miles) from the reactor site, iodine-131 ceases to be the main problem, partly because it decays very quickly, and the other relatively volatile but longer lived fission product, caesium-137, becomes important. Interestingly, the expected number of deaths from a reactor accident in the immediate neighbourhood (15 to 20 miles radius) arising from iodine-131 is roughly the same as those due to caesium-137 in the wider zone. But since the wider zone has an area 500 times that of the inner zone and hence a population roughly 500 times greater, the individual risk from a reactor accident is lower by one five hundredth, and well below the threshold of concern as defined in this section (that this factor of 500 is the same as that encountered above for the difference in exposures to routine releases of radioactivity between local residents and the population at large is not wholly coincidental).

Outside the OECD: Chernobyl

However, all this assumes that reactors are always built to meet the Farmer criteria or something similar. In the OECD countries, there is no

---

25 Bethe, *The Road from Los Alamos*, pp. 206, 217.

real evidence that reactor safety standards are significantly worse than the Farmer criteria. Indeed, safety is possibly on an improving trend, to the extent that improvements can be made retrospectively to older designs (this has fortunately been true, as hinted above, of US reactors since the Three Mile Island accident). Outside the OECD things are different. The Chernobyl accident, it will be recalled, represented (at a minimum) the largest accident that Farmer could imagine and was expected by him to occur only once in ten million reactor years. That is to say, in a world with 200 reactors built to Farmer safety standards, such an accident could be expected to occur only once in 50,000 years. In practice, with, on average, about 200 commercial nuclear reactors in operation since 1956, there has been one such accident already.

Statistically speaking, the fact of the Chernobyl accident could mean that a very rare event has indeed occurred once and that in itself is no evidence for its being less rare than estimated by the Farmer criteria. But in practice nobody could be blamed for perceiving it differently. In fact, it seems clear that the Chernobyl reactor was designed without the air-tight containment shell obligatory for commercial reactors in the OECD countries and was almost certainly therefore not designed to Farmer safety standards or anything remotely comparable.

Resistance to nuclear power on environmental grounds and the hardening of this resistance after the Chernobyl accident is not to be wondered at especially where populations living near nuclear facilities are concerned. Local populations are expected to tolerate discernable increases in the hostility of their immediate environment on behalf of their fellow citizens, who on average live further from nuclear installations and do not have to bear this tax in kind.

Progress in France

What is the way forward, if the hurdle posed by environmental considerations is not to prove insuperable? There would seem to be two mutually compatible possibilities for progress. The more obvious is to recognise that the Farmer criterion is probably too lax and should be tightened by a factor of ten. Similarly, permitted routine releases of radioactivity from nuclear reprocessing have also been too high, especially when water-borne routes are involved.

The second possibility, which can be pursued in parallel with the first, seems to have been tried out with some success in France. The relative success of France in making the transition to maximal nuclear substitution for fossil fuel owes something to an official recognition that populations living close to a nuclear facility should simply be compensated for the risks they run on behalf of the national community. This is version of the principle that the polluter should pay. Thus one reason why the French authorities are faced not by protest groups but by local representatives volunteering nuclear waste disposal sites is that central government rewards the inhabitants of the locality chosen. Thus, according to Kemp:[26]

> the three small communities close to the new site [for shallow disposal of nuclear waste] in the Aube [department about 100km south-east of Paris] will receive a capital payment of 30 million francs (1984 prices) plus 1 million francs per annum. These are seen as 'natural' economic benefits ... to help with the local infrastructure, the provision of better medical services and school buildings, for example ...

Any awkwardness that some sort of bribe may be involved is dispelled by the fact that it is not unusual in France for local firms to make contributions to regional exchequers. In other countries compensation of this kind is not unknown but it is always disguised as something else. In Britain, the compensation is the spurt to the local economy consequent on the employment generated by the construction of the nuclear facility in question. The difficulty here, of course, is that in localities where employment is already high this is a mixed blessing. In any case the boost to local employment is strictly temporary since the manpower required in the construction phase of any nuclear facility is very much greater than that needed to service its day to day operation. The French approach avoids both of these drawbacks.

An ideal solution for Britain where nuclear reactors are concerned would be to compensate the locality by providing cheap domestic and industrial heating using hot water from the steam turbines at the nuclear power station which would otherwise simply be lost to cooling towers or to the sea. The elegance and economy of such a proposal (for CHP – combined heat and power) are almost overwhelming. For one thing, the practicable reach of the piping that would be involved is only about 30 kilometres

---

26 Ray Kemp, *The Politics of Radioactive Waste Disposal*, p. 97.

from the reactor, which more or less exactly covers the zone most likely to be affected in the event of an accident. On top of this, here is a method of compensation which will reduce overall demand for energy: it is an energy conservation measure. On the other hand it has to be conceded that there is a suspicious neatness about the proposal (also an awkward 'not invented here' aspect), which would maybe guarantee its acceptance in Singapore, but which would be unlikely to survive the rough and tumble of norm setting in Britain.

Of course this would not even be an option where other sorts of nuclear facility were involved, such as a waste depositary, where something closer to the French model might be more appropriate. Even so, it is improbable that any compensation scheme could be introduced in Britain solely for nuclear construction work. It would be better to admit that all major energy schemes have adverse environmental effects falling chiefly on the well-being of the locality affected by their operation. Arranging French-style compensation in these cases too would be equitable. It would also be educational in that it would demonstrate that nothing, nuclear included, is perfectly safe.

Public confidence in British nuclear industry not high

Naturally, it cannot be supposed that what works for France would automatically work elsewhere. In Britain public confidence in the nuclear industry cannot have been helped by its failure to achieve the efficiencies in generating electricity from nuclear reactors achieved in France. Williams tells a dismal story of vacillation over the appropriate design of reactor and sudden shifts and reversals in strategy.[27] Where France depends exclusively on the PWR design of commercial reactor, Britain employs Magnox (with no two of the nine Magnox stations built to the same design), advanced Magnox in the form of the AGR (with greater consistency in design, but with puzzling discrepancies – the two 2 unit AGRs at Heysham in Lancashire are built with design differences) and the PWR at Sizewell B. It has even seriously toyed with a third design based on heavy water as moderator. Other countries, too, with different economic arrangements, will not find it possible to generate nuclear electricity as cheaply as the French where government ownership means

---

27 Roger Williams, *The Nuclear Power Decisions: British Policies, 1953-78*, (London, Croom Helm, 1980).

lower borrowing costs for construction than the private sector would face. It is these low costs which in part make it possible for the French to afford compensation payments.

Even so, no one would quarrel with a nuclear reactor design strategy that sought to incorporate the best safety science gleaned from the experience of other countries. Incorporating the best practice in trans-science too might not be a bad idea.

The adverse environmental impact due to nuclear power whether arising from routine operations or accident, in its physical manifestations, is largely a domestic affair. In other words, abjuring nuclear power nationally on environmental grounds, as the Swedes for instance appear to have done, is not normally vitiated by the possibility that neighbouring states may decide differently. What adverse environmental impacts nuclear power may have are, as we have seen, almost invariably felt most strongly in the near vicinity of the nuclear installation. Normally the precautions states take to protect their own populations will mean that neighbouring states also automatically benefit. The one glaring exception to this general rule was virtually foreclosed in 1984 when Britain stopped dumping nuclear waste at sea. A slight loophole remains with ongoing Irish objections to the small British discharges of liquid low level waste into Cumbrian coastal waters. Only where states are clearly negligent in terms of protecting their own populations might a problem arise, as arguably was the case with the Chernobyl accident.

A future problem

A second exception, academic in current conditions but one which would become more important in the event of the large scale expansion of nuclear power mooted in the previous chapter, towards a global installed capacity of 3000 Gw(e), is the routine releases of gaseous low level nuclear waste from reprocessing plants and to a lesser degree reactors. Currently the global atmospheric and oceanic dilution of these gases (which include, ironically, radioactive carbon dioxide, although in wholly insignificant amounts in global warming terms) means that their contribution to radioactive exposures amounts to less than one per cent of the natural background.[28] But with an expansion of nuclear power coupled with the

---

28 Extrapolating from a table presented by Johns, 'Environmental pathways of radioactivity to man', p. 206.

long radioactive lives of these gases, this figure will rise. Britain, for instance, now very much a net exporter of these gases, will become an importer too were the nuclear industries of other countries to expand along the lines suggested. For the world-wide installed capacity of 3000 Gw(e) postulated earlier, together with matching reprocessing capacity to extract the plutonium produced, world-wide exposure as a result will rise to about 8 per cent of average natural exposures to radiation.

There is no technical difficulty involved in trapping these gases before release, simply a lack of incentive hitherto to incur the economic penalties involved. An expansion of nuclear power will produce that incentive, but translating the incentive into action will not be straightforward since internationally collective action (the kind obviously required) poses new problems of its own.

Conclusion

Whilst it is possible that it is too late to do anything about it and the British public may have lost faith in nuclear fission power irretrievably, the explanation for the failure to set acceptable norms for nuclear power in Britain is surprisingly simple. Parts of the public were simply being asked to accept without any compensation risks that were sufficiently comparable to other daily risks to life and limb for them to be unignorable.

Instead of the two categories of risk-proneness British nuclear planners have always implicitly assumed existed, there are three, as seems to have been known in France for a long time. One, numerically the smallest, is the employee of the nuclear industry. He or she knowingly faces higher health risks and is tacitly or explicitly compensated for this. Another, the largest, is the member of the general public living more than twenty miles or so from a nuclear installation. He or she is not exposed to significantly greater risks by virtue of the existence of the nuclear power industry. The third, middle, category is made up of persons who live near nuclear installations. Most do not particularly choose to do so. But all are subjected, as a result, to a new risk to well-being, large enough to be noticeable, at about 10 per cent of the risks already encountered in daily life. Yet no compensation of any kind is offered.

Relating this failure to our earlier discussions of norm-setting, it should not be seen as a failure to be aware of the usefulness of the Vickers's feed forward that can be obtained by the use of models. The implicit British model that there were only two categories of persons exposed to nuclear radiation from the nuclear power industry, rather than three, was at least a model. The influential Flowers report also provided a model for the nuclear waste disposal programme. In both cases, however, the model was a bad one.

Oddly enough, the two bad models were bad for almost opposite reasons. The Flowers report seems to have given insufficient weight to scientific advice: the decision to give priority to finding a site for disposal of high level waste which was only going to be needed (because there was so little of it, relatively speaking) long after sites for intermediate and low level wastes is, as we have said, a puzzle. On the other hand, failure to acknowledge that persons living in the vicinity of a nuclear installation were neither average members of the public nor employees of the nuclear industry seems to have been due not to too much scientific input but to too much input from scientists, many of whom in the nuclear industry had come to see nothing untoward in being exposed to radiation well in excess of background levels. Following the models, then, conferred no advantage over simple learning from experience. This has proved such a slow procedure that doubt has crept in as to whether norm-setting will be possible at all. Even if, in the end, too much confidence has already been lost and nuclear fission fails to gain acceptance in Britain, the eventual long term alternative of nuclear fusion power may find similar norm-setting questions being asked again, at some a future date.

The failure to set norms does not mean that norms are left unset. Rather the norms that are set are those that are inherent in the situation and usually less desirable than those that might have been set otherwise. For Britain and a number of other countries it is possible, perhaps probable, that the default norm for nuclear energy will be that nuclear energy will be abandoned entirely. The knock-on effects of this will be a greater vulnerability amongst importing states to future contrived shortages of fossil fuel and the loss of a partial substitute for polluting sorts of fossil fuel.

The pattern of success and failure amongst states in setting norms for domestic discharges of waste from nuclear energy programmes defies easy categorisation. What can be said is that failures probably outnumber successes. The connection between nuclear power and nuclear weapons may have contributed to the apparent inability or unwillingness of governments to learn from each other in the business of norm-setting. Publics, by contrast, have not been slow to draw inferences concerning the safety of national nuclear installations from the safety records of those overseas.

Norm-setting for nuclear energy is a domestic story, or a series of domestic stories with indirect international consequences. But, as we have already suggested, if somewhat against the odds nuclear power were to be taken up by more states than present to somewhere nearer the limits of its capacity to substitute for other energy sources, it would create a new international environmental problem, and it is with this that we begin the next chapter.

Appendix:Radiation and Health[29]

The unit of radioactivity is taken in this chapter to be the curie. For historical reasons associated with the radioactivity of radium, an element discovered by Marie Curie, it corresponds to radioactive decay occurring at a rate of 37 billion nuclear disintegrations a second. Each disintegration will be accompanied by the emission of at least one energetic particle or X ray photon. The curie (Ci) is being displaced by a more modern unit, corresponding to one nuclear disintegration a second. This smaller unit is the becquerel ((Bq) – Curie was Becquerel's pupil).

A lump of radioactive material may throw off radiation (emissions) corresponding to a large number of curies. The danger this presents to humans will obviously depend on how near persons are to the source of emissions; how well the air absorbs the emissions; and how harmful to human tissues the emissions in question are.

To pursue the metaphor equating radioactivity with heat, a high curie count might be supposed to be the equivalent of a high temperature.

Exposure to a hot object will lead to heat being transferred to the person concerned, depending on the length and type of the exposure, and, where external, the distance between the person and the source. The amount of radioactive exposure equivalent to the amount of heat absorbed by the human body is measured in a unit called rads.

But plainly the actual harm done to a person from exposure to a hot object depends on more than just the temperature of the object and the length of the exposure, it also depends on the kind of hot object in question. Exposure by swallowing scalding hot food might do more harm than external contact with an iron grid at the same temperature and for the same length of time. Similarly with radioactivity. The same amount of rads can have different effects depending on its source. A small amount of rads from an alpha particle source is very dangerous, being equivalent to 20 times the amount from a strong X ray source. But to be harmful, since alpha particles are easily absorbed by any sort of matter, the source of alpha particles has to be inside the body – either breathed in, or swallowed.

To allow for the different biological effects, the absorbed radiation dose

---

29 See Samuel Glasstone (ed.), *The Effects of Nuclear Weapons*, (Washington D.C., USAEC, 1962), pp. 577, 580: Gonzalez, 'Radiation Safety: New International Standards', pp. 2, 11: Saunders and Wade, 'Radiation and its control', pp. 1, 49.

is measured not in rads but in rems.

In very round order of magnitude terms, for a radioactive source emitting strong X rays in the form of gamma rays, a person standing 1 metre from the source of one curie radioactivity for one hour will receive a dose of about one rem ('roentgen equivalent man' – Roentgen was the discoverer of X rays). Standing ten metres away will result in a dose of one hundredth the amount.

The rem (usually as millirem or one thousandth of a rem) is the unit used in this chapter for prolonged exposures to low levels of radioactivity.

Just as the curie is being displaced by the becquerel, the rem is being replaced by the sievert. An exposure of 100 rems is equivalent to one sievert; an exposure of 100 mrems, 1 mSv. The rad is being displaced by the gray (Gy) in the same ratio.

5 International Collective Action

Abstract discussion by itself is easily misunderstood (or even not understood at all). The abstract ideas that are the topic of this chapter are to do with the nature of international collective action to set norms for sustainable exploitation of common sinks or common sources. But they are not presented alone. In the present chapter they are prefaced by a semi-imaginary historical example which is used, alongside passing references to real historical examples, to give a little body to the otherwise somewhat spectral abstract ideas. In an immediately succeeding short series of chapters, illustrative reinforcements follow, on two occasions exclusively employing actual cases, and on a third looking ahead to collective action to control global warming.

Global radioactive waste

In the event, unlikely or not, of a large expansion of civil fission-based nuclear power, a new global environmental problem would arise, as we saw at the end of the preceding chapter. There would eventually be a build-up, at the global level, of the radioactive gases that are currently routinely released in very small quantities from nuclear power plants and reprocessing facilities. The radioactive products which eventually may pose an environmental problem on a global scale are carbon-14, released as radioactive carbon dioxide; krypton-85; and tritium, which forms, and is partially discharged as, radioactive water. The simple technical reason for this is that these gases quite quickly become evenly distributed throughout the planet.   At present this produces dilution of their concentration to insignificantly low levels (compared to the natural background). But with an expansion of nuclear power to, say, ten times the present level, the atmosphere as a sink for these gases starts to become saturated in the sense that their concentration starts to rise to a point where their associated radioactivity becomes a significant addition to the natural background.

Currently, operators of nuclear facilities calculate, we may quite confidently assume, that the cost of trapping these gases is too high in relation to any good that will be done, so well does the dilution process do its work. This might seem unobjectionable. But in the future, should the concentration of these gases start to build up to levels representing a danger to human health, operators of nuclear facilities even when agreeing about the dangers will still normally feel no incentive to do anything about it. Why should this be so?

The simple answer is that no operator of nuclear plant will act unilaterally (we may take it that operators of nuclear plant within any one state are represented internationally by the national government), because the cost of acting will be felt nationally and unilaterally whilst the benefits will be shared globally. Paying out from national resources to benefit other states who may be seen as economic competitors is not something governments would normally find easy to explain to their domestic constituency. And if nuclear power is particularly widespread, even these benefits may be a drop in the ocean compared to the scale at which these radioactive gases are being released by others. Imagine a state with one per cent of the world's nuclear power installed and with the installation of nuclear power globally growing at one per cent per annum. A unilateral decision to meet the costs of fitting its own nuclear plant with means to trap the gases would involve real costs incurred but in exchange for a small benefit that would moreover be entirely nullified in twelve months.

The situation is even worse than so far portrayed. Suppose an increase had taken place in the amount of nuclear capacity installed world-wide and that the build-up of radioactive gases had reached a significant level. Suppose further that this was universally acknowledged and recognised as the case (i.e. there was no scientific uncertainty about the matter). Suppose also that there was complete agreement that taken as a whole, the cost of trapping the gases was small in relation to the costs incurred in treating persons for the cancers they were experiencing as a result of the increased radioactivity. Imagine as a consequence that an international agreement was arrived at banning or at least limiting the release of these gases. This outcome would be desirable, no doubt, but it would not be stable: in other words it would not obviously be a sustainable solution.

Cheating and free-riding

The reason is simply that once such an agreement was reached, the incentive to stick to it would be extremely weak. Any one participating state might easily calculate that if it cheated on the agreement and carried on emitting these gases, it could save itself money (by not fitting or operating the gas-trapping devices) whilst hardly hurting either itself or the rest of the world at all, given the diluting properties of the atmosphere. It could calculate further that the rest of the world was not going to tear up the agreement just because one state out of many was not playing by the rules. This sort of defection from this sort of agreement, when successful, is usually described as 'free-riding'. But if one state could calculate this way, so could others, and the agreement would be in an unstable condition.

The above is an illustration of a more general phenomenon already referred to in Chapter 2. When market conditions are absent, so is the hidden hand that tends to harmonise collective and private (or in this case national and international) interests. Where global resources are held in common, whether as sinks for pollution as in the above case or as sources (e.g., the oceans for fish), considerable political effort is normally needed to effect the necessary harmonisation. In the case of a common source we may simply suppose that fishing states had agreed, in the light of experience and with the guidance of appropriate scientific models, how much fish of a particular species could be caught each year without diminishing the catch available in succeeding years. This would almost invariably require the fishing states to set a quota for the permissible catch. But any one state when only one of many will be tempted to exceed its quota. In so doing, it will increase its income confident that its small crime could not much affect the survival of stocks nor indeed the price obtainable for the fish. But if one could reason this way, so could others. The agreement would be unstable.

Olson's themes

The problem of setting environmental norms in the above kinds of circumstances and analogous problems in domestic and international political economy can be effectively tackled using a series of insights normally credited to Mancur Olson.[1] Not so much Olson himself but more particularly his later followers have tended to employ mathematical methods in the presentation of their ideas. This has definite advantages in some circumstances but will not be attempted here. Instead Olson's main themes will employed in a context informally designed to demonstrate their plausibility.

According to a recent study by one of Olson's chief disciples, Todd Sandler,[2] Olson's basic themes are:

1. Group size is in part a root cause of collective failures (to secure collectively desired ends).
2. Group asymmetry (i.e. when group participants are unalike in some significant characteristic) is related to collective failures, with larger members of the group carrying a disproportionate share of the costs of the group.
3. Collective failures may be overcome by arranging for members of the collective to receive additional benefits (over and above those provided by the successful action of the collective itself and for this reason sometimes referred to as sidepayments) which may be denied them in the event of their defecting from the collective action. Collective failures may also be overcome by 'institutional design'.

Olson sums up his Theme 2 by saying that there is a 'systematic tendency for the exploitation of the great by the small'.[3] In fact, if extended to

---

1 Mancur Olson, *The Logic of Collective Action*, (Cambridge, Mass., Harvard University Press, 1965).

2 Todd Sandler, *Collective Action: Theory and Applications*, (Hemel Hempstead, Harvester Wheatsheaf, 1992), pp. 8, 9.

3 Ibid., p. 9.

mean also the exploitation of the many by the few, as we shall see it also encapsulates Theme 1.

We have already illustrated how indeed one participant amongst many in an arrangement to set an international environmental norm could all too easily behave as Olson's Theme 1 suggests. But if we supposed that the number of participants in the arrangement was small rather than large, Olson also leads us to think that the prospects for a stable outcome might improve.

Group size

To see this, consider the smallest possible arrangement of the sort being discussed: this would contain only two participants. If moreover they were of equal weight (the situation a symmetrical one, in other words), neither could assume that a unilateral, though perhaps conditional, suspension of emissions into a common space would be totally pointless, i.e. without significant (and more or less immediate) beneficial effect to their own population, unless annual emission rates were rising extremely rapidly from one year to another. Thus, in 1995 when the USA and the European Union each accounted for about 1/3 of installed global nuclear capacity, a unilateral US move to fit its nuclear plant with devices for trapping radioactive gases would have brought tangible benefits to the US population. Quite soon, a third fewer people than before would be at risk from cancers induced by radiation from this source. But this assumes that global expansion of nuclear power was occurring, if at all, at a slow rate. As of 1995, this assumption would be correct. But if it were rising at 10 per cent per annum (the sort of rate of increase we suggested earlier as necessary if nuclear were to become a worthwhile substitute for fossil fuel), a US self-denying ordinance would create benefits for only about 4 years, after which the situation – for the USA – would be worse than before. This is because the pollution would be no better and money would have been spent in vain.

But in conditions of static or slowly rising demand, a conditional unilateral move in the expectation of reciprocation would in such circumstances seem like an obvious first step to a formal agreement. As we see below, the first step towards an agreement is often the most difficult. At the same time, unless there was a bias towards action sooner rather than later, perhaps in the form of an acceptance of the precautionary principle, it should be recognised that we are also saying that the opportunity for collective action may be most easily grasped when the apparent need for it is least, i.e. when the pollution load and hence the 'problem' was growing only very slowly, if at all.

Interestingly, the same analysis concerning the possible usefulness of a unilateral gesture does not do equal service where the commons in question is a common source, of fish, say. In the corresponding case of two equal and dominant fishing states, irrespective of the state of demand, a unilateral gesture would produce nothing tangible to the state making the gesture in return for its sacrifice.

Once any sort of collective agreement is reached, as already noted, the most obvious cause of breakdown in a large multilateral arrangement is an expectation by a potential cheat that an act of cheating on the agreement could be overlooked: first of all it might not even be noticed, secondly even if it were it might well be condoned. In an agreement between two a defection would be more likely to be spotted: the procedures available to either side for gathering information about compliance with the agreement (usually described as verification procedures) would have the benefit of being able to concentrate on only one target. In addition, condoning in such a case would seem inherently improbable, given that it would amount to the other party continuing unilaterally to limit its emissions/extractions in the face of evidence that its opposite number was happy to exploit its misplaced trust, contributing nothing to the resolution of a common problem whilst blithely taking advantage of the other side's unselfishness.

To put things a little differently, an agreement between two would be relatively stable compared to an agreement among many in that defection from the agreement – because of the higher probability that it would be detected and responded to – would be deterred more effectively.

Assuming that there is nothing analytically special about the two-party case which prevents our being able to think of some real life cases as being intermediate between the two party and the many party extremes, and second, assuming adequate verification, it is reasonable to suggest that other things remaining unchanged, an arrangement between a comparatively small number of equal participants will be more stable than an arrangement involving a larger number, just as Olson suggests. The scope of the many to exploit the few, in other words, is limited when the grouping is limited.

Regional versus global

In practical international environmental politics this has two consequences. One is that regional agreements (where the technical nature of the problem is such as to permit a regional approach, as is the case with acid rain (or its precursor gases) which rarely carries more than a few hundred miles from its point of origin), because they involve a limited number of participants, may be easier to achieve than global kinds which will normally have a much larger number of participants. The second consequence is that even global arrangements, where these are called for, will be more stable where the number of independent participants remains, for some reason, low. In practice, unless we lift our simplifying assumption of equality between the participants, this can only be achieved in one way. That is for states to negotiate as federated groups rather than as individual sovereign entities (the reasonable question of why the federated group should be itself stable enough to participate as a group is parried, at least, by the previous argument relating to number). Arguably, this was the case over the treaties to limit damage to the ozone layer caused by emissions of CFCs, where, as we shall see in Chapter 7, negotiations at least in the beginning were essentially between the US and certain allies, on the one hand, and the European Community on the other.

If we relax the condition of equality for the moment, another method of restricting the number of participants in a global treaty is to strike out for a treaty whilst the problem in question still has a regional or selective character and before it becomes truly global. Again, there was something of this quality about the attempts to protect the ozone layer, in that north Atlantic states, by and large, were the main producers of CFCs and their populations in the front line of risk from a damaged ozone layer. It would also apply to our (still fictional) treaty reached to stop countries with nuclear power programmes discharging radioactive gases into the atmosphere, should it be agreed before the turn of the century, say, whilst the number of such countries is still rather small. Since most of these countries, moreover, are in the Northern Hemisphere, and truly global atmospheric mixing of these pollutants is quite slow, the parallel with protection of the ozone layer is a good one.

Institutional design

The above manouevres to keep the collective small do not perhaps quite fall within Olson's 'institutional design' (Theme 3) remedy for instability: it is difficult for example to redesign a problem as regional when it is not. But institutional design can take other forms. The most obvious aspect of institutional design is that an arrangement reached by the collective should include provision for verification. This may mean no more than a facility for the receipt and storage of national data relating to progress achieved towards meeting the targets required by treaty for reductions in emissions/extractions. Smallness helps here too. It may not do much to keep down the overhead cost of the verification bureau (which has to be met by the participants in the arrangement) but it will improve its effectiveness. States with their ears to the ground will automatically know more about what their neighbours may be getting up to than they will of fellow participants in an arrangement situated a continent or more distant.

But institutional design can be even more ambitious. So far we have spoken in terms of a single agreement. This means that many of the potential participants will not know in advance as much as they might like about the risk-taking or risk-avoiding tendencies of their fellow participants, specifically in terms of their degree of inclination to cheat (or not) on an arrangement in the expectation that they will get away with it. But if the objective of a single agreement could be sub-divided into a number of intermediate milestones in the form of partial objectives reachable in a succession of smaller agreements, movement in certain circumstances can be made easier. It is easier to chance your arm when the stakes are comparatively small. (An arbitrary sub-division into successive steps towards the whole would not do nearly as well, there would typically be argument over how this should be done, and hence delay – natural sub-divisions are what is needed.)

A particularly important circumstance arises where a significant number of potential participants in an arrangement are risk-averse, with the main obstacle to a successful agreement coming at the beginning (once an agreement is reached, the same risk-avoiders will be among the arrangement's most reliable members). Risk-avoiders may refuse to countenance an agreement because of their fear of being cheated and being exploited by a risk-taker. If the first step can be made a small one, the risk-avoiders are being asked to chance very little (in the case of radioactive gases, the first step might be to tackle only the cheaply curable krypton-85 problem). A successfully implemented first step will then reassure participating states sufficiently to encourage them to proceed to the next step, and so on.

Taking a complex issue one step at a time, provided the whole process is not too long drawn out, increases the chances of the participants actually being able generally to learn something from experience – to apply corrective (negative) feedback, in other words. Successive steps then need not replicate earlier steps mechanically but may be adapted to take account of everything that may have been learned from earlier steps, not just about where fellow participants stand on the risk-taking: risk-avoiding spectrum. The smaller the steps taken, the easier in principle is it to learn from them. Otherwise, as Vickers points out:[4]

> The more complex the situation in which we act, the less verifiable by experience is the effect of our own actions and inactions ... [experience] may or may not tell us something about the effect of our own would-be remedial actions in the past; for these may return for judgement so long after the event and so intermixed with other more important variables as to give us neither confirmation of the past nor guidance for the future.

Scientific uncertainty

Additionally and importantly, risk-avoiders will normally need assurance on one other matter which may be in doubt: the true extent of the environmental problem posed by the matter in hand. In other words there is often scientific uncertainty attaching to the scale of the problem posed (for instance, in this case, quite how many cancer deaths will arise globally because of tritium emissions, given that tritium has quite a short half-life (12 years) and may accordingly be specific in its effects as between the Northern and Southern Hemispheres).

In addition there is usually a related lack of certainty about the most appropriate technical response. In this case it will not merely be a matter of the cheapest and most effective design of traps for capturing the radioactive gases but could include choices concerning the design of nuclear reactor, since there will be some variation in the amounts of gas released as between the various types. It could even go further and stoke up the reprocessing debate, since reprocessing plants will be prominent emitters of radioactive gases. And whilst not arising in this case, an appropriate technical response will often involve a search for a substitute process to the one now under a cloud. The availability and cost of

---

4 Geoffrey Vickers, *The Art of Judgement: A Study of Policy Making*, (London, Methuen University Paperback, 1968), p. 73.

substitutes may not always be clear. In the present example, risk-avoiders will want to avoid taking expensive precautions against discharges of tritium only to be told eventually that the danger to health was actually minimal (or that there was a much cheaper method of filtering out tritium).

Again, the step-by-step approach allows progress to be made in advance of scientific certainty, provided the initial movement towards a full agreement is not taken as a signal for the suspension of further scientific investigation.   Indeed part of the institutional design of the initial agreement might usefully include the apportioning of funds for further basic scientific investigation (normally a very cheap enterprise compared to the economic stakes involved in environmental protection agreements, although the tendency for all committees to devote time to issues in *inverse* proportion to their budgetary implications is a warning against complacency on this point). A basic scientific enquiry in this case would look into the global atmospheric circulation of tritium.   Given that profitable sales should accrue to whoever comes up with effective tritium filters, applied science can be left to market forces.

As we saw in Chapter 1 there invariably is much to be said for avoiding delay in setting environmental norms. The virtues of the step-by-step approach certainly include an ability to reduce the height of the hurdles in the way of starting negotiations. And unless the problem being dealt with is itself growing at a rapid rate, a successful first step will normally buy time for subsequent steps. In the context of environmental commons problems one of the advantages of making an early beginning to a solution is that the problem will not at this stage be growing at the high rate it will eventually reach if nothing is done.

The step-by-step approach does not, then, seem to carry with it many disadvantages, but this can only be said with complete confidence once we have explored the consequences of abandoning the assumption made so far that we are dealing with negotiations between equals. One advantage of this assumption is that it has allowed our analysis to proceed without the necessity of discussing the nature of the bargain eventually agreed between the participating states. Equality means that the benefits of the agreement are simply shared equally.

National inequalities

Now, speaking of equality around an international negotiating table is not quite as unrealistic as it may sound. States aware of the possibility of international negotiations for the orderly exploitation of a commons may postpone participation until they feel more confident that they can enter the negotiations as more of an equal with other participants. This may simply create delay, as in the radioactive gases problem where a state may attempt to hold back negotiations until its own nuclear programme was up and running. Alternatively and not necessarily to be associated with much delay, a small group of states (with only small nuclear power programmes, say) could form an alliance or federation for the tactical purpose of negotiation.

Nonetheless it is a striking characteristic of international politics that states are very much unalike in their military, geographical, demographic and economic attributes. Certain combinations of these attributes can give states that possess them, or rather their governments, the sought-after capacity to extend their reach beyond domestic boundaries as a result of the influence they have over other states' policies. Or, in other words, some states are simply more powerful than others. It is inevitable that international negotiations in practice will reflect these inequalities, if only in the obvious benefits in negotiation a unitary large state will enjoy over a tactical grouping of about the same size made up of smaller states.

How far are these power differences likely to qualify the conclusions reached above concerning the achievement of an arrangement for the orderly exploitation of a commons? Olson suggests that now some participants are 'great' whilst others are small, it is the former who will be taken advantage of, or free-ridden upon.

We can understand Olson's point by first recapitulating what has been said already. A fundamental source of instability in a collective undertaking for environmental protection (among equals) is the temptation, which increases in line with the number of participants, for one participant to free-ride – to cheat on the arrangement in the expectation that the other parties will be prepared to live with that. Where the arrangement involves non-equals, two things then follow. First, comparatively weighty (i.e. great) participants are in a sense at a disadvantage in that they cannot calculate with the same confidence that smaller parties can, that they may be able to free-ride. Unlike the defection of a small party, their defection is almost sure to be noticed (verification and detection will scarcely be an issue) and is unlikely to be shrugged off by the other weighty parties who may indeed be expected to react in some dramatic way as to impose a cost on the defector, even to the extent of tearing up the agreement. So, as Olson suggests, by comparison with an arrangement between equals, where non-equals are involved the free-riding problem is simplified. In other words tendencies to free-ride will also be unequal. They can be anticipated to be most strong amongst the smaller parties involved.

Discouraging free-riders

Secondly, the passive discouragement of free-riding among the smaller parties (which is the product of the probability that the defection will be detected and the unspecified but probably none too serious penalties exacted) can now be added to considerably. Free-riding means having your cake and eating it – enjoying the benefits of an environmentally safer world where discharges of radioactive gases from nuclear power plant are banned, whilst contributing nothing to the achievement of this desirable state of affairs, by deciding not to pay the costs of curbing your own emissions. Positive discouragement means presenting a would-be free-rider with a bill for any delinquent behaviour, with a view to deterring it from happening in the first place. Credible deterrence of a small potential defector cannot be got by a threat to tear up the arrangement. But if the weightier members of the arrangement were to contribute towards a central fund that was then disbursed to smaller members for as long as they remained members in good standing and not otherwise, free-riding would acquire a real cost – the loss of contributions from the central fund.

It might reasonably be conjectured that the central fund arrangement will itself be unstable, breeding its own free-riders. This is an argument for keeping the number of contributors to the fund small (which may not be very difficult). In turn, of course, this will tend to keep the value of the fund small whilst enlarging the number of potential beneficiaries of the fund. Bearing in mind that not all contributors to the fund, even, will be of equal weight, problems over bargaining amongst contributors to the fund can be anticipated (but the smaller the fund, the more restrained and the sooner resolved squabbling over contributions will be).

Bargaining and political 'height'

This is not quite the end of the story. It might be thought that bargaining over contributions to the central fund would be fairly trivial. Enormous sums will not normally be involved. All are benefiting from a successful arrangement and contributions to the fund might properly be scheduled by ability to pay, with largest payments coming from the richest states, as in contributions to the running costs of the United Nations. But this would not take into account the possibility that some central fund members will be gaining more from the whole arrangement than others. The nearer the subject matter of the arrangement touched on the relative power of the contributors, the more problems this would create for the central fund. A useful shorthand terminology describes this sort of subject matter as 'high politics'. Very often, by comparison with other areas where international collective action is sometimes deemed appropriate, for example in matters relating to the control of armaments, environmental issues are thought of as low politics. But some environmental issues are 'higher' than others.

As a set of examples we can put forward, in ascending 'height': CFCs and the ozone layer; carbon dioxide and global warming; the problem discussed above of radioactive gases.

The logic at one level is simple. The production of CFCs has never involved more than a tiny fraction of any state's manpower or capital resources. On the other hand, carbon dioxide emissions are intimately tied up with the production of energy, and the availability of energy (as the oil crises of the 1970s showed) is a central issue for the functioning of the economy of most states. And whilst the emission of radioactive gases is only in a small way tied up with energy, even with the sort of expansion of nuclear power mooted in Chapters 3 and 4, all states with nuclear weapon programmes will either emit some of these gases as part of their weapon production process, or be reluctant to allow international verification that they have ceased to do so. What may be less simple is that power is about perceptions and what may be seen by some as a matter of low politics may to others not seem quite as low. Furthermore, circumstances also matter. What was seen as high politics during the Cold War may not be seen as quite so high today. The economic strength of a state (say the size of its surplus of disposable economic resources or the tax base of its government) has become a relatively more important index of power, closing the gap with the military index, perhaps even superseding it. And to take an example from conservation, a catch of fish from a common sea may be low politics to one state, representing a very small proportion of national income or employment, but the same tonnage of fish taken may be high politics to another whose economy may be much more dependent on fishing (as a proportion of employment and capital investment).

Hegemony

The extreme case of a collective arrangement made between non-equals arises when one state is possessed of very much more weight than any of the others. Now the central fund referred to above disappears or rather becomes identified with the national Treasury of the leading power, or hegemon, to use the term of art.[5] This may not be a stable state of affairs in that once more we are in the presence of costs being carried by one whilst procuring benefits for the many. Some of these benefits, again, will accrue possibly to rivals and competitors and improve, therefore, their position relative to that of the hegemon itself (this will be more or less important, of course, according to the height of the politics involved). An oligopolistic hegemony may be more sustainable than a monopolistic one: the central fund or hegemonic grouping can be too small as well as too large and presumably there is therefore one size which will be optimum.

Otherwise the position of the hegemonic group is not unreasonable. It is protected from excessive calls being made upon its fund by two things. First, it helps that whilst potential free-riders are numerous, they are small and have not formed themselves into a negotiating group. Were they to do so, they might be able to bargain more out of the central fund but as a group they would not always be able to imply a threat to free-ride as convincingly as before (the small may exploit the great – the not so small will have a harder time of it trying that on). Tactical alliances amongst potential free-riders will be compatible with retaining the threat to free-ride only when the individual participants in the alliance are particularly 'small' in the Olson sense.

It should not be unusual, therefore, for the central fund managers to be able to shape their schedule of disbursements almost unilaterally, restricting payments only to those who are in a practical position to free-ride, in proportion to the size of the impact their free-riding would make and explicitly ear-marked for reducing their capacity to do so (the negative feedback quality of the last of these conditions will be noted). Thus, in the case of radioactive gases emitted from nuclear power plant, the fund should be used to pay for the fitting of gas traps to the chimneys of nuclear plant.

---

5 For a brief exploration of the meaning(s) of this term, see Joseph S. Nye, 'The Changing Nature of World Power' in Charles W. Kegley and Eugene R. Wittkopf, (eds), *The Global Agenda: Issues and Perspectives*, 4th edition, (New York, McGraw-Hill Inc., 1995), pp. 111, 113.

Naturally the institutional design feature of a verification procedure will play a significant part here in confining transfers from the fund only to states that have signed up to the arrangement and abided by the rules.

The second safeguard the hegemonic group possesses against excessive inflation of the central fund is that they will not allow it to cost them more than would their fall-back position, which would be to let the arrangement collapse and use the funds that would otherwise have protected the treaty against free riding to pay for national, i.e. non-collective, responses to the problem in hand. In the present example the natural national response would be to fund additional medical research and care for cancer patients.

So far, the inequalities between participants have been referred to by quite deliberately using the rather neutral, even vague, terms of weighty, great or small, following Olson. It turns out that what in fact is meant precisely by such terms is extremely important.

Meaning of size

What differentiates the great from the small in the preceding analysis of the problems and possibilities of collective action is simply the proportion of the total pollution added to a common sink, or proportion of the extraction total taken from a common source, attributable to the state in question. Where a state ranks significantly higher than the average on this score it is in this context great. Olson's aphorism about collective action meaning exploitation of the great by the small simply means that whilst a small state may get away with free-riding this is not an option for a weighty state because its anti-social activities are so gross as not to have much chance of escaping notice or of being tolerated.

In matters of pollution, since pollution in the sense of production of waste materials and energy correlates closely, if not exactly, with intensity of economic activity, and intensity of economic activity is measured by gross national product, weight in this context will correlate fairly closely with national wealth. Thus the hegemonic group will on the whole be wealthier than the others and accordingly well able to afford a worthwhile central fund to deter free-riding.

This explains, in passing, the tendency for international environmental negotiations over pollution questions to acquire some of the character of negotiations over development and development aid, since the source of the common fund and its destination find precise parallels in aid questions.

This is not necessarily an advantage from the perspective of securing a stable arrangement to curb pollution. The hegemonic group will contain states who already give international aid, both multilaterally and on a national basis.   Those that are sensitive to power differentials will normally be keen to retain a healthy proportion under national control. Participation in the hegemonic group on the other hand is contingent on being prepared to increase (if only slightly), in effect, multilateral donations.

It also matters that the fund should promise real transfers. If hegemonic members of the central fund meet their obligations by dipping into their ordinary aid budgets, this obviously portends for at least some parties to the arrangement outside the hegemonic group only very small or even negative nett payments from the fund, threatening to destabilise the whole structure. Development considerations, albeit from a different perspective, also argue against negative sanctions for the deterrence of free-riders, such as trade barriers lowered against the guilty. This not only firstly hurts the hegemonic group along with the target states and secondly lacks the useful negative feedback that comes from targeting payments from the fund to tackling the physical source of the pollution, but it also aims for stable norm setting in the matter of pollution at the expense of destabilising the automatic norm setting of market relationships in matters of trade.

But where extraction from a common pool is concerned, as in deep-sea fishing, there are no grounds for anticipating that the hegemonic group will be made up of wealthy states. Over the two years 1991–93, most sea fishing was done by China at an annual average catch of 8.7 million tonnes, 10.5 per cent of the world total. The second largest catch was taken by Japan, at 8.3 million tonnes; the third largest, by Peru, at 7.4 million tonnes.[6] Over the same period, Peru was the second largest recipient of international economic aid in Latin America and Japan the world's largest donor of aid.[7] In other words the three leading fishing states included one representative from the OECD, and two from the less developed world.

This explains why development issues are normally absent from the search for arrangements to control deep sea fishing (and whaling). More importantly it also emphasises the difficulties there may be in setting up a central fund or similar positive sanction against defection from the

---

6 *World Resources 1996–97* (New York, Oxford University Press, 1996), pp. 310, 311.
7 Ibid., p. 169.

arrangement and indicates a stronger likelihood that the hegemonic group, if formed, will have to rely on the less satisfactory negative sanctions (e.g. trade barriers).

In the pollution analysis it was not claimed that emissions of pollution would tally exactly with national wealth. It was also assumed, rather than argued, that the adverse effects of pollution were felt uniformly. In the case of emissions of radioactive gases this would be true objectively in that the same proportion of each country's population would be affected; no national or ethnic differences in human susceptibility to the effects of radiation are known of. But we put forward the proposition in Chapter 4 that it may be the level of radiation relative to the natural background that matters, and different countries certainly have different natural radiation backgrounds.

How is our analysis altered if in the search for greater realism we allow states to differ not just in national wealth but also along two further dimensions?[8]   One of these new dimensions allows for variation in the size of the individual state's contribution to the pollution load – some states may have no programme of nuclear power at all, others with more or less comparable national incomes may have large amounts installed. The second dimension allows for variation in a state's perceived vulnerability to their own and others' pollution.

Pollution responsibility and pollution sensitivity

These two new dimensions allow us to place real states, then, broadly into one of four categories. Where states are all emitters of waste (in proportion to their GNP) and also equally affected by pollution (with the same proportion of their populations exposed to additional cancer risks), this is the category already discussed.

States with disproportionately low emissions, but still highly sensitive to the emissions of others will be strongly supportive in principle of almost any arrangement to cut emissions. They will benefit greatly but have to pay very little or nothing towards it. An obvious comparison here would be between France and Italy – not much difference in national wealth but

---

8   For a pioneering (and slightly more complex) analysis of the importance of other sub-divisions of states in addition to the simple hegemonic/non-hegemonic groupings, in our terminology, see Martin List and Volker Rittberger, 'Regime Theory and International Environmental Management', in Andrew Hurrell and Benedict Kingsbury, (eds), *The International Politics of the Environment*, (Oxford, Clarendon Press, 1992), p. 101.

a huge difference in emissions of radioactive gases.

States with both low emissions and low sensitivity to the emissions of others will be unconsciously supportive of an arrangement to cut emissions because subtracting such 'indifferent' states from the class of all states reduces the negotiating total amongst whom an arrangement has to be reached. This is simply Olson's Theme 1 again.

The fourth category is more interesting: large emitters, all with low sensitivity to the pollution consequences of their own or others' emissions. If such states are at the same time economically relatively weak with large GNPs and populations but small national incomes per head, the problem is not too serious. Indeed, the combination of low sensitivity to home-produced and external pollution on the one hand and poverty on a per head basis on the other will not be terribly uncommon, since it is almost invariably the case that populations become more environmentally sensitive subjectively as they become more prosperous. Such states can often then be regarded as belonging to the same category as other potential free-riders (they become honorary small states) and compensated for the costs of cleaning up. But if they are not poor on a per head basis something else has to be done.

An example precisely within the radioactive gases context is not easy to think of, but much actually depends on the exact nature of the pollution problem. Thus, Britain is not particularly sensitive to its own or anyone else's discharges of sulphur dioxide and nitrogen oxides – precursors of acid rain – because of the direction of the prevailing winds (the size of Ireland's GNP and hence emissions of these gases is too small to signify here). But these same winds make Britain's emissions a serious problem for other states in western Europe. Precisely analogously, the same set of circumstances also arises whenever a river passes through more than one state, with the river not untypically treated as a convenient receptacle for the disposal of waste. The state furthest upstream need not be hurt either by its own disposal of waste into the river nor by what any dumping states in the lower reaches may get up to.

Bargaining over more than one thing

In a case like this the only way forward would seem to be through linking progress towards collective action in one area (where Britain, in the acid rain example, would get a rather bad bargain) with progress on another, where Britain was better placed. But there is obviously no guarantee that this could be managed within a reasonable lapse of time if everything was done on a strict step-by-step basis. Perhaps it is right to conclude that larger steps where more than one pollution issue may be handled at the same time will occasionally be justified. This is less risky than it may sound. The common sense belief that a small agenda is always more easily negotiated than a larger one should not be applied unthinkingly on behalf of the step-by-step approach. It is a commonplace of the bargaining literature that bargains over one thing alone can actually be more difficult to reach than bargains involving more than one thing.[9] The difficulty about bargains to be reached over one thing (in, for the moment, the simplified setting of two bargainers, individuals, companies or states) means that what one gives up the other simply acquires.

In the European acid rain illustration (taken up in much greater detail in Chapter 7), given that collective action would be undertaken by a group of regional states many of which had already built up a fund of mutual confidence via their membership of the European Union, a step-by-step approach (still valuable when we are dealing with scientific uncertainty, even when political confidence-building is not an issue) would still be feasible. Britain in such circumstances would be more willing to trust that its bad bargain of today would be compensated by a better bargain in the future.

The fourth category case of a large emitter of pollution indifferent to the effects of both its own waste products and the waste products of others has its parallel in the world of extraction from a common source. Once more this is a regional matter where states may extract fish or water from an international river, with the state furthest upstream often wholly indifferent to the extraction activities of its downstream neighbours.

Further institutional design and the first move

We have not completely finished saying what 'institutional design', part of Olson's Theme 3, can contribute to overcoming 'collective failures'.

Especially where comparatively high politics is involved and where the

---

9   The homeliest illustration of this can be seen in car sales. Most of these actually involve the sale of two cars. The buyer usually has an existing car to 'trade-in' for a price (within limits) to be determined whilst simultaneously buying a new car from the dealer also at a price to be determined. A classic of the non-quantitative bargaining literature, but from which this example is not drawn, is Howard Raiffa, *The Art and Science of Negotiation*, (Cambridge, Mass., Harvard University Press, 1982).

potential participants in an environmental agreement are therefore likely to be more than a little concerned about relative benefits and costs, institutional design can help with the further obstacle to progress here which takes the form of a special difficulty attaching to making the first move. A first move in the form of an initiative by a state calling in good faith for an arrangement to curb emission of radioactive gases may be a long time coming, because to make it would be seen as a sign of weakness on the part of the promoter (who would be aware of this). Where it was made, then, there would be a tendency for it to be perceived as lacking in good faith and therefore propagandist in intention.

One way of getting over this obstacle is to have the first move made exogenously by someone or something with standing but without an axe (or with an entirely different sort of axe) to grind. This could even be a prominent individual, or private grouping, or a member state of the UN too small to feature in power calculations. But the obvious facilitator will be a international institution of some kind that is already in existence (otherwise the new first move would be for the creation of the organisation, which would face the same frictional difficulties as any other first move). It would neither lose face nor court suspicion by seeking to initiate international discussion of an environmental issue. Governments making favourable responses to such an initiative can easily then preface their statements by disclaimers (heartfelt or otherwise) indicating that action is being supported in the name of all mankind (or the 'international community').

Similarly, where the politics involved is comparatively high there may be further advantages in there being clear water between the institution and the governments of the powerful states. The simplest way to achieve this would be for the secretariat of the institution to be drawn from countries that do not themselves figure prominently in the power calculations of powerful states.

Naturally, other factors will also help determine the nature of the secretariat. In environmental issues, familiarity with the scientific and economic backgrounds of the matter and being in good standing with the respective epistemic communities will be essential, but this is not a particularly restrictive condition (compared to a very high political matter, the control of nuclear weapons, say, where genuine expertise outside the ranks of nationals of the leading powers scarcely exists). Recalling Vickers's warning about the suspicion with which science is viewed in the less developed world and the comparatively recent and incomplete conversion of many in the less developed world to market economics, deliberately drawing the secretariat from the less developed world might be particularly productive.

Regime formation

The processes just described whereby international norms for environmental protection may be set constitute what we have neutrally described as arrangements or agreements between the participating states. What we call arrangements are equivalent to what List and Rittberger define as international regimes. Following but emending Krasner's much quoted definition which describes regimes as 'sets of implicit or explicit principles, norms, rules, and decision-making procedures around which actors' [states' – singly or in groupings] expectations converge in a given area of international relations', they add the requirement that there should also be evidence of Krasner's 'principles, norms etc.' being adhered to in practice.[10] In effect this corresponds to asking that the arrangements be structured so as to be self-sustainable. What we have looked at so far in this section have simply been the apparent pre-conditions for the formation of such arrangements (which List and Rittberger agree is *the* important question), with some regard paid to how far the pre-conditions may be sensitive to the kind of arrangement under consideration and how far of general applicability.

Summary and conclusions: sinks versus sources

Since our discussion was built around Olson's Themes, our conclusions can be no more than variations on them.

One linking strand between these variations relates to possible differences between collective action to set norms for the exploitation of a common sink (pollution of the atmosphere or the seas) for the disposal of waste, and collective action to set norms for the exploitation of a common source (harvesting the seas for fish or whales).

Olson's First Theme concerning the importance of number is fully endorsed, irrespective of whether a common sink or a common source is

---

10 List and Rittberger, 'Regime Theory and International Environmental Management', pp. 89, 90.

involved.   So regional arrangements or regimes for the sustainable exploitation of either are more likely to be formed and to persist than global regimes, other things being equal.   But even here, the variation on the First Theme that identifies as a particular advantage of small numbers the incentive for one of a small number sometimes to act unilaterally in a matter of environmental pollution (with a possibly beneficial catalytic effect on collective action), does not find any echo in conservation (the exploitation of a common source).   This suggests at a minimum there is more likelihood of delay in setting norms for the latter than for the former.

Olson's Second and Third Themes concerning both the difficulties presented for collective action by the presence within the collective of large and small participants, plus the route out of the difficulties the same asymmetry offers, are also applicable to both the sink and the source problem.   But here, the escape route of a central fund set up to discourage free-riders is much more obviously applicable to matters of pollution than to matters of conservation.   This is simply because in the latter case, we cannot normally expect that the larger participants will be in a position to make useful contributions to the fund.   Therefore, asymmetry is more of a problem for the setting of conservation norms than it is for pollution norms.

Olson's Theme 3 also speaks of institutional design – the possibility of designing arrangements carefully so as to minimise the barriers to and hazards of collective action.   One of these, a system for verifying that participants to the arrangement were adhering to their undertakings, has been reputably claimed elsewhere to be more easily applicable to the monitoring of a conservation arrangement.   If this were true, it would offset the pessimistic appraisals that we are beginning to accumulate concerning the setting of sustainable norms in the latter case.

But it does not seem to be true.

Certainly, Weale would maintain that getting away with discharging radioactive gases into the atmosphere, for example, whose diluting effect dissipates not only the gases but also the evidence of the misdeed, is relatively easy.   He argues that it would be harder to cheat successfully on a fishing agreement, say, when the fish illegitimately caught in excess of an agreed quota are presumably, however briefly, in the possession of the violator.[11]

---

11 Albert Weale, *The New Politics of Pollution*, (Manchester, Manchester University Press, 1992), p. 194.

Whilst this may be true as far as it goes, there is a counter-argument that is at least as strong. At bottom, this says that it is always easier to verify a complete ban on something rather than some permitted upper limit, or ceiling. Many anti-pollution arrangements have at least the ultimate intention of eradicating the pollutant altogether (as with CFCs) – so *any* detected, anywhere, at the end of the day, is *prima facie* evidence of cheating. By contrast, conservation agreements by their nature wish to set as high a ceiling as possible, on a catch of fish say, compatible with sustainability. A slight breaching of this overall ceiling could easily be lost in the background (even sustainable ceilings will fluctuate because of natural phenomena), but still represent a worthwhile 'extra' catch to the cheating state.

In sum, verification considerations do not alter our conclusion that by its very nature collective action is probably easier when the problem is one of pollution than when conservation is the issue.

This conclusion is reinforced when we look more closely at the motivations of the participants in collective action to control the exploitation of a common source in the next chapter.

6 Living Resources

Sustainability in setting pollution norms is about sustaining collective action in the face of private incentives to cheat. If this is achieved the problem is essentially solved. Other things staying the same, the collective interest is for less pollution rather than more, although the cost of removing the last unit of pollution will always be greater than the cost of removing the first.

But sustainability about setting extractive norms is only in the first place about solving the collective action problem: in the second place it is also a question of where the best interests of the collective (of fishing states, say, now operating as a stable unit) would seem to lie. The problem of sustainability is only solved if the collective of fishing states see it as in their interest that they stay in the fishing business indefinitely. This need not necessarily be the case.

Interest rates and sustainability

To understand this, it is simpler first to consider not the collective action of a group of fishing states but the activities of a single fishing state, with its own supply of fish (taken say, by a nationalised fishing fleet from a small inland sea). Is overfishing possible in this case? The answer would seem to be in the affirmative.

We can imagine that the fish in the sea have a certain market value. We can assume that left to themselves the stock of fish in the sea can maximally increase in number and hence in value by, say, 15 per cent a year (although at some point, like all life, the fish in question will reach the carrying capacity of their environment and stop increasing in number). Whether or not it makes economic sense to aim to fish the sea indefinitely (catching 15 per cent of the population annually) or net them all as quickly as technology will allow depends simply on interest rates. If interest rates are higher than 15 per cent, catching as many fish as possible quickly and putting the proceeds in interest bearing deposits will produce a higher income than fishing sustainably would. Accordingly it would be the rational thing to do.

Of course 15 per cent is a rather high rate of interest and it would perhaps be an unusually heavily indebted government, with an unusually poor international credit rating that would find the cash in hand more attractive than the fish in the sea. What nonetheless remains in some circumstances a possibility for fish becomes more of a probability whenever we are dealing with a living resource whose maximum rate of increase is much smaller. Populations of whales and other marine mammals (as sources of food, pelts etc.), left to themselves, seem to have a natural growth rate peaking at about 5 per cent.[1] Something similar is true for elephants (as sources of ivory), since natural growth rates of populations seem to correlate inversely with the size of the organism. And forests, as sources of timber and shelters for potentially exploitable flora and fauna, can often be sustainably harvested only at similarly slow rates.

Whilst most species of fish are given a sort of protection by the fact that they become more difficult to find the fewer there are, the same is not true to the same extent of whales, and not true at all of elephants and forests (forests are not typically common sources, in that national ownership is usually pretty clearly defined, but it is convenient to postpone discussion of this distinction). So it does not need interest rates to rise very high for exploiters of the latter three classes of living resource to be tempted to

---

1 Colin W. Clark, 'Bioeconomics', in Robert M. May (ed.), *Theoretical Ecology*, (Oxford, Blackwell Scientific Publications, 1981), pp. 398, 399.

abandon sustainable harvesting in favour of rapid exploitation, possibly to extinction.

The tendency to over-exploit marine mammals, and to a lesser extent, fish, or for the ivory trade to drive elephants to extinction is not, then, only a failure of collective action, it is also a failure of market-based regulation.   The villain of the piece is usually seen to be the suspect already identified – the interest rate – with the tendency for high interest rates to promote short-run considerations at the expense of the longer term.   Explanations for the failure of the market to harmonise what may be desirable in the long term with what seems attractive in the short term usually maintain that an individual exploiter will almost always face higher interest rates than society as a whole would, since there is more risk to the lender in the former case than there would be in the latter.[2]

There is nothing particularly novel about this: well-established governments with a strong predilection for working with the grain of market forces have been aware of it for years.   The British government used to give concessions on taxation to private owners of forests in an attempt to encourage conservationist attitudes by in effect easing the anti-conservation pressure from interest rates.   In Britain and elsewhere, taking forests into government ownership (governments can normally borrow money significantly more cheaply than anyone else in society) is also seen as a solution.   In 1996, half of all British woodland was still owned by government.   In the USA, at the peak of the deregulation fashion in the 1980s, 'about a third of all commercial forests [were] publicly owned, most by the federal government but some by states …'.[3]

The international parallel of domestic society is the market-based international trading system.   There may easily be a mismatch between the rate of exploitation of a living resource appropriate to the welfare of the international trading system as a whole and that most appropriate to the welfare of the owner of the resource.   Anti-conservation pressure from interest rates is felt most strongly by those countries in a high state of international indebtedness and experiencing difficulty in servicing these debts – in short, countries with poor international credit ratings who face

---

2   See Robert M. Solow, 'The Economics of Resources or the Resources of Economics', in Robert Dorfman and Nancy S. Dorfman, (eds), *Economics of the Environment*, (New York, W. W. Norton and Company, 1972), p. 363.

3   Roger A. Sedjo and Marion Clawson, 'Global Forests', in Julian L. Simon and Herman Kahn, (eds), *The Resourceful Earth: A Response to Global 2000*, (Oxford, Basil Blackwell, 1984), p. 140.

particularly high rates of interest on their international borrowing because of the high perceived risk of default on their debts. Thus the US government is able to borrow hard currency on the international market much more cheaply than, say, the Brazilian government could. Forests or fish or animal stocks under the national control of states with poor international credit ratings are therefore the most at risk from over-rapid exploitation.

Now, the interest rate problem does not arise only with living resources. The owner of a mine or oil well would seem to be in a very similar predicament, except that the portability of the capital involved will be very low compared to that of a logging company, and itself an inducement therefore to deplete the mine slowly. Internationally, moreover, the problem arises only in a weakened form because for historical reasons, minerals and oil have long been under the control of monopolistic or near monopolistic bodies. In the case of minerals we are speaking of a comparatively small number of multinational mining corporations. In the case of oil we are speaking, since the 1970s, of the OPEC governments and before then of the seven major multinational oil companies. Although even with oil, periods of low international interest rates, as we saw in our discussion of nuclear power, will tend to encourage oil producers to pump at lower rates than normal.

On this analogy, it seems reasonable to suggest that a more sustainable exploitation of living resources might also follow from some form of international collective action. Catching all the fish tomorrow and putting the profits into interest bearing stocks could now seem much less attractive. For one thing, compared to a private (national) owner of fish, the collective (international) owner is in more of a monopolistic position: conceivably this of itself could be translated into lower effective interest rates. A pooled grouping of even individually poor financial risks would present a lowered risk to a lender. But interest rates would not be the whole story. A more conservationist policy would now seem more attractive for a range of other reasons. Firstly, the maximum short-term catch could now be so large (as a proportion of the total catch of the species in question) as to swamp the market and depress prices. Secondly, the subsequent winding down of the fishing fleet, i.e. exiting from the business, would be costly – the market for surplus and, to some degree at least, specialised fishing vessels etc would be limited. Thirdly, the alternative of sustainable fishing is itself more attractive, in that to the degree it has a monopolistic position, the collective can have more certainty about the prices its catch will fetch and should normally be able to keep fish prices high.

Fish

Arguably the most important upshot of the UN Conference on Law of the Sea (UNCLOS, 1972-1983, but not ratified by the USA until 1994) was the green light it gave to states with coastlines to assert exclusive economic control of waters up to 200 miles (nautical) off their coasts.[4] From the discussion above, it will be clear that the implications of such a step (underlining national ownership of fish stocks at the expense of common ownership) were not necessarily conservationist. But it tidied up a disorderly pattern of inconsistent national claims to territorial waters that had begun to emerge just after the Second World War. Individual states in Latin America had started the trend in reaction to the new tendencies of long distance fishing fleets from the Northern Hemisphere to intrude upon what had been regarded as southern fishing grounds.

Fish do not invariably swim over enormous distances. Pelagic or surface-dwelling fish such as herring or mackerel are long distance swimmers, with tuna and swordfish notoriously so, but demersal species (bottom-dwellers) such as cod, haddock and flat fish are comparatively immobile. But even for demersal species, exclusive economic zones are not quite the same as inland seas. Their natural habitat could easily span two or more adjacent exclusive economic zones (EEZ) and even straddle the 200 mile limit between the domain of EEZs and the open seas. Orderly fishing would seem almost invariably to require that a number of neighbouring fishing states form a collective (a further advantage of so doing would be the shared cost of a verification system that would monitor not only cheating within, but also poaching in the collective's waters by outside fleets).

Our treatment of Olson's Themes would suggest that such regional arrangements, with their naturally small numbers of national participants, at least where demersal species were concerned, ought to be relatively stable. But there is obviously a limit to the feasibility of forming such

---

4 For an optimistic and informative appraisal of the achievements of the UNCLOS, see Ronald Barston, 'Law of the Sea: Issues and Practice', in Ronald Barston (ed.), *International Politics Since 1945*, (Aldershot, Edward Elgar, 1991), pp. 133, 161.

collectives. Straddling species, as indicated above, present a problem. So do very migratory types of fish. Whales are themselves highly migratory, although the Southern Oceans are the main catching grounds. But these same oceans gird the Antarctic land mass which has no EEZ waters guarding its fringes at all (there is a whaling sanctuary, created in 1994 by the non-whaling (preservationist) members of the IWC).

A very full study by Peterson of international fisheries (including whaling and sealing) divides the conservation problem as a practical matter into pre- and post-1977, the date he prefers for the emergence (*de facto* if not *de jure*) of EEZs.[5] He notes, as a reading of Olson would lead us to expect, that prior to 1977 that there was a marked inverse correspondence between the success of international fishing regimes and their size. He cites the North Pacific Fur Seal arrangement with only four participating states (Canada, Japan, USA, USSR) as an outstanding success story, but the various Atlantic fishing regimes, with 15 or 20 participants and the International Whaling Commission with, at the time, 12, as failures. Accordingly, he sees the emergence of EEZs as likely to contribute to better prospects for conservation because they will normally obviate the need for very large and unstable groupings.

EEZs twenty years on

Our own conclusions are somewhat less optimistic. As Peterson would agree, whales and tuna, because of their great mobility, may not benefit at all from the EEZ revolution. But even when less mobile species are at issue, as we have seen, there may be economic circumstances (pressure from interest rates) in which a regional fishing arrangement made up of only a few participants and comparatively stable then in the Olson sense, unless it had a near monopoly of the species in question, could still rationally chose to overfish.

Indeed, latest estimates of the state of world fish supplies, 20 years on from the birth of EEZs, are gloomy. Assuming as we must that recorded catches have been dropping because stocks of fish are falling and not due to the success of conservationist policies, the global catch, which increased by five times between 1950 and 1989, fell during the 1990s. The

---

5 M. J. Peterson, 'International Fisheries Management', in Peter M. Haas, Robert O. Keohane and Marc A. Levy (eds), *Institutions for the Earth: Sources of Effective International Environmental Protection*, (Cambridge, Mass., MIT Press, 1994), pp. 249, 305.

correctness of this assumption is put beyond doubt by the rash of disputes between fishing states (including Canada's quarrel with Spain over Atlantic straddling stocks in 1995, and the long-running intra-European Union quarrels over national quotas) which have at their core a shortage of fish. Landings of Atlantic cod which had stabilised, seemingly, at 2.5 million tonnes a year have declined during the 1990s to less than half that figure.

The global position would be worse had there not been a rise in fish farming, which now amounts to nearly 20 percent of total fish supply, with half of this, according to British government sources, coming from fish farms in China.

In 1992 the Rio Conference (UN Conference on Environment and Development (UNCED)) agreed a programme of further political action on the fishing problem. This was in response to concern that EEZs were being overfished. There were also growing pressures by fishing states, whose own EEZs were inadequate, to fish in international waters but on the boundaries of others' EEZs (in or not far outside of which the habits of fish, in any case, which lead them away from the very deepest waters, incline them to congregate).

In August 1995 the Rio-inspired UN Conference on Straddling and Highly Migratory Fish Stocks held in New York came up with solutions in the form of essentially enhanced verification provisions. States belonging to regional arrangements were given more authority to place inspectors on board suspect vessels within the zone of the arrangement. Relatedly, the duties of states to collect and share scientific data relating to the condition of their fishing stocks were stressed. And very much in keeping with the observation made above concerning the tendency of poor or at least highly indebted states in some circumstances to overfish for economic reasons, a non-mandatory call for aid from rich to poor to enable the latter to meet their verification obligations was assented to.

Whilst then there are problems with setting norms for fishing and optimism may be misplaced, failure is not a foregone conclusion. Certainly the problems encountered by the European Union states are not encouraging from the perspective of stable regional arrangements being reached in other parts of the world, where broad political relations between neighbouring states may be intrinsically far worse. But from the perspective of the Olson Themes, the European Union is a large body. Moreover, the interest shown by non-regional states in sailing close to the wind by fishing intensively on the boundaries of regional EEZs should stimulate regional cooperation, rather than the reverse. And 80 per cent of all fish stocks do seem to be contained within EEZs.

Whales

Whales are not fished much within EEZs and indeed are migratory on a large scale. This would seem to rule out collective action naturally centred on a small number of participants. Moreover, whales, or some important species at least, increase in number naturally very slowly (at around 5 per cent a year for the larger species). Thus even if a collective could be effectively formed there would be a danger that it would not see its interest as lying in a conservationist direction at all.

Patricia Birnie's tightly packed account of the attempts by the International Whaling Commission to set sustainable norms for whaling (upon which most of the following discussion is based) tells a story of near comic dimensions.[6]

If 1977 was Peterson's watershed year for setting fishing norms, 1972 and the Stockholm Conference (UN Conference on the Human Environment (UNCHE)) of that year, according to Birnie, marked the real turning point for the setting of whaling norms.

But attempts to set sustainable norms for whaling go back many years before that. The International Whaling Commission itself was founded in 1946, an event described by Clark as the first official act of the newly founded United Nations,[7] as a reaction to the failure of an earlier much less formal international agreement concluded between whaling companies in 1931.

The IWC regulations were along more modern lines. Norms would be set with the assistance of scientific principles. It would have its own secretariat, statistical records were to be kept, voting procedures among members (now governments) were laid down for the changing of regulations and quotas would be set to prevent over-whaling. However, little good was done and stocks continued to fall. By 1965 the stock of blue whales seems to have fallen below 10,000, whereas the optimum stock (that which would provide the maximum sustainable annual catch)

---

6 Patricia Birnie, 'Environmental Diplomacy' in Barston, *International Politics Since 1945*, pp. 255, 259.

7 Colin W. Clark, 'Bioeconomics', p. 399.

was perhaps 75,000.[8] Participating states voted themselves quotas that were too high, scope to do so being provided by scientific uncertainty. Verification that the quota was not being exceeded was in any case weak, with no provision for mutual inspection of catches. Worse still, the quota was a blanket figure with no attempt to allocate whaling states individual sub-quotas. The obvious way perhaps of fixing national quotas would have been to set them in proportion to the average catch of whales by the state in question over the previous five years, say. But this may have been ruled out by the exceptional circumstances of the recent years of war and before that, of economic depression. Whatever, and however plausible, the excuse, this failure to set quotas at the national level had serious consequences. With only a global quota there was every incentive for whaling states annually to catch whales as fast as possible in a sort of gold rush so as to have as much of the quota for themselves as could be managed. Anything less likely to encourage states to wind down their fleets or to desist from modernising them, or indeed to make it probable that quotas would not be exceeded, is hard to imagine.

To add to this list of problems, whaling was also being carried out by states that were not even members of the IWC but presumably selling their catches wherever they could find a market.

'Save the whale'

But by 1972 it was apparent that something rather unusual was happening. Domestic pressures to 'save the whale' had begun to be felt by a number of whaling states who responded by accepting voluntary bans on commercial whaling. The USA virtually abandoned commercial whaling in 1971 (excepting only whaling by Alaskan aboriginal communities). The Stockholm Conference called for a temporary suspension of all commercial whaling for ten years. Whaling for scientific, i.e. non-commercial, purposes was left untouched in the interests of developing better and more realistic models of the lifestyle of particular species of whale to facilitate the setting of sustainable norms for commercial catches in the future.

Within the IWC, the membership was starting to grow in size and alter in composition. A number of formerly keen whaling states, such as the USA, had become, in Passmore's term, preservationist (conservationist, in our and Passmore's usage (but not, unfortunately, always for other

---

8 Ibid., pp. 397, 398.

authors) means having an interest in catching whales but on a sustainable basis: preservationist means having no interest in commercial whaling but a keen interest in the indefinite survival of the animal for its own sake).[9] Non-governmental environmentalist organisations (Green NGOs) with preservationist goals managed to persuade previously disinterested states to join the Whaling Commission under the preservationist banner with the aim of creating a preservationist majority within the IWC (its voting rules required a three-quarters majority of members for rule changes). The Whaling Commission at the same time apparently constructively sought to enhance its monopolistic position. It tackled the problem posed by whaling states that were not members by prohibiting member states to trade in whales and whale products and whaling technology with non-members.

This was quite in tune with the times. The European Community banned its member states from trade in whales and whale products. In 1975 a wholly distinct international treaty, the Convention on International Trade in Endangered Species of Wild Flora and Fauna (CITES) came into force. It puts species at risk under one of two headings, which take the form of Appendices to the treaty, one, preservationist, banning commercial exploitation of the species in question, the other, conservationist, restricting it. Whales, according to species, were entered in both Appendices. Unilaterally, the US government took powers to exclude from fishing in the US EEZ, states that seemed to be endangering the survival of certain species recognised as under threat by the CITES or departing from the norms of an international fishing arrangement.[10]

The reaction of Japan (which as a big whaler narrowly avoided becoming a target of the US legislation, the US Supreme Court eventually ruling in its favour) to the IWC's prohibitions was to take it upon itself to go on an IWC membership drive among states outside the Commission's membership that shared its own strong commercial interest in whaling.

The battle for votes in the Whaling Commission between the preservationists and the rest gradually moved in favour of the former. In 1981 the IWC voted that sperm whales should not be caught, i.e. a quota of zero was set. In 1982 a vote was passed outlawing all commercial whaling from 1984–85 for a period of five years in the first instance.

The few keen whaling states now left in the IWC but outvoted did not take this lying down. At first they sought to keep within the rules. Japan,

9 John Passmore, *Man's Responsibility for Nature*, (London, Duckworth, 1974), p. 73.

10 Birnie, 'Environmental Diplomacy', pp. 256, 257.

Norway and Iceland (and possibly but covertly the USSR too) continued to whale, claiming that the objective was scientific research. But in 1991 Iceland stated its intention to sever its membership of the Whaling Commission, and formed a breakaway whaling organisation with Norway.[11] Japan stated its intention of doing for the Pacific what the two Nordic states had done for the Atlantic.

Elephants

Coming, in terms of our analysis, somewhere intermediate between fish and whales, are African elephants. By an argument paralleling that for bottom-dwelling fish, the conservation of African elephants would also be assisted by the formation of a collective among the neighbouring states where they form a natural part of the fauna. This would be favoured by the tendency of wild herds not to be punctilious about observing national boundaries. Nor would there be excessive risk in this case of the collective being too large from the Olson perspective.

If the collective then had a monopoly or near monopoly of the ivory trade, whilst there is no guarantee it would still be small enough to avoid problems of the kind Olson identifies (there are five neighbouring African elephant states, called the 'range' states, plus Kenya), there would be a chance of it.

Such a collective is possibly in the process of formation. Like whales, African elephants have also come under the wing of CITES, but that does not mean that setting conservationist norms has proved easy. Member states of the CITES (which is a body with global membership) continue to quarrel about the ivory trade, or in terms of the CITES agreement itself, into which of the two Appendices to place the African elephant.

In Lean's words, 1989 was crisis year for CITES.[12] Southern African states with elephants wanted trade to continue, as did the main customers for ivory products, China and Hong Kong. But in 1989 the vote was to stop the trade. Interestingly this was accompanied by an apparent drop in demand for ivory, and the vote was ratified three years later. But the drop in ivory demand seems to have been temporary. The range states have

---

11 Geoffrey Lean and Don Hinrichsen, *Atlas of the Environment*, (Oxford, Helicon Publishing, 1992), p. 164.

12 Ibid., p. 148.

formed a pro-trade group to lobby for change within CITES. The group, called SACIM (Southern African Central Ivory Marketing) has some of the features necessary to make it effective, but not all. It is small (Zimbabwe, Malawi, Botswana, Namibia). South Africa is not a member. Were it to join, it would seem to be a candidate for a hegemonical role, but in fact it possesses relatively few elephants of its own. Nor does SACIM have a monopoly: Kenya and Tanzania stand outside as anti-ivory trade elephant states.

Forests

A particularly interesting question of conservation arises in the case of forests. Forests are not naturally a collective action problem since they are usually national property. Forests embody four kinds of resource: timber; subsidiary and often complementary species of flora and fauna residing within and often dependent on the forest, also with a modern market value of some kind as a store of biodiversity; a presumably benign climatic influence at regional and local levels; and a benign contribution to global flows of carbon dioxide to and from the atmosphere. Only the last of these is irrelevant to a national owner's comparison between the returns to a conservationist policy with those from one of more immediate exploitation, since the forestry policies of a single state would have a negligibly small effect on the global flows of carbon dioxide. A possible exception to this rule was the former USSR, which in 1990 had within its boundaries about one fifth of the world's woodlands.[13]

The choice facing the national owner of a forest is still influenced by interest rates. On the one hand, the forest may be sustainably farmed for the flow of income generated by felling trees for timber. Doing this sustainably means felling trees at no more than their natural replacement rate (probably rather slow). But a steady state forest will also yield rent obtained from exploitation of the store of biological diversity (species of flora and fauna) to which the forest is a natural and possibly unique home. Both sorts of income depend on a slow rate of felling because deliberate replanting without disturbing the equilibrium between the forest and the subsidiary flora and fauna could be difficult. On the other hand, the forest may be speedily cleared for what it will fetch in timber. And once cleared

---

13 *World Resources 1996–97*, p. 219.

the formerly forested area may be converted to productive cropland, although excessive deforestation might in turn put at risk the value of the crops which may be grown, because local climate patterns could have altered in an adverse direction with the removal of the forest.

Interest rates will affect the decision taken in the usual way. A climate of high interest rates will tilt the decision towards rapid exploitation: low interest rates towards conservation. To the extent that tropical forests are under the control of governments facing high interest rates, they are the most vulnerable to excessively rapid depletion.

Nonetheless there is still an analogy to be made between forests on the one hand and fish and elephants on the other in that tropical forests tend to span national boundaries. This makes it reasonable to think that regional collectives for sustainable exploitation even of forests may have some success, for essentially the same reasons that apply to fish and elephants. But as soon as they are formed, with the various advantages they bring in their wake, they are as vulnerable as any large collective to free-riding. And the collective in this case may indeed be rather large. Tropical forests which are in addition potentially valuable stores of biodiversity are found in three continents.

Forests and Rio

That there are problems in setting norms for the sustainable development of forests is generally recognised. The Rio Conference on 1992 had forests on the agenda under two headings – biodiversity and their role in regulating the flow of carbon dioxide to and from the atmosphere.

Under biodiversity, it was claimed at Rio that at the current rate at which forests are being cleared in the less developed world, one third of all species within them could be lost over a period of thirty or forty years. An international agreement to set norms for sustainable exploitation of forests, or the first step towards such an agreement was reached under the name of the Framework Convention on Biodiversity (FCBD). It was signed by 153 states plus the European Community.

The FCBD has two parts. Countries are asked only to catalogue their stock of species and to set a baseline for conservation, but no timetable is asked for. The sting comes in the second part. The developed world agree to foot the bill for at least some of the cost of this information-gathering exercise. However, they also agree to share with the less developed world profits derived from the sale of new products derived from the genetic storehouses of the South.

The US government balked at this provision on the grounds that no entrepreneur is going to take the risk of exploiting these resources if they cannot be assured of profit at the end of the day for themselves. It did not sign the Convention.

As can be seen, the Convention only faintly resembles the model for sustainable development of forests as outlined above. The grouping of forest-rich states seems to be the largest one possible. It has started showing signs that it may indeed be too large, since some Latin American forest-rich countries have already concluded separate deals with US chemical/pharmaceutical companies who provide funds for conservation in exchange for permits to 'mine' the forest. Perhaps for bargaining purposes, forest-rich states also allied with the rest of the less developed world, with a promise of financial reward for the latter to buy their support.

In Chapter 2 we noted that environmental norm setting would be more effective for being in sympathy with market norms as far as possible. We also noted that the 'competitive' or anti-regulatory attitudes intrinsic in market norms are not easily harmonised with the more collective responses appropriate to the setting of environmental norms. On biodiversity, at Rio the forest-rich states did not take the obvious quasi-market (income-maximising) route of forming a monopoly and auctioning access to the forests to the highest bidder. Equally, the US government found the collective action aspects of the Convention as difficult to swallow as it had those of the UNCLOS in 1982. At that time what stuck in the US craw was the suggested international profit-sharing scheme for the exploitation of the mineral resources of the sea bed (lying outside EEZs). Evan Luard, who was later to become a Foreign Office Minister in a British Labour government, wistfully described the draft arrangements for this as a form of 'world socialism'.[14] The Reagan administration agreed entirely and accordingly withheld the US signature from the UNCLOS treaty.

However, the FCBD is a first step. If UNCLOS is any guide, the USA may even eventually retract some of its objections in exchange for alterations being agreed at least in the interpretation of the Convention.

---

14 Evan Luard, *The Control of the Sea-bed*, (London, Heinemann, 1977), p. ix.

Forests and CO$_2$

Even less success attended the attempt at Rio to arrive at an international agreement to tie down forest-rich states in the less developed world to managing their forests consistently with controlling emissions of carbon dioxide. In the steady state, forests neither add carbon dioxide to nor subtract it from the atmosphere. Dead and decaying trees do give up some carbon dioxide but new growth absorbs it. Expanding forest coverage, through new planting, will bring about a net absorption. But burning forests to create crop land, even when done inefficiently, will add large bursts of carbon dioxide to the atmospheric load. The attempt at Rio mainly on the part of the developed world to arrive at a Forest Convention to try and limit the freedom of the less developed world to burn forests did not get far. A mutual promise to think about the matter further was all that was achieved. We return to this question in more detail in Chapter 8.

Olson and living resources

Where the problem for collective action is one of conservation of a living resource there are often two problems to be solved. One is the set of problems addressed by Olson's Three Themes in the previous chapter so that collective action may be proofed against free-riding. As we have seen, achieving this is no simple matter, even for the control of pollution which generally seems easier to achieve than collective action on behalf of conservation. The second set of problems is the temptation that high interest rates may present even to a successful collective to abandon sustainable harvesting or farming of the living resource in favour of plundering the resource to near exhaustion as soon as possible (complete exhaustion cannot be ruled out either, but it will often be defended against by the greater costs involved in exploiting resources as they become more inaccessible as a result of scarcity. Of course, the point is that whilst a conservation norm may in this way be set automatically just this side of complete exhaustion, it is a default norm, less desirable than one setable at least in principle through political intervention). As we have seen, analogous temptation exists when the resource is inanimate. But, apart from the practical point that reasonably successful international collectives already exist for the extraction of minerals and oil, there are in addition back-stops.   The sea-bed and Antarctica both in all probability contain large quantities of hard minerals and even oil which have not even begun yet to be exploited.   There are no such back-stops for living resources.

If conservation of common and/or living natural resources, as we maintain, does seem to present special difficulties in theory, this in itself may explain the particular difficulty in practice of setting norms for the exploitation of living resources.

Preservationism the solution?

Luke Martell, in a careful exploration of alternative explanations for the undeniable fact that environmental or green politics has made more impact on the domestic political scene of some societies than on that of others, does not rule out the deceptively simple explanation that 'environmentalism is a response to environmental problems'.[15]   This is another way of saying, possibly optimistically, that politics (in this case green politics) is a bit like economics.   In a free market, demand is apt to be met.   Or, politics abhors a vacuum.   The additional input of environmental politics that the special problems of conservation may call forth is what we have already referred to as preservationism.   This, it will be recalled, is simply a refusal to admit that the sustainable harvesting of certain living resources can ever be organised, no matter how much ingenuity may be expended in coping with Olson's Themes and the curse of interest rates.   Instead, conservation as a goal is abandoned in favour of preservation – no harvesting at all.

Passmore accurately refers to the clash between conservationists and preservationists[16] as having the intensity of a civil war.   Turbulence and what has been described as polarisation of positions can easily be understood.   A widespread upsurge of 'save the whale' feeling can only provoke whalers to be even less conservationist than they had been previously.   If one's market is about to disappear, this is not the time to be holding back and underfishing.   All of which proves the preservationists' case.   Similarly, boycotts of timber from tropical forest sources or boycotts of ivory from African elephants directly diminish the interest of the owners of these resources in conservation.

From a pessimistic appraisal of where collective action may be at its

---

15 Luke Martell, *Ecology and Society: An Introduction*, (Cambridge, Polity Press, 1994), p. 131.
16 *Man's Responsibility for Nature*, p. 73.

most difficult, we now turn to two cases of apparently successful collective action – the steps taken to control the damage to ozone layer caused by CFCs and related chemicals, and the control of lower atmosphere pollution in Europe.

7 The Stratosphere and Lower Atmosphere

This chapter deals with two almost exactly contemporary efforts made, during the 1970s and 1980s, at international environmental norm setting. Both deal with the pollution of the atmosphere, one the erosion of the ozone layer, the other the pollution of the lower atmosphere, particularly above Europe, by industrial waste gases. The similarities and differences as between the two cases are instructive in their own right but need also to be read with the next chapter in mind, which goes on to look at the unsolved atmospheric pollution problem of global warming.

I

The ozone layer

Introduction

The story of the reaching of international arrangements to control the emission of pollutants damaging to the ozone layer has been the subject of a number of previous studies.[1] The version given here attempts to place itself at the median point of other accounts, a number of which have been coloured by an illuminating tendency to re-fight the conference chamber debates in publishers' book-lists.

Conservation and preservation issues are a matter of biology and ecology. The pollution of the atmosphere which threatens the ozone layer is a matter of chemistry. Here, a particular class of industrial gases (CFCs and certain others), on being released into the atmosphere interferes with an important natural continuous chemical reaction that takes place 15 miles up in the stratosphere. There, where the air is thin, oxygen is exposed to powerful sunlight that actually causes the oxygen molecules to break up and reform again but in such a way as to create a distinct compound of oxygen known as ozone (a molecule made up of three atoms of oxygen rather than the common two). The ozone too is broken up into oxygen again by the same sunlight in a continuous self-balancing process. In being broken up in this way, the ozone actually intercepts ultraviolet (UV) radiation from the sun that would otherwise reach the surface of the earth in harmful quantities.

$$\text{Sunlight}$$
$$|$$
$$O_3 <> O_2 + O$$
$$|$$
$$Cl$$

Figure 7.1 Stratospheric ozone chemistry

In the natural state, the amount of ozone present is just sufficient (life on earth has evolved in the presence of the appropriate amount of UV – a very small amount – that the ozone layer has always let through). However, Lovelock points out that life on earth taken as a whole must be tolerant of pretty large variations in the amount of UV radiation that

1 See, R. E. Benedick, *Ozone Diplomacy: New Directions In Saving The Planet*, (Cambridge, Mass., Harvard University Press, 1991); Nigel Haigh, 'The European Community and International Environmental Policy', in Andrew Hurrell and Benedict Kingsbury, *The International Politics of the Environment*, (Oxford, Clarendon Press, 1992), pp. 228, 249; Edward A. Parson, 'Protecting the Ozone Layer', in P. M. Haas, R. O. Keohane and M. A. Levy (eds), *Institutions for the Earth: Sources of Effective International Environmental Protection*, (Cambridge, Mass., MIT Press, 1994), pp. 27, 73; Ian H. Rowlands, *The Politics of Global Atmospheric Change*, (Manchester, Manchester University Press, 1995); Caroline Thomas, *The Environment in International Relations*, (London, Royal Institute for International Affairs, 1992).

penetrates to the surface. He notes that UV intensities at tropical latitudes – not known for their inhospitability to life – are naturally seven times those at the poles (because the typically glancing sunlight at polar altitudes has to penetrate a thicker cross section of the ozone layer).[2]

The actual concentration of ozone in the stratosphere is really very small, about 10 parts per million of air. Incidentally, if this same concentration of ozone were present lower down, where life is situated, it would be fatal. Ozone is more reactive than oxygen and is actually quite poisonous. It is manufactured widely in industrial quantities for use, amongst other things, as a disinfectant in public swimming baths as an alternative to chlorine.

If the stratospheric concentration of ozone were to drop much below 10 parts per million, however, this would be dangerous. UV radiation would not be as fully intercepted. The additional amounts that would now reach the surface of the earth would damage plants and animals. Animal life, including human life, would suffer from increased incidence of eye diseases and skin cancer. Lovelock himself points out that in the comparative absence of migration, human life and, it should be added, customs, have adapted to the level of UV radiation appropriate to the latitude of residence.[3] The truth of this is certainly seen in reverse, almost, when immigrants to northern climes from more southerly homelands can suffer from illnesses related to inadequate exposure to ultraviolet radiation (e.g. rickets due to a lack of Vitamin D, which is synthesised in the body under the action of sunlight and not always readily obtainable from dietary sources).

We might think simply on the basis of common sense that such a small amount of ozone in exactly the right place doing this key job would be rather vulnerable and indeed this turns out to be the case.

CFCs

The problem, as we have seen, is a class of industrial chemicals called CFCs (chlorofluorocarbons).

This class of chemical was developed on an industrial scale in 1930 by

---

2 James Lovelock, *The Ages of Gaia*, 2nd Edition, (Oxford, Oxford University Press, 1995), p. 158. The factor of 7 is purely illustrative and increases with nearness to the poles. See R. P. Wayne, *Chemistry of Atmospheres*, (Oxford, Clarendon Press, 1991), p. 155.

3 *The Ages of Gaia*, p. 159.

the US General Motors company in response to a need for environmental protection of a sort. Up until that time the working fluids available for refrigerators were rather reactive, indeed poisonous but chemically simple and familiar compounds – either ammonia or sulphur dioxide. The search for a chemically inert and hence safer and non-inflammable working fluid led to CFCs.

After the Second World War, further uses for CFCs were found. Refrigerators, domestic and industrial, expanded into air conditioners in houses, factories and cars. CFCs are also good solvents and this helps make them particularly good cleaning fluids for electrical circuit boards. More notoriously, their very chemical inertness made them a suitable propellant gas for aerosol containers which became an increasingly popular method with consumers for dispensing everything from furniture polish to artificial cream.

Two types of CFC were originally developed: CF_2Cl_2 and $CFCl_3$, more usually referred to in shorthand as CFC-12 and CFC-11 respectively.[4] From an initial production rate of a few hundreds of tons a year of CFC-12 in the 1930s, peak annual production was reached in 1974 at half a million tons. Total production up to 1990 came cumulatively to about 10 million tons. Similar production figures apply to CFC-11.[5]

If CFCs were perfectly inert, they would still be a problem in that drifting about in the atmosphere they add strongly to the greenhouse effect, actually trapping heat that carbon dioxide is incapable of doing. In fact, they are not perfectly inert and gradually decay in the atmosphere, although they remain there for as long as 100 years before that happens. The way in which this decay proceeds is that at the height of the stratosphere the CFCs come under the influence of strong sunlight, including UV action, which causes them to break up and release atoms of chlorine.

In the stratosphere the chlorine (Cl) reacts with the free oxygen on the right hand side of the equilibrium process (Figure 7.1) for the natural synthesis and dissociation of ozone. The balance of this process is now

---

4 Naming of CFCs, as CFC-11 (one-one), for instance, is done for convenience. The chemical formula is translated for easier oral communication according to the following rule. The prefix CFC is followed by a three digit number. The first is the number of carbon atoms in the compound, LESS one. The second digit is the number of hydrogen atoms, PLUS one. The third digit is the number of fluorine atoms. When the first digit is zero, it is omitted. Thus $CFCl_3$ is CFC-11 and CHF_2Cl is CFC-22. See Wayne, *Chemistry of Atmospheres*, p. 160.

5 Wayne, *Chemistry of Atmospheres*, p. 167.

disturbed, there is less oxygen on the right hand side and in order to try to make up the balance more and more ozone dissociates.   Thus the amount of ozone at any one time is decreased and more and more UV radiation is allowed through.

The presence of CFCs in the atmosphere was reported first by Lovelock and colleagues in 1973.   The amounts present were large and corresponded more or less to the total quantity that had ever been manufactured. Aerosol uses relied, of course, on CFCs being squirted into the atmosphere, but leaky commercial refrigerators and the deliberate breaking up of old domestic refrigerators and air conditioning units ensured that CFCs everywhere sooner or later reached the atmosphere.   Only one year later, the US scientists Molina and Rowland identified CFCs as a threat to the ozone layer, using theoretical arguments very much more detailed and sophisticated than the crude outline given above (showing, for instance, that one atom of chlorine can do very much more damage to ozone production than the simple model above would seem to suggest).

It is an interesting sidelight on the scientific uncertainty relating to the effect of CFCs on the ozone layer that Lovelock himself was not originally convinced that there was any great urgency about the matter.

Ozone and Concorde

It is also the case that the waters, so to say, had already been muddied. In 1970 attention of the atmospheric physics and chemistry communities had been drawn to the possible vulnerability of the ozone layer to exhaust gases emitted by long range supersonic aircraft which fly at stratospheric altitudes.   The problem gas involved seemed to be nitric oxide.   This provisional finding coincided with two linked political debates: the internal US debate over the possible development of a US supersonic transport aircraft and the granting of landing rights in the USA for the Anglo-French Concorde.   Subsequent scientific enquiry over the next decade indicated that the Concorde, at least, presented a significantly smaller risk than had originally been suggested.[6]   This episode was to colour CFC diplomacy because the commercial success of the Concorde depended on the north Atlantic route and on its being granted extensive landing rights in the USA and on US airlines buying it.   These hopes were

6   Wayne, *Chemistry of Atmospheres*, p. 158.

dashed and the Concorde programme turned into a large-scale commercial failure, with only a handful of aircraft kept flying by the two national airlines on a subsidised basis. In Britain and France, a suspicion gained ground that the original (exaggerated as it turned out) claims that Concorde damaged the ozone layer had been a little too convenient for US aircraft manufacturers, after Congress had denied them the funds to develop a supersonic transport aircraft of their own.

Skin cancer

The environmental consequences of damage to the ozone layer that had the most immediate political impact was the predicted rise in skin cancers. Because, as we have seen, the effective thickness of the ozone layer depends on latitude, the amount of ultraviolet radiation penetrating to ground level in the northern parts of the USA, for instance, will always be smaller than that for the southerly states. Skin cancer incidence should therefore be greater in the south than the north (given the essential geographical homogeneity of US population), which is indeed what medical statistics show. On this basis, a 7 per cent thinning of the ozone layer (originally predicted to occur by 2015 if CFC use remained unchecked) is calculated to produce an annual additional 20,000 cases of skin cancer among the US population, against a natural background of about 500,000 cases. Whilst the proportion of these new cancers taking the form of the dangerous melanoma type seems to be open to doubt,[7] it will be noted that our order of magnitude test would suggest that such an environmental impact, at 4 per cent of background, would probably be seen as significant.

US aerosol ban

The debates over supersonic passenger aircraft had sensitised the US public and to a lesser extent the publics of other north Atlantic states who were more or less neutral in the Concorde debate. Soon after Rowland and Molina had apparently identified CFCs as the real villain, a strong public reaction set in. Aerosol containers began to be boycotted by US consumers and were being left on the supermarket shelves. The US company DuPont, at the time responsible for a quarter of the world

---

7 Ibid., pp. 152, 153.

production of CFCs, was soon selling very little for aerosol use and so was not seriously hurt when in 1978 the US government banned CFCs in aerosols in the USA (the ban was actually on 'non-essential' aerosol uses of CFCs).[8] That substitutes for CFCs in this particular role were plentiful helped make this decision relatively easy, although aerosols did constitute nearly a half of the domestic market for CFCs, with refrigeration second in importance, accounting for about one third. There were no obvious substitutes for CFCs in refrigeration: returning to ammonia or sulphur dioxide would not have constituted a step forward even in environmental terms.

At all events, this was a unilateral action. According to Rowlands, in 1974, prior to the ban, the USA and the European Community between them were responsible for three-quarters of the world production of CFCs.[9] Each camp was producing virtually the same absolute amount for aerosol use – three-quarters of European production, a half (of the somewhat larger) US production total. So the US action meant a drop of more than one third in short-run CFC releases to the atmosphere. Since world demand for CFCs at the time was not growing quickly, we can see that the extra costs to US manufacturers of producing new aerosols may not have been understood as disproportionate to the benefits. This is after taking into consideration the fact that the benefits could not of course be captured by the USA alone, and that the inhabitants of other parts of the world would also benefit from the respite granted to the ozone layer.

The US initiative was followed over the next two years by Canada, Sweden and Norway – a grouping of countries half-seriously named 'Candanavia' after their tendency to find themselves on the same side of a number of international issues, not just the environmental kind. Their unconditional coupling with the US position would have cost them little in industrial discomfort, since they were not major CFC producers. Their positive motivation may have stemmed from an original heightened awareness that their geography laid them open to the consequences of a damage to the ozone layer caused by supersonic passenger aircraft on the busy north Atlantic routes. The tendency for thinning of the ozone layer by CFCs to be more marked in polar and near polar latitudes was not confirmed until several years later.

---

8 Rowlands, *The Politics of Global Atmospheric Change*, p. 104.
9 Ibid., pp. 104, 105.

European response

As we have seen, the other main producer of CFCs in the world apart from the USA was the EC. In fact the two were commercial rivals, or at least their home chemical companies were. The EC public and official view at the time of the US unilateral ban was that US public fears were exaggerated, in a manner all too reminiscent of the Concorde episode, and that there could be sinister commercial motives behind them. This is precisely the sort of suspicion unilateral moves are apt to excite in collective action situations. CFCs were proportionately a much more important part of the EC economies than of the USA (50 per cent more important, in terms of persons employed, but still, of course, a very small part of total economic activity). In addition the EC countries had a large export market in CFCs and aerosols, again unlike the USA whose CFC market was almost wholly self-contained. Within the EC, Britain and France were the leading sceptics as to the US position. The Concorde business predisposed them to scepticism but it had also led the two countries to encourage scientific enquiry into the chemistry of the ozone layer, which did not go all the way with US scientific thinking and provided a basis for a more principled challenge. Britain, moreover, was a leading producer and exporter of CFCs.

Nonetheless, the EC was a coalition of 12, not two. Even in the late 1970s it included countries that had begun to share some of the US doubts over CFCs, Holland and, with growing conviction, Germany (actually by this time the largest EC CFC producer). Eventually the EC moved somewhat in the US direction but not very far. In 1980 the EC announced a Community-wide cut-back in CFC aerosol use from the 1976 level by 30 per cent and a freeze on production capacity for CFCs as of 1980.

Now, the 30 per cent reduction in aerosol use from the 1976 level was a very small sacrifice since unilateral action, mainly in Germany, had seen the EC-wide usage decline by 26 per cent already. The announced cap on production capacity is also sometimes portrayed, mainly by US analysts, as equally cynical. It is true, for example, that production capacity for CFCs was at the time under-used (plant lying idle etc.) and actual output of CFCs could be much increased (by as much as 60 per cent) even without any increase in production capacity.

On the other hand, a cap on production capacity capped all EC production of CFCs and not just the aerosol uses the USA and 'Candanavia' had focussed on. It had a precautionary quality too in that it was a ban taken in advance of the emergence of obvious CFC substitutes for non-aerosol uses (refrigerants, circuit board cleaners). In truth, it was an illustration of something that the original US ban had itself illustrated – restraint in the production of an environmentally suspect thing is always easier when demand for that thing has already turned down. In the EC case, demand seems to have turned down in sympathy with the business cycle. But a production limit had other merits besides. Environmental legislation limiting production rather than use of CFCs lends itself much more easily to verification, since there are comparatively few production centres.

The road to Vienna

In 1980 the centre of gravity of agitation to protect the ozone layer shifted away from the USA and towards the UN Environmental Programme (UNEP) directed by M. Tolba. This signalled a slackening in momentum, partly because scientific uncertainty about the effects of CFCs on the ozone layer was not being dispelled very rapidly, but more importantly because of a change in US administration. The Reagan years symbolised in a fairly acute form the collision between the competitive instincts of market economics and the more collective responses required for environmental protection. We have already noted that in 1981 the US government reversed its historic position on the Law of the Sea conference, decrying the arrangements reached for the international exploitation of the sea bed as socialism.

However there was a difference here that proved to be crucial. It was in the interests of US business that there should be *international* CFC regulation. There already was domestic US regulation which was never going to be reversed, so they were operating at a disadvantage with their international competitors who did not have such strong or even any domestic restrictions on their doings. So the pro-business side of Reaganism came into conflict with the anti-regulation and anti-internationalist sides and by the end of 1983 it came out ahead, just.

In 1983 the USA joined the Toronto group ('Candanavia' plus Finland and Switzerland) in pressing for a world-wide ban on 'non-essential' aerosol use of CFCs, which would hurt the large EC export market. The EC responded, predictably, with its production cap idea, which if accepted globally would hurt US manufacturers who had no spare capacity for CFC production so that all additional world demand, when the business cycle turned, would have to be met from Europe's under-used factories.

Meanwhile the UNEP working party on protecting the ozone layer with the guiding themes of buying time until the scientific picture became clearer and of accelerating the same scientific understanding proposed an international convention that did not even attempt to reconcile the US (more accurately, Toronto group) and European positions.

The so-called Vienna Convention, which was signed in 1985 by the USA and Europe and the Toronto group (plus the then USSR, a smallish CFC producer, Egypt – Tolba's home country – and some Latin American states) committed signatories to very little.

Essentially all it required was that signatories take appropriate measures to protect the ozone layer and to participate in further scientific research as well as data collection and exchange on production and use of CFCs. Also added was an authorisation for UNEP to prepare the ground for a future binding agreement by 1987.

The Antarctic 'hole' in the ozone layer

Shortly after the Vienna Convention was signed, a team of British scientists led by Joe Farman (the importance of nationality should be evident) disclosed that they had found a substantial thinning (a 'hole'in popular parlance) in the ozone layer above Antarctica. They said that they had found that springtime ozone levels, which they had been measuring since the 1960s, were now about one half of what they once were. The Antarctic, under the international treaty of 1959, had been sanitized of international competition and was (and remains) home to a number of national scientific geophysical bases. Stratospheric ozone happened to fall within the scope of the sort of thing British scientists had been monitoring fully consistently with the original national requirement for knowledge about the stratosphere in the days of high hopes for Concorde.

It turns out, although this was not appreciated immediately, that even a relatively small drop in ozone concentration world-wide can be detected at the South Pole as a result of the magnifying effect of weather conditions above the Antarctic during winter. What happens is that part of the atmosphere is temporarily as it were held in a large natural test-tube, not mixing with the rest, and in the dark of Antarctic winter nothing much happens either to CFCs or ozone. Along comes the sun at springtime, in flashes the ultraviolet radiation, chemical reactions take place and before subsequent mixing with the rest of the atmosphere occurs, the amount of ozone present high above the South Pole can be measured from the ground.

Now it is fair to point out that the effect of these findings on pushing the Vienna Convention along to the Montreal Protocol, which was added to it in 1987, is in dispute. It is said by Benedick, who was the US negotiator at Montreal, that their significance had not really been absorbed by the time of the Protocol.[10] However, we can take it that the period between Vienna and Montreal did see a growing conviction in scientific circles that the ozone layer really was threatened probably by CFCs and similar compounds. And there is no doubt that the British origin of the ozone layer hole findings added to their credibility, since Britain seemed an inherently unlikely source, hitherto publicly doubting on scientific grounds the need for any urgency over the ozone layer.

Montreal Protocol

The Montreal Protocol actually committed states to concrete steps towards the phasing out of CFCs, and was negotiated in the context of a larger group than Vienna. Participants now included Japan and some less developed countries. The old transatlantic quarrel over consumption vs production was bargained away. States would have to control not production but adjusted production, which was defined as production + imports − exports (for the USA, which did not trade internationally much in CFCs, this meant production, pretty well – a US concession). But there was a European concession to match it. The Europeans wanted originally only a freeze on production (this was a step forward from the old freeze on production capacity), with possible small cuts in the future. The US position was to start with a freeze, but showed a willingness to contemplate future cuts in production as high as 95 per cent. This created European suspicions that US manufacturers must have already cleared the decks for the production of substitutes for CFCs in refrigerator applications. Nonetheless the Europeans compromised. There was to be first a freeze at 1986 levels in place by 1990; a 20 per cent cut in 1986 levels to be in place by 1994; and a 50 per cent cut in place by 1999. The

---

10 Benedick, *Ozone Diplomacy: New Directions In Saving The Planet*, p. 20.

CFCs covered were CFC-11, 12, 113, 114, 115.[11]

Secondly, controlled chemicals went beyond CFCs to include halons, used in fire extinguishers for instance.

The importance of ODP

Thirdly, controlled chemicals were now identified by an ODP number (ozone depleting potential) and it was cuts in total ODP adjusted production that mattered. Some CFCs had more than double the ODP of others and some halons ten times the ODP of CFCs. This was an important step. It was made possible by increased scientific understanding of the link between particular types of CFCs and their impact on the ozone layer. The ODP number relates the harmfulness of a CFC or related compound, weight for weight, to the harmfulness of CFC-11, which is assigned the ODP score of 1. The score is made up of a rising scale for how many chlorine or bromine (even more ozone-depleting) atoms the compound in question has and an allowance for how long the compound stays in the atmosphere. CFC-11 (ODP 1) has a residence time of 60 years: CFC-22 (ODP 0.04), 17 years.[12]

This refinement in understanding obviously opens the door to the use of near substitutes for CFC-11 and CFC-12 in refrigeration and cleaning roles. Bargaining at Montreal was also made easier through permitting signatories to reach their adjusted production levels by restricting only their ODP total. How the total was reached would be within the state's own discretion.

Fourthly, controls were put on imports and exports of CFCs and of items using CFCs where non-parties to the treaty were concerned.

Fifthly, special provision was made for less developed countries. It would have been absurd to ask them to freeze production at 1986 levels and then cut from there. Most of them had no production at all. Thus they were permitted ten years free of restrictions during which they could increase production up to around the sort of per head level the developed world would have by 1997. After that time they had to implement a programme of cuts like everyone else.

Sixthly, Montreal set up a committee of technical specialists – Panel for

---

11 Edward A. Parson, 'Protecting the Ozone Layer', Haas *et al.*, (eds), *Institutions for the Earth: Sources of Effective Environmental Protection*, p. 44.

12 Wayne, *Chemistry of Atmospheres*, pp. 165, 167.

Technical Assessment – which was given the job of recommending appropriate substitutes for controlled chemicals in line with the advance of scientific understanding.[13]

Why the progress since Vienna? No doubt, better scientific understanding played a part. Whether the actual discovery of the hole in the ozone layer over the Antarctic was itself really significant may be in doubt, but as Parson makes clear, there was a scientific turning point in 1985.[14] Before that date the scientific community seemed to be unable to come to a settled view, with frequent changes of mind and reversals over the effects of CFCs on stratospheric ozone. After that date, there was a settled view that the effects were indeed damaging, most remaining doubts being in the direction of wondering whether the effects were not being underestimated.

But there had been other changes. The EC had probably moved politically as Germany became progressively greener in outlook and more influential in Brussels, compared to the UK and France. The USA may have been paradoxically strengthened by Reaganism. One can often drive a harder bargain internationally when one has an apparently difficult domestic client to be satisfied. Certainly the USA was ruthless, officially encouraging, possibly paying for, US green non-governmental organisations to stir things up in Britain in favour of the US position. There was an official British government complaint to the USA about this in 1987. EC doubts were also partly bought off by Montreal recognising Brussels as an international actor and allowing it to act on behalf of its member states with regard to certain obligations of the Protocol.

Post Montreal

Montreal was not the end, more the end of the beginning. New scientific evidence of a most alarming kind began to flood in. First of all, a new 1987 Antarctic study showed that the extent of ozone depletion measured above the South Pole was even greater than British scientists had thought and that there were abnormal amounts of chlorine in the stratosphere. Worse, there was evidence that the ozone layer had already started to thin over populated parts of the Northern Hemisphere. No thinning in the ozone layer was discovered in 1988–89 by an Arctic expedition, although

13 Rowlands, *The Politics of Global Atmospheric Change*, p. 119.
14 'Protecting the Ozone Layer', p. 28.

they did discover abnormal amounts of chlorine. (The Arctic is somewhat less vulnerable than the Antarctic because it is not quite so cold, normally, and the nett effect of low temperature is to accelerate the ozone depleting effect. The Northern Hemisphere winter of 1996, which was unusually cold, did however see record drops in Arctic ozone levels.) Ozone over southern Australia and New Zealand was already 10 per cent down by the end of the 1980s.

All this seemed to galvanise the EC into thinking that Montreal was not enough. Interestingly, the UK began to take a leading part. In September 1988, Mrs Thatcher spoke of her government's extraordinary interest in saving the ozone layer and announced a conference to speed things along to be convened in London. That there was a European election due in months and British opinion polls were already showing strong Green Party support (they got 15 per cent of the vote in 1989) had of course absolutely nothing to do with this.

The London conference on the ozone layer took place in 1990. It tightened up Montreal significantly and in several ways. Important new signatories were brought on board, China and India. Controls were extended to new compounds with big ODP and tightened. CFCs-11 and 12 were to be phased out altogether by 2000, as were halons and a number of other chemicals not mentioned at Montreal. Even a watchful eye was to be kept on hydrochlorofluorocarbons, HCFCs (e.g. CFC-22) touted as substitutes for CFCs. Arrangements were made more attractive for less developed countries, with a special fund created to assist them through their ten year period of grace, and improved promises of technology transfer. The USA was only unwillingly brought to pay for the lion's share of the fund. Life was made less attractive for non-signatories by prohibitions on signatories trading banned substances with them.

In 1992, in a further review, in Copenhagen, the basket of controlled chemicals was enlarged again, timetables for phasing out further tightened but with additional concessions provided for signatories from the developing world. By the end of 1993 the Protocol had more than 100 parties.

Assessment

It is tempting to regard the whole process as a model undertaking. Restrictions on CFCs were introduced step-by-step. Unilateral action began the process, and was taken in just the sort of circumstances one might predict. Negotiations were begun soon enough so as to involve only a small number of parties which increased the chances of a deal being struck. Sidepayments were devised to ensure the adherence of smaller producers to the arrangement. These act like glue for parties to the arrangements but also act like magnets for potential small parties undecided about joining. Production limits are the best controls from the verification aspect.

But unqualified congratulation would be out of place. Parson certainly takes a dimmer view, claiming that the Protocol and its subsequent reviews represent 'the right measures enacted too late'.[15] Certainly delay is the bane of environmental norm setting. In this case, the residence time of the now-banned CFCs 11 and 12 in the atmosphere is so long that concentrations will remain above the 1970s level, where they stood when Lovelock first detected CFCs in the atmosphere, well beyond the first half of the 21st century. Added to which, more recent measurements of ozone layer thinning over the Antarctic correspond to rates of depletion of ozone far in excess of those predicted by the scientific models that informed the Protocol.[16] Had the Protocol been achieved earlier, the overshoot would have been smaller and the number of skin cancer cases observed and lying around the corner substantially fewer.

Parson regards the long gap between the US unilateral aerosol ban and the Vienna Convention as the period of avoidable delay. But there is no shortage of plausible explanations. Scientific uncertainty stayed high until 1985. It was the first consequence of there being two well-funded schools of scientific enquiry on either side of the Atlantic able to back up their temporarily contradictory claims. On the whole, better science is eventually likely to emerge from two well-funded schools of enquiry than from one, but this may involve delay. Relatedly, substitutes for CFCs in non-aerosol uses could not be identified until the science was clearer. In addition, by the start of the 1980s the domestic political climate in the USA and Britain was better attuned to the 'deregulation' of economic activity than to its regulation (on the other hand, the very opposite was true of Germany). On top of which, the legacy of the quarrel over Concorde fuelled trans-Atlantic suspicions. Although without the stimulus of the earlier debate over supersonic transport aircraft, it is possible that

---

15 'Protecting the Ozone Layer', p. 72.

16 Wayne, *Chemistry of Atmospheres*, p. 168 and p. 171.

scientific understanding of the ozone layer would have been even slower in coming. Finally, the criticism of Parson and Benedick (less balanced in the case of the latter, although aimed possibly more at the post-Vienna period[17]) of delay due to time spent clarifying the status of the EC as a negotiating party, is not obviously justified. By condensing 12 negotiating parties into one this is more likely to have been a small investment in time that repaid itself several-fold.

II

The second half-chapter moves the scene to the lower atmosphere and from a metaphorical political position half way across the Atlantic to a scene somewhat further to the east.

Lower atmosphere pollution

Introduction

At regional levels, the burning of either oil or coal injects sulphur compounds into the lower atmosphere (from sulphur impurities in the raw material – there can be as much as one tonne of sulphur in every 40 tonnes of coal or 60 tonnes of fuel oil: even desulphurized petrol contains a kilogram of sulphur in every thousand gallons).[18] On a world-wide basis the burning of fossil fuel injects sulphur into the atmosphere at 70 per cent of the natural rate (the latter set by volcanic eruptions and sea-spray, mainly). The percentage of the natural regional rate can, of course, often be very much higher. Still at the regional level, all burning of fossil fuel releases into the atmosphere soot (particulates) and other products of incomplete or inefficient combustion. At the same time, high temperature combustion processes also create oxides of nitrogen, injecting these into the atmosphere at 10 per cent (at a minimum) of the natural rate.

These regional pollutants are regional in that their effects are localised within a few tens to a few hundreds of kilometres of the source and this in turn is simply because their time of residence in the atmosphere is very

---

17 Benedick, *Ozone Diplomacy*, pp. 94, 97.

18 Wayne, *Chemistry of Atmospheres*, pp. 238, 242. Wayne's account of air pollution (pp. 237, 263) is closely followed here.

short (a few days) and there is a corresponding limit to how far they may be spread on the wind. It is also a characteristic that their damaging effects to the habitat are more often due to their presence in combination rather than as individual pollutants. It is also typical that the products of chemical reactions involving the pollutants are themselves a source of damage. This is true of the former smogs of London where soot and sulphur dioxide (both mainly from the combustion, domestic and industrial, of coal) in combination in 1952 led to about 4000 premature deaths. It is true of the modern smogs of Los Angeles, and of a number of European cities during the summer, where nitrogen oxides arising mainly from the internal combustion engines of motor vehicles plus hydrocarbons from incomplete combustion of petrol in the presence of sunlight creates a health-threatening rise in ozone concentration at ground level.

Acid rain

It is also true of acid rain. Two regions of the world have been affected particularly by acid rain, the north-eastern USA and adjacent parts of Canada and in Europe, Sweden and southern Norway.

Natural rain is already slightly acid, but a rise in acidity at ground level (in streams and lakes) in the regions mentioned has been observed involving sulphuric acid (from sulphur dioxide), nitric acid (from nitrogen oxides) and hydrochloric acid (from reactions in the atmosphere involving sulphuric acid and salt – the latter from the sea). This has had damaging effects on buildings, grasses and trees and fresh water fish stocks. Chiefly as a result of deliberate policy to diminish the immediately local effects of large scale burning of fossil fuels, electricity-generating power stations and other industrial scale fossil fuel furnaces in OECD countries have for many years been fitted with tall chimney stacks. The effect of these is to reduce the concentration of pollutants in the immediate vicinity of the power stations by dispersing them on the wind. But the effect is also in some cases simply to export the pollutants on prevailing winds beyond the international borders of the country in question.

According to Wayne:[19]

More than 70 per cent of the sulphur in the atmosphere over Sweden is thought to

19 Wayne, *Chemistry of Atmospheres*, p. 249.

be anthropogenic [originating from human economic and social activities], and, of this load, 77 per cent may originate outside Sweden. Britain and the Ruhr valley, together with some Eastern Bloc [Central European] countries, are cited as sources of the foreign sulphur.

All fossil fuels are implicated in regional pollution. As already indicated, coal is by and large (joule for joule) a dirtier fuel than oil and oil dirtier than natural gas (methane). But even the burning of natural gas at power stations is likely to produce nitrogen oxides and soot, although modern designs should be able to minimise this.

Indeed, just as car engines and exhaust systems can be designed to minimise the emission of partly burnt fuel in the form of volatile organic compounds (using so-called catalytic convertors) careful design of power plants can arrange for pollutants to be extracted from chimney gases by chemical 'scrubbing'. Unfortunately, this adds possibly about 10 per cent to the cost of electricity produced by this method. And this creates a dilemma for some states. As noted above, the atmosphere over Sweden is polluted with anthropogenic sulphur to no greater a degree than the global average. But the crucial point for the Swedes is that the anthropogenic sources for this sulphur lie almost exclusively outside Sweden. If Britain, lying upwind of Scandinavia, finds that the bulk of sulphur dioxide and nitrogen oxides produced by its fossil-fuelled power stations is deposited outside British territory, its motivation to install expensive scrubbers is weakened.

LRTAP

Our penultimate historical example of norm setting deals with regional atmospheric pollution in Europe, where the quality of the environment in one state is partly determined by the policies or lack of them followed by its neighbours to control the emissions of regional-range pollutants from (chiefly) the combustion of fossil fuel. Heavy reliance is placed on the encyclopaedic and stimulating account due to Marc Levy.[20]

The three particular pollutants which have attracted the attention of European governments are sulphur dioxide (SO_2), nitrogen oxides (NO_x)

20 Marc A. Levy, 'European Acid Rain: The Power of Tote-Board Diplomacy', in Peter M. Haas, Robert O. Keohane and Marc A. Levy (eds), *Institutions for the Earth: Sources of Effective Environmental Protection*, (Cambridge, Mass., MIT Press, 1993), pp. 75, 132.

and volatile organic compounds (VOCs).   VOCs enter the atmosphere partly from the incomplete combustion of some fossil fuels, and partly from the evaporation of certain industrial chemicals. They are implicated in causing deterioration in the quality of the lower atmosphere, including brokering the production of ozone at low levels. But both sulphur dioxide and nitrogen oxides are produced by the combustion of fossil fuel and lead to the production of acid rain.

Nordic concerns

In 1968 a Swedish scientist, Oden, concluded that acidification of Swedish lakes with consequent damage to fish stocks was occurring as a result of wind borne 'exports' of SO_2 and NO_x produced by large fossil fuelled power stations outside Sweden. Britain and central Europe were the chief suspects.   The Swedish and Norwegian governments brought their anxieties on this matter before the 1972 Stockholm Conference, which was not even attended by the USSR or its East European allies for Cold War reasons connected with the vexed question of the diplomatic status of East Germany.   Other European governments at Stockholm were somewhat sceptical of the Nordic claims.

Nonetheless the well-established OECD group of Western industrialised states sponsored a study of boundary-crossing air pollution in Europe. In 1977 it published results showing that it was so extensive that almost half of the Western European states participating in the enquiry, as a result of wind patterns actually were subject to more pollution from the activities of their neighbours than as a result of their own actions. Again, as non-members of the OECD, the Warsaw Pact group did not participate. The Nordic case was established at least in principle.   Britain, the largest exporter of SO_2 and NO_x in Europe and upwind of almost everyone, was the most reluctant to accept the OECD findings. The pollution monitoring centres created by the OECD were hived off from the OECD itself in 1978 and given a separate existence as EMEP (Cooperative Programme for Monitoring and Evaluation of the Long-Range Transmission of Air Pollutants in Europe).

By the middle of the 1970s, detente, i.e. a partial easing of Cold War antagonisms, had made some progress, particularly in Europe. A typical Soviet preference for gestures of international friendliness which would not put at risk the correlation of forces and with an eye, as always, to the possibility of inserting a political wedge between Western Europe and

North America, led the USSR in 1975 to sponsor the creation of new international organisation called the Conference on Security and Cooperation in Europe (CSCE; after the end of the Cold War to be transmuted into the OSCE – Organisation for Security and Cooperation in Europe). All European countries were meant to join: Western suspicions of Soviet intentions led them successfully to insist that the USA and Canada join too. In 1976 the Soviets proposed a meeting of parties to discuss a range of 'low politics' issues, which was narrowed down by the nearest thing there was at the time to a CSCE secretariat (in fact the UN Economic Commission for Europe – ECE) to the air pollution question.

First step

In 1979 the Long Range Transboundary Air Pollution Convention was signed by 33 states. It was to do with principles rather than specifics (rather like its CSCE mother-body). It identified this class of pollution as an international problem and obtained pledges that steps would be taken to reduce it. But parties also agreed there should be a process for collecting and distributing national data on pollution creation, flows etc. Data were to include material on carbon dioxide emissions, as well as the three regional pollutants, SO_2, NO_x and VOCs.

It was a first step, but of a peculiar kind. It had 33 parties, but seen as a Cold War document, the effective number of parties was perhaps three or four – the two alliances of East and West plus the neutrals. Sweden, of course, was a neutral. It was an agreement about more than one thing, which, as we have seen, need not be a disadvantage. For many or most it was a detente document as well as an environmental protection agreement. The USA could have had no very strong interest in it outside the detente context.

Germany and the sulphur protocol

For the Nordics, perhaps also for Canada, it was an environmental protection document and their attempts to have the LRTAP commit signatories actually to reduce pollution emissions made only small progress until 1982. At this point West Germany put pressure on its more laggard European Community partners when it sided with Sweden and Norway in asking for a second step in the LRTAP process, in the form of commitments to specific cuts in emissions of sulphur dioxide. The proximate cause of the German move was the discovery that the Black Forest had apparently been damaged by acid rain. In 1985 a Sulphur Protocol to the LRTAP was signed, committing the 21 parties to 30 per cent cuts on sulphur dioxide emissions from a 1980 baseline to be achieved by 1993.[21]

France had no real difficulty in following Germany. Its extensive and growing reliance on nuclear power meant promising to cut sulphur dioxide emissions was easy, since few extra costs would be incurred thereby.

The USA did not sign (it was later to pass domestic legislation setting limits on sulphur dioxide emissions similar to those required by the Protocol). There had been a deterioration in detente since 1979 and whilst the second Cold War which had broken out in the intervening period was past its peak, the connection between LRTAP and high politics which had helped its birth had become a handicap in its adolescence. The US attitude, seeming to distance itself from a large number of other NATO members, even Canada, would have been no reason for the USSR not to sign: quite the reverse. The Soviets however were allowed to sign up to a cut in 'exports' of sulphur dioxide, not production. Since the USSR exported very little, because of the direction of prevailing winds, but produced a great deal, this was a particularly easy control to accept. But permitting cuts of this kind within the Sulphur Protocol could not have done anything for the verifiability of the Protocol. National production targets are much more reliable and inherently difficult to falsify.

The dirty man of Europe

In more ways than one, Britain was at the opposite pole from the USSR. The spurning of the Protocol by the USA was itself a reason for Britain to do likewise in Cold War terms. But in any case the bargain being offered was a particularly poor one. Britain was a major exporter of sulphur dioxide but not much hurt by either its own or others' emissions. The costs involved in meeting the 30 per cent target would have been high (the order of magnitude seems to be about £1 billion[22]), borne by Britain, and the benefits would have gone elsewhere – chiefly to the Nordic countries. Britain refused to sign and in so doing won its 'dirty man of Europe'

---

21 *World Resources 1992–93*, (New York, Oxford University Press, 1992), p. 199.

22 1991 pounds sterling. Interpolating from a table provided by Levy, 'European Acid Rain', p. 104.

badge. Other non-signers were mostly small European states. Since the Protocol contained no central fund for the dissuasion of free-riders, the magnetic effect such a fund might have had on smaller potential parties was also absent.

A further reason for Britain's reluctance to sign was its concurrent involvement in a closely parallel set of international negotiations within the European Community. These stemmed from a German proposal that EC member states should accept the same tight emission standards for fossil fuelled power stations (the so-called Large Combustion Plant Directive) that Germany had unilaterally already accepted in 1982 in reaction to the Black Forest alarm. Had Britain agreed to the LRTAP Sulphur Protocol it would have found itself naked in the EC conference chamber in discussions of the Directive, which covered both SO_2 and NO_x emissions from power stations. Even here it was short of allies (Spain excepted), but the rich spread of intra-Community negotiations at least opened the possibility of Britain obtaining special treatment over the Directive in exchange for granting concessions somewhere else on the huge EC negotiation menu. It did indeed obtain easier terms for the implementation of the Directive, which came into force in 1988.[23]

Nitrogen oxides

The next step in the LRTAP process was taken in the same year, with the signing of the Nitrogen Oxides Protocol (we shall postpone discussion of whether this 'step' was part of a step-by-step process). Like sulphur dioxide, nitrogen oxides are implicated in the production of acid rain and like VOCs also implicated in the production of ground level ozone, a key ingredient of modern smogs. The chief source of nitrogen oxides is the exhausts of motor vehicles, and this was to prove the main difficulty in negotiations. In a manner reminiscent of the early stages of negotiation of the Montreal Protocol (signed the previous year), one side wanted, seemingly, large cuts in NO_x emissions, with the other side warily looking for something more modest. The equivalent of the Toronto Group, wanting large cuts (30 per cent), was Germany and the Nordics. The equivalent of Brussels in the Montreal setting was in this case the rest of

---

23 See Nigel Haigh, 'The EC and International Environmental Policy', in Andrew Hurrell and Benedict Kingsbury, (eds), *The International Politics of the Environment*, (Oxford, Clarendon Press, 1992), pp. 237, 238.

Europe, who suspected that German enthusiasm stemmed from a confidence that their motor manufacturers would find the fitting of the necessary catalytic convertors easier than their competitors in other parts of the EC. Incidentally, the equivalent of the less developed states, which in Montreal terms had no or very little CFC production capacity, was a number of East European states, just beginning to enter the motor age in earnest.

In the event, as with Montreal, a compromise was reached. The Nitrogen Protocol required parties only to freeze emissions at 1987 levels (by the year 1995). Whilst something resembling a central fund was created, mandating transfers of technology for controlling NO_x emissions, this was not sufficient to sway all East European doubters. Interestingly, the Nitrogen Protocol also allowed states who felt they could go beyond a freeze, optionally to sign up in addition to a promise of a 30 per cent cut in emissions by 1998. Twelve of the 27 parties did so, including Germany and the Nordics. Britain did not do so and had allies on this occasion from Eastern Europe and North America.[24] With the beginning of the end of the Cold War in sight, the USA and USSR both signed up to the freeze. It is not clear that the Nitrogen Protocol has verification provisions fully appropriate to its more difficult subject matter. There are far more motor vehicles than there are fossil fuelled power stations.

VOCs

By the time the VOC Protocol was signed, in 1991, the political map of eastern and central Europe was changing rapidly, so much so that their governments were too provisional or too new to participate effectively. As a result only 21 states signed the Protocol. Again there was convergence on the 30 per cent figure, with all but 5 states agreeing to a 30 per cent cut in their VOC emissions to be reached by 1999. The selection of the base year from which cuts were to be made was left to the individual party, provided the base year was between 1984 and 1990. Bulgaria and Hungary, the only east European states involved, were allowed instead to opt for a freeze only, along with Greece. Canada and Norway, as exporters of very little VOC, obtained a dispensation reminiscent of that granted to the Soviets in the Sulphur Protocol, permitting them to restrict

---

24 The usually reliable *World Resources 1992–93*, p. 199, seems to err when it characterises these 12 as the EC 12.

their reductions in VOC emissions to border areas.

Assessment

Parts of the above tell a familiar story. The initial step involved, in effect, few negotiating parties. The availability of appropriate substitutes and remedial technology helped determine the order in which further steps towards a complete agreement were taken. The sulphur dioxide matter is clearly the easiest to tackle from these aspects (replacing one type of coal with another, or even more so substituting natural gas for coal, can cut sulphur dioxide emissions instantly, although as with fitting chimneys with chemical scrubbers, these options all represent additional costs). Curbing the emission of nitrogen oxides not only required the introduction of catalytic convertors for motor vehicles but also engine designs that tolerated non-leaded petrol so as not to poison the catalysts (this latter less demanding than it seems because lead in petrol produces environmental damage on its own account and, moreover, almost entirely within national boundaries). Where the scientific model was clearest, there the steps towards political progress were easiest: on this basis, action on VOCs was predictably the most delayed. Unilateral or quasi-unilateral action helped produce collective responses, and this was taken by a state both polluting and being hurt by pollution on a large enough scale (Germany) to obtain some worthwhile national benefit from its initiative. The very bad bargain facing upwind Britain was indeed a problem and one that was solved by enlarging the bargaining agenda.

Added to which, the steps that were taken were progressive. The Nitrogen Protocol was an advance in that something resembling, albeit faintly, a central fund (for the dissemination to weaker signatories of technical advice and help) was added. Even the apparent retrogression in number of signatories as the LRTAP Convention moved on to the Sulphur Protocol was more apparent than real. The Convention was signed as a Cold War document, involving only three parties; East, West and the neutrals. The Protocols were signed in a rapidly evolving political climate. As Cold War groupings dissolved, there were now more signatures to be secured than before and most of them were. Finally, these curbs on national freedom to burn fossil fuel were accepted at a time that was propitious in one sense. In Western and Eastern Europe, if not in the USA or USSR, the LRTAP Protocols were agreed during a period when use of fossil fuel and hence emission of pollutants was diminishing, if only marginally.[25] This was a result not of the Protocols but of structural changes in Western economies towards less energy-intensive activity.

Other interpretations

And yet this is only one reading of events. Levy's own reading admits of more altruism in international politics, or at least in its lower variants, than we normally give credit for. He sees the parties as engaged in mutual education and mutual moral blackmail. An awareness of the damage being done by the boundary-crossing pollutants is gradually disseminated. For some states this awareness is enough for them to take action, for their own good and that of some at least of their neighbours. Publicity for what they are doing is disseminated at the same time, partly with the help of NGOs. States that do nothing are then shamed into action.

It is not claimed that our reading is any more compelling than Levy's (in fact, there are points in common). It is immediately conceded, for instance, that the original smallness of the negotiating group for the Convention owed virtually nothing to the nature (regionality or otherwise) of the pollution problem at hand. This could be read as a warning that easy references to the regionality of certain environmental protection issues run the risk of allowing politics to be obscured by geography.

But Vickers's warnings about the difficulties of learning from experience are taken seriously, as applying to observers of events as well as participants in them. The experience of LRTAP is consistent with Levy's interpretation of events and doubtless other equally plausible interpretations could be found. But it can also be understood in terms of our model based on Olson's Themes. By virtue of its speed and completeness we can regard the LRTAP process, like Levy, as a success. Its success we would choose to attribute to its regional nature. Remaining weaknesses can be put down to the fact that it was a regional process taking place in extremely trying circumstances. From the start, the USA, Canada and the USSR were involved, as we have seen, chiefly for Cold War reasons. After the ending of the Cold War, the largely peaceful but far reaching political convulsions in Eastern Europe and the Soviet Union distracted

---

25 *World Resources 1992–93*, p. 317.

successor governments, rather leaving the OECD members to make the LRTAP running themselves.   In other words the membership of the collective was severely affected by exogenous concerns.

Learning from LRTAP

What can be learned from LRTAP, on the other hand, is that whilst science and economics play an important part in norm setting, the best may sometimes be the enemy of the good. This was not so obviously true of the Montreal Protocol process (although Parson might disagree). But progress in LRTAP seemed to depend on a crudeness of approach. First of all, a target of 30 per cent reductions seems to have become a norm. It seems to have been suggested by the Nordics as early as 1980. Germany went further in 1982 when it mentioned 50 per cent as a target (of course, base years and time allowed to reach the target may have also varied). Germany eventually jobbed back to the 30 per cent figure. It is clear that the figure was arbitrary, although readers with a taste for numerology will note that the EC had offered to make a 30 per cent cut in aerosol use, also in 1980, as a contribution to saving the ozone layer.

Because 30 per cent was agreed to more or less arbitrarily in the Sulphur Protocol it became the target, now less arbitrary precisely because of the precedent, in subsequent protocols. It was not a norm set scientifically, based upon 'critical loads' or what levels of sulphur dioxide European forests and lakes could tolerate. Nor was it particularly in line with market norms. Ideally, after some weighting for wind patterns, the states party to the arrangement where cutting sulphur dioxide emissions could be done most cheaply should have been those that accepted the largest cuts.

On the other hand, it had the advantage of simplicity, predictability of outcome from the verification aspect, and an appearance of equality of sacrifice or contribution to the collective good. In addition, waiting for better scientific modelling which would have encompassed critical loads, wind patterns, and economic impacts would have created further delay. In any case, there is no reason why more sophisticated norm setting should not take place after the 30 per cent cuts are in place. After all, this is one of the main virtues of the step-by-step approach.

8 Global Warming

Introduction

We began this three-chapter section of the book dealing with Olson's Themes and their applications with a semi-fictitious example of a global pollution question: the dissemination and slow accumulation on a global scale in the atmosphere of radioactive gases released by the routine operation of nuclear power plant. We end with a wholly real question: the dissemination and slow accumulation on a global scale in the atmosphere of carbon dioxide from fossil fuel combustion. The consequent build-up of carbon dioxide in the atmosphere increases the heat-trapping properties of the atmosphere significantly, leading to a rise in ground level temperatures. In turn, this will lead to an expansion of the volume of sea water, i.e. a rise in sea levels. It will also alter climates, which will on average be warmer.

Carbon dioxide is a natural constituent of the atmosphere and of the oceans. Its concentration in the atmosphere is tiny by comparison with oxygen and nitrogen and seems to have remained reasonably steady at between 270 and 290 ppm (parts per million) for most of the past 10,000 years (the evidence for this comes from Antarctic ice layers, which contain records of atmospheric composition, reminiscent of the way that tree rings can contain records of climate).

The atmospheric reservoir of carbon dioxide loses gas naturally to participate in the growth of plant life which employs carbon dioxide and sunlight in the process of growth, releasing oxygen in the process. Animal life, in the process of breathing air, transforms oxygen into carbon dioxide which is exhaled and released to the atmosphere. Equally, as plants and animals die and decay carbon dioxide is returned to the atmosphere.

By 1989 total anthropogenic release of carbon dioxide as a result of burning fossil fuels and deforestation had reached about 27 billion (i.e. thousand million) tonnes per year.[1] Natural flows of carbon dioxide to and from the atmosphere, which are approximately equal in each direction, amount to about 700 billion tonnes per year.[2] This puts anthropogenic release at about 4 per cent of the total. Only global flows are significant in this case since the residence time of carbon dioxide in the atmosphere is of the order of a hundred years or more. While there is certainly a very marked regional variation in the quantities of anthropogenic carbon dioxide released into the atmosphere, it eventually exercises its effects globally or virtually so.

The cumulative impact of anthropogenic release on the amount of carbon dioxide in the atmosphere, which began essentially with the Industrial Revolution, has amounted to a gradual increase from its earlier steady value of around 280 ppm at the end of the eighteenth century to about 350 ppm at the end of the 1980s.

The polluting effect of this build up of carbon dioxide is indirect. Along with other constituents of the natural atmosphere including ozone and water vapour, carbon dioxide plays a part in maintaining the average earth temperature at its present value. Like water vapour and ozone (to a smaller extent), carbon dioxide does this by allowing visible light from the sun to penetrate the atmosphere and heat the earth but is opaque to some of the longer wavelengths via which the warm earth would otherwise radiate its heat back into space. For this reason these gases are referred to as greenhouse gases (see Appendix 2 to the present chapter). Increasing the concentration of any one of these greenhouse gases – in this instance, carbon dioxide – would appear to run the risk of enhancing its greenhouse

1 *World Resources 1992–93*, (New York, Oxford University Press, 1992), pp. 346, 347.

2 John Houghton, *Global Warming: The Complete Briefing*, (Oxford, Lion Publishing, 1994), p. 30.

effect and causing a rise in the average temperature of the earth.

Scientific uncertainty

There is no disagreement within the epistemic community of atmospheric physicists and chemists concerning the above. Neither is there disagreement that other gases released by anthropogenic activities such as methane (from industrial and agricultural sources), nitrous oxide (industrial and agricultural sources) and chlorofluorocarbons (CFCs – solvents, pressurisers, refrigerant gas) are also greenhouse gases. There is equally agreement that a clear statistical correspondence exists between recorded past atmospheric concentrations of carbon dioxide and records of the mean temperature of the earth, provided we are speaking of time scales of the order of 100,000 years into the past. It is also agreed that on time scales of tens of years or more that there are substantial lags or delays in the details of what the warming process means for the global climate pattern. The lags arise from the part played by the oceans. An imaginary instantaneous addition of heat to the earth would have immediate effects but the long run alteration to the climate would only become apparent once an equilibrium had been reached between the oceans and the atmosphere since both play a part in determining climate patterns. Reaching this equilibrium would take decades. Consequently, the full effects on the earth's climate of releases of greenhouse gases that have already occurred may not yet be apparent.

If there is no scientific uncertainty at the qualitative level, it shows up at the quantitative level as soon as there is a requirement to attach figures to the temperature rises likely to be experienced should current trends in the emission of greenhouse gases continue.

As luck would have it, the obvious testbed for a detailed model of global warming – the recent historical record – is untrustworthy. An overall increase in average global temperature of 0.5 degrees centigrade since the beginning of this century has been recorded. A good model should be able to correlate this with the known increases in atmospheric concentrations of greenhouse gases over the same period. Unfortunately, doubt has been cast on the accuracy, or at any rate comparability, of the land or sea-based readings that older records of temperature are based on, when set against those recorded by modern satellite-based systems. Since the late 1970s, the latter have detected *week by week* fluctuations in average global temperatures of 0.5 degrees centigrade, thereby casting more doubt on the reliability of the trend figure.[3]

Missing CO$_2$

The core uncertainty attaching to the warming model is connected with carbon dioxide itself. As already noted, reliable records show that in the absence of anthropogenic release of carbon dioxide the amount in the atmosphere stays remarkably constant. Since the Industrial Revolution, the amount has started to rise. It is possible to measure with good accuracy actual annual increases in the amount of carbon dioxide in the atmosphere. The same is true for increases in the amount held by the oceans.

Naturally, the total of these increases should equal the amount of carbon dioxide released from anthropogenic sources. This too can be accurately assessed, at least as far as releases from the burning of fossil fuel go (global statistics are good here). Figures for releases from the burning of forests are less reliable. But even allowing for the latter, it turns out that there is still some carbon dioxide unaccounted for. To be exact, just over 20 per cent of the carbon dioxide anthropogenically released apparently goes missing. It may be that it gets absorbed by unrecognised healthy increases in plant growth, or that forests are expanding in some parts of the world faster than estimated. Indeed, both or even neither may be responsible. But this unresolved puzzle is the core weakness of the current scientific model and it contributes to the large error brackets that have to be attached to quantitative predictions.

A different kind of uncertainty, although still of political significance, concerns the pattern of international responsibility for the threatened global warming. About one sixth of total anthropogenic emissions of carbon dioxide comes not from the burning of fossil fuel (chiefly in the developed world) but from changes in land use – a chain of events beginning with deforestation – mainly (virtually 100 per cent) in the LDCs. Whilst there is scientific uncertainty over the details, replacing self-renewing forested areas permanently with land given over to agriculture (crops or grazing animals) reduces the amount of carbon dioxide locked up in each hectare within the bodily mass of the plants concerned. It is true that allowance has to be made for the fact that some of this carbon dioxide remains locked up (in the form of carbon compounds) as trees are felled but then transformed into furniture or (often more temporarily) paper. Allowance

---

3 R. P. Wayne, *Chemistry of Atmospheres*, (Oxford, Clarendon Press, 1991), p. 413.

has also to be made for the fact that even when 'slash and burn' methods are used to clear the forested areas, the burning is usually quite inefficient, leaving a lot of carbon dioxide (as carbon) still locked away indefinitely in the form of charcoal. Allowance has even to be made for the probability that in the Northern Hemisphere, land use is changing in the opposite direction, with an expansion of forest cover.[4] But the net global effect of changes in land use is to make a minor but quite definite contribution to the atmospheric load of carbon dioxide.

Other greenhouse gases

A related complication for the assigning of political responsibility comes from the existence of other anthropogenic greenhouse gases besides CO_2. Methane (CH_4) concentrations in the atmosphere appear to have been steady at about 0.7 ppm from pre-historical times up until the end of the 16th century.[5] Arctic ice records show that levels then began to rise, slowly at first but subsequently more rapidly. By the early 1990s concentration in the atmosphere had reached double the prehistoric level, to stand at 1.7 ppm. Since 1965, concentration of methane in the atmosphere has risen at an annual rate of 1.7 per cent, which means a doubling time of 40 years. Whilst the concentration of methane in the atmosphere is minute compared with that of carbon dioxide, it is about one hundred times, volume for volume, more effective as a greenhouse gas. If the increase in carbon dioxide concentration from its pre-Industrial Revolution level has caused a temperature rise of just over 0.5 degrees centigrade, the increase in methane concentrations since the 16th century has produced a rise of about half of that.[6]

The early date at which rises in methane concentrations in the atmosphere started to appear is a clue as to its origins. By far the largest single anthropogenic source of methane is agriculture, with domesticated livestock and paddy-field rice growing about equally responsible and together accounting for about one half of total emissions. The other half comes mainly from fossil fuel production (coal mining, plus leaks, accidental or deliberate, during oil and natural gas production) but with a large input too from the decay of municipal solid wastes. Roughly

---

4 *World Resources 1992–93*, p. 353 and *World Resources 1996–97*, pp. 218, 219.

5 Wayne, *Chemistry of Atmospheres*, p. 411.

6 Ibid., p. 411.

speaking, global responsibility for methane emissions divides equally between the OECD countries and the LDCs.

Another minor greenhouse gas somewhat similar politically and in terms of its greenhouse effect physically to methane is nitrous oxide. It is naturally present in the atmosphere to a small degree as a result of the action of certain plants that synthesise it, for its fertilising properties, from atmospheric nitrogen and oxygen. But human activities, not only the manufacture of fertiliser but going beyond this to a variety of other industrial activities, are releasing N_2O into the atmosphere at a rate approaching 50 per cent of the natural flow.[7] This is leading to a rise in atmospheric concentration of about 0.25 per cent per year. The breakdown of international responsibility for N_2O release is not perfectly clear. But as we have hinted, the pattern is probably similar to that for methane. It resembles methane too in that as a greenhouse gas, volume for volume it is 100 times more powerful than carbon dioxide.[8]

The final complication is presented by a class of entirely synthetic chemical compounds known collectively as chlorofluorocarbons (CFCs) originally developed prior to the Second World War as a safe refrigerant fluid for domestic use to replace the rather poisonous ammonia-based and sulphur dioxide-based working fluids. We have dealt with these gases in Chapter 7 in the context of their threat to the integrity of the ozone layer. But CFCs are also powerful greenhouse gases, even more so than methane (volume for volume, typically some thousands of times more powerful than carbon dioxide).

Whilst, as we have seen, emissions of CFCs have been the subject of international control since 1987, these compounds stay in the atmosphere for tens of years. In addition, some types of CFC which have been less severely controlled because they are calculated to do comparatively little damage to the ozone layer, are still powerful greenhouse gases. In 1989, global responsibility for CFC emissions rested almost exclusively with the OECD countries.

Toronto and the IPCC

According to Rowlands, the year in which global warming forced itself

---

7 Wayne, *Chemistry of Atmospheres*, p. 411.

8 Using information provided in graph form by Houghton, *Global Warming*, p. 44.

onto the international agenda was 1988.[9] This was the year of the Toronto conference of the World Meteorological Organisation on the 'implications for global security' of man-induced atmospheric changes. The remit of this mainly scientific meeting covered both ozone layer and global warming issues. In spite of scientific uncertainties concerning the extent of the links between a build-up of greenhouse gases and changes in climate, it issued the so-called Toronto target, recommending a global cut in annual emissions of CO_2 of 20 per cent below the 1988 figure to be reached by 2005.[10]

The year of the Toronto conference saw the establishment of an international study into scientific and other aspects of global warming; the Intergovernmental Panel on Climate Change (IPCC). This body was sponsored by the World Meteorological Organisation and the UNEP. One of the IPCC Working Groups focussed on scientific aspects. Not surprisingly, its main scientific manpower was drawn from the meteorological specialists of the developed world, but 'a Special Committee on the Participation of Developing Countries was created in 1989 to ensure the active involvement of representatives from the [less developed] world.'[11]

The IPCC Working Groups issued their first reports in 1990.[12] In general there seemed to be virtually full scientific agreement over the broad picture, i.e. there is not much scientific uncertainty over the qualitative aspects of the scientific model. More uncertainty attached to specifics. Thus carbon dioxide, methane, CFCs and nitrous oxide are all confidently identified as greenhouse gases. Interestingly, whilst there is, as foreshadowed above, some uncertainty as to how their respective contributions should be weighted in order to create a composite 'Greenhouse Index', the uncertainty is of manageable dimensions. (A Greenhouse Index gives, wrapped up in a single figure, a measure of how much overall a particular state's industrial and agricultural activities may

9   Ian H. Rowlands, *The Politics of Global Atmospheric Change*, (Manchester, Manchester University Press, 1995), p. 74.

10 Wilfrid Beckerman, 'Global Warming and Economic Action', in Andrew Hurrell and Benedict Kingsbury (eds), *The International Politics of the Environment*, (Oxford, Clarendon Press, 1992), p. 271.

11 Rowlands, *The Politics of Global Atmospheric Change*, p. 75.

12 A good digest is given by Matthew Paterson, 'Global Warming' in Caroline Thomas, *The Environment in International Relations*, (London, Royal Institute of International Affairs, 1992), pp. 155, 198.

be contributing to global warming. It is closely analogous to the 'ozone depletion potential' figure for national releases of CFCs and similar ozone layer-damaging gases). Nor is there any disagreement about the built-in lags involved in the link between the emission of greenhouse gases into the atmosphere and the eventual warming of the globe. Because of the oceans, if it was desired that global warming should be reversed, a reduction in emissions would of course be necessary, but the benefit would take twenty years to appear in the form of the first reductions in temperature.

Global warming: IPCC predictions

The central predictions of the model used by the IPCC are usually couched in terms of the climatic consequences of a doubling of the atmospheric content of carbon dioxide (or the equivalent, allowing for the presence of other greenhouse gases) from its 1990 level. Without any political preventive action, this would occur within about 100 years. This is the so-called 'business as usual' scenario, based on an assumption that annual emissions of carbon dioxide will carry on rising at current rates of increase, so that they will be three times 1990 levels by the year 2100. This is reasonably consistent with, if slightly more optimistic than, the figure of 1.8 per cent per annum for the rate at which global energy consumption is rising. The temperature prediction is a 2.5 degrees centigrade rise in average global temperature by the year 2100, or a $1°$ C rise in average global temperature by 2030. Error brackets (reflecting uncertainties in the model) of plus or minus 40 per cent attach to these temperature predictions.[13]

The working groups ventured into greater detail. Qualitatively, polar regions would warm, in winter, by more than the global average. But their quantitative predictions of this effect for 2030 illustrate the uncertainties very nicely. For the central region of North America, average winter temperatures will rise $3°$ C, plus or minus $1°$ C (in other words it could be as high as $4°$ C or as low as $2°$ C). The summer temperature rise will be $2.5°$ C, plus or minus $0.5°$ C. For the sub-Saharan region of the Sahel in Africa, warming will be $2°$ C plus or minus $1°$ C.

Of course, within the margin of error, all three predicted temperature

---

13 Houghton, *Global Warming*, p. 80.

rises could be the same, at 3° C, although this is rather unlikely.

The actual measured rise in average global temperature since the turn of the century is 0.5° C. As we have seen, this instrument based measurement may not itself be trustworthy, but it falls within the range of what the model would predict. The predicted extra rise in polar temperatures has not been observed at all but (see the illustration in the preceding paragraph) this too falls within the range predicted.

Uncertainties also attach to the rise in sea levels consequent on global warming. The best estimate is a rise of about 6 cm per decade, with an error of plus or minus about 50 per cent. The error bracket is a shade greater than that attaching to the predicted temperature rise, because whilst there is a one to one correspondence between a warmer ocean and the increased volume it occupies (the whole acts as a giant thermometer, literally rising as temperature rises), the redistribution of water between atmosphere, sea and land will not be all one way. Whilst there will be melting of glaciers, which will also cause sea levels to rise, there may be higher snowfall in the (normally rather dry) polar regions, consequent on the probable greater warming expected there.

The latest update from the IPCC in 1996 does not propose much change in the above predictions, indeed none at all within the margin of error stated. But it has reduced its central prediction for the rise in average global temperature by the end of the next century from 2.5° C to 2° C. This is because it previously underestimated the cooling effect caused by the presence of sulphate pollutants (from the burning of fossil fuel) in the lower atmosphere.[14]

The chief practical effect of the imprecision of the model for international politics is that the model is too imprecise to allow predictions to be safely made about the different impact global warming will have on states by virtue of their geographical location. As we have seen, North American and sub-Saharan African temperature rises could be the same. Only at the very highest level of aggregation is it possible to say something. The figures given above for expected temperature rises in North America and North Africa were higher than the global average predicted figure because the IPCC model postulates temperature rises in the Southern Hemisphere at about half those for the North, as a result of the circulation pattern of the oceans.[15]

---

14 *World Resources 1996–97*, p. 317.

15 Houghton, *Global Warming*, p. 84.

Political responses

Paterson reports that in parallel with the original IPPC findings, a number of states volunteered unilateral or regional commitments to freeze or cut back on their carbon dioxide or greenhouse gas emissions.[16] By early 1991, when international negotiations began on the Framework Convention on Climate Change, seventeen OECD states including EC states and Japan had undertaken to freeze their carbon dioxide emissions at a variety of base years (but mostly between 1988 and 1990) by a target date of 2000 (in some cases 2005). The EC countries took 1990 as their base year and 2000 as the target year. Conspicuously absent from this list, at least in spirit, was the USA. It refused to countenance limits on carbon dioxide emissions, claiming that its commitments under the Montreal Protocol and the drop these would mean in US emissions of CFCs would automatically freeze its total greenhouse gas emissions (measured by its Greenhouse Index) at the 1990 level by the year 2000. Of course the limits other OECD states accepted on their CO_2 emissions were in addition to Montreal curbs on their CFC emissions.

The USA defended its semi-detached position partly by reference to the sensitivity of its economy to levels of fossil fuel use and partly by citing uncertainties in the scientific model of global warming. There can be little doubt that the comparatively high energy intensity of the US economy (a measure of the sensitivity of a national economy to price changes in energy, e.g. as a result of a tax on carbon dioxide emissions) did indeed play a part. US energy intensity in 1993 was 16 units (megajoules of energy consumed per 1987 US dollar of gross national product); the EC was about 10; Japan stood at 6.[17]

US caution received some justification with the publication of the 1992 follow-on report of the IPCC, which was less definite than its predecessor concerning the goodness of the scientific model, although it confirmed the projected temperature rises to be anticipated in the absence of controls.

The Framework Convention on Climate Change (FCCC) signed at the Rio 'Earth Summit' in 1992 obtained the signature of the USA only because its provisions regarding the curbing of emissions of greenhouse gases are deliberately weak. In this respect it is more a statement of principle than a set of specific obligations and highly reminiscent of the

---

16 See fn 12, p. 180.

17 *World Resources 1996–97*, pp. 286, 287.

1979 LRTAP Convention.

FCCC contrasted with Montreal Protocol

The negotiation of the FCCC included, not unexpectedly, a marked development dimension. Surprisingly, the tacit analogue seems to have been the Montreal Protocol. Like the pollution of the ozone layer, pollution of the atmosphere by greenhouse gases was something for which the developed world was taken to be largely responsible. It was for the industrialised states to take remedial action. It was equally up to them to find the means to allow the newly industrialising states to short circuit the conventional development route which would involve the burning of large amounts of fossil fuel. US reluctance to contemplate the transfer of funds implied by this claim further differentiated its stance over the FCCC from that of most other OECD states.

In 1995, at the Berlin Climate Summit (essentially a review conference of the FCCC), the same themes were expressed. Developing countries, with India, China and Brazil in the lead, obtained a reaffirmation that the FCCC does not bind them to do anything beyond making an inventory of their greenhouse gas emissions and received confirmation that the entire onus for actually limiting emissions should be placed on the shoulders of the developed world. For their part, the developed states undertook nothing stronger than their original Rio pledge to make an effort to stabilise their emissions of non-CFC greenhouse gases at the 1990 level by the year 2000.

It is tempting to speculate that US disengagement from global warming issues, apart from occasional and sometimes well directed sniping at the quality of the scientific model, has in turn contributed to the poverty of the working political model. In fact, as we shall see, the problem scarcely resembles the ozone layer problem at all. If there is an historical parallel, perhaps the closest is the LRTAP. But to see this, it is necessary to go back to first principles.

At first sight, global warming might seem to be closely similar to the semi-fictitious radioactive gases example we began with, but there is one important difference. Certainly, all states with coastlines will need to attend to their sea defences. Some rich states with comparatively small lengths of coastline may not find this especially burdensome, since there is broad scientific consensus that even if nothing is done to check emissions of carbon dioxide, by the middle of the 21st century rises in sea level will amount only to tens of centimetres (25 cms is the best estimate[18]).   At the same time, all states will be affected by climate change.   In some cases this will be beneficial, in others, harmful. Scientific models, as we have seen, are too crude to be able to specify how and where the dice will fall, with the exception that the Southern Hemisphere as a whole will receive less warming than the Northern.

Beckerman makes the crucial point that states with relatively small agricultural sectors will scarcely be affected in the purse one way or another, since (tourism apart) agriculture is the only activity whose productivity depends on climate.[19]   States with large agricultural sectors will be affected, but unpredictably.   In effect they will be compulsorily entered into a strange redistributive lottery, out of which they could emerge either as winners or losers, with the magnitude of the winnings comparable to the magnitude of the losses.

First approximation

To a first approximation, we can say that global warming is caused by a single pollutant, carbon dioxide, and that states emit carbon dioxide roughly in proportion to the size of their gross national product, since energy use and GNP are closely correlated. The effects of global warming will be to create changes in climate and rises in sea levels. The estimated rise of 25 cms by the middle of the 21st century is based on the assumption that current trends in global energy use will not alter. States will be hurt by global warming partly according to how vulnerable they are to climate change and that in turn depends upon the relative size of their agricultural sector. Statistically speaking, where GNPs are small, the relative size of the agricultural sector of the national economy is large. Again statistically speaking, the impact of a rise in sea level will vary from a minor inconvenience to a national disaster depending mainly upon the length of the state's coastline relative to its GNP.

If for the moment we forget about the rise in sea levels (it turns out that this is not a serious oversimplification), from the point of view of collective action it follows that there are only two classes of party to a potential arrangement for the curbing of CO_2 emissions. One is the party

---

18 Houghton, *Global Warming*, p. 91, with an allowance for the 1996 sulphate correction.

19 Beckerman, 'Global Warming and Economic Action', pp. 262, 264.

of large emitters which being rich and hence relatively non-agricultural is virtually unaffected by the consequences of its emissions: the other is the low emitters which are severely at risk from the activities of others. This is the reverse of the ozone layer problem. There, the large emitters of CFCs were precisely the states most at risk from the immediate consequences, chiefly because of their high latitudes.

LRTAP closer parallel

The LRTAP parallel is much closer. Low emitters of carbon dioxide are the equivalent of the Nordic states grappling with the effects of acid rain for which others are chiefly responsible. The large emitters are the equivalent of Britain, badly affecting others whilst almost unaffected itself. There is a difference in that the vulnerable group are vulnerable as a class only. As already noted, at the present level of scientific understanding it is impossible to forecast the climate changes consequent on global warming in sufficient geographical detail to identify precisely which agricultural states will be damaged severely, which not at all, and which actually helped.

On this basis we have an unpromising outlook for collective action. The large emitters would be required to meet the considerable costs involved in cutting down on their use of fossil fuel, with the availability of substitutes limited and additionally in the case of nuclear power politically moot. The benefits on the other hand would go to the small emitters of the agriculturally-dependent less developed world, who would be spared mandatory entry into a climate lottery from which they could as easily emerge losers as winners.

But the first approximation picture turns out to overstate the bleakness of the situation.

The first approximation identified polluters with carbon dioxide production from the combustion of fossil fuel and related the latter directly to size of GNP. The size of GNP, in turn, was related inversely to the size of the state's agricultural sector. A closer investigation shows that this is not the whole story, for two reasons. First, it is not only rich states that emit large amounts of carbon dioxide from industrial sources. Secondly, as we know, industrial carbon dioxide is not the only contributor to global warming.

Greenhouse index

In the same way that the Montreal Protocol saw different CFCs categorised according to their ozone depleting potential (ODP), so it is possible to do something similar with greenhouse gases to arrive at a Greenhouse Index.   Giving carbon dioxide an index of 1, the Intergovernmental Programme on Climate Change (IPCC) put CFC-11 and CFC-12 as greenhouse gases at approximately 6000 and methane at approximately 20 (the score for methane is greater than that for carbon dioxide because it is, as we have seen, simply a more powerful greenhouse gas, 100 times, volume for volume, more powerful than CO_2. But its residence time in the atmosphere is much shorter, which then pulls down its overall Greenhouse Index rating). There does not seem to be complete scientific consensus over the exact weightings to be applied when constructing a Greenhouse Index, but the order of magnitudes seems more or less agreed.[20]   However, apart from these minor technical disagreements, the Greenhouse Index still has to be employed carefully in that the CFC contributions to the Index of individual states emitting these gases will change rapidly as the Montreal Protocol takes effect (although it certainly does not follow that CFCs with low ODPs automatically have low Greenhouse Indexes). Finally, the Index takes into account carbon dioxide and other gases released from non-industrial sources, including burning of forests. Another reason for employing the Index carefully is that some of these non-industrial data will be rather poor.

Thus, when states are ranked according to their overall contribution to global warming, via the Greenhouse Index, more poor states appear high in the list than our first approximation would have suggested. Partly, as we have seen, this is because some of them do emit large amounts of carbon dioxide from industrial activity: partly it is because some of them are large emitters of carbon dioxide, methane and nitrous oxide from agricultural and related sources.

Exposure index

The first approximation took no account of the exposure of states to rises in sea level. In this regard, the first approximation was a good one. As we show below in Appendix 1, states vulnerable to climate change because

---

20 *World Resources 1992-93*, p. 207.

of their large agricultural sectors tend also to have long coastlines relative to their GNP. This is a curious coincidence. There are, however, some exceptions to this rule and in a mirror image of the Greenhouse Index, which we call the Exposure Index, it is possible to make an allowance for these exceptions.

The table in Appendix 1 compiles a simple composite index for the vulnerability of a state to global warming. This Exposure Index has three equally weighted ingredients: the percentage of the state's GNP due to agriculture; the length of its coastline relative to GNP; and the proportion of its population living in coastal zones. The appendix gives more detail as to how this is done. The resulting Exposure Index (which of course does not have the same official status as the Greenhouse Index) ranks states not very differently from how they would be ranked on the straight comparison of the size of their agricultural sectors. But the ranking is not quite the same and the adjustment, like the adjustments occasioned by the Greenhouse Index, give us our second approximation (Canada would be well down the exposure list by size of agricultural sector alone, but its huge coastline pushes it up the Exposure Index).

As Table 8A.1 shows, the top twenty contributing states to the greenhouse effect contain a number of states highly exposed to the consequences of the global warming for which they (by virtue of belonging to the top twenty emitters) bear a strong element of responsibility.

So, the second approximation, by going beyond the broad statistical outlines of the first, indicates that gloominess concerning the prospects for an arrangement to control global warming may not be completely appropriate. The top ten contributors to global warming contain five states from the less developed world:[21] China, India, Brazil, Mexico and Indonesia. The top ten most exposed states to the effects of global warming, measured using the Exposure Index, contain four states from the less developed world: China, India, Brazil and Indonesia. The eleventh most exposed by this criterion is Mexico.

So, the exposed five, taken as a group, become the equivalent of Germany in the LRTAP process – an author, but not the only author, of its own misfortunes. The huge tail of much less populous poor states with large agricultural sectors and long coastlines and emitting virtually no carbon dioxide are the LRTAP equivalent of the Nordic states – virtually dependent on the actions of others to get them out of a hole. At the very

---

21 Since 1994, Mexico has formally been a member of the OECD.

end of this tail sit the group of states which are, or are composed of, small islands. These have combined themselves for purposes of negotiating a global warming control arrangement as the Alliance of Small Island States (ASIS).[22]

The remainder of the big ten emitters are the parallel of Britain in LRTAP – threatening a great deal of damage to others whilst remaining largely (if not quite wholly) unaffected itself.

Germany was the first in LRTAP to respond positively to the plight of the Nordics. What incentive have the exposed five for behaving similarly over global warming?

One sort of incentive derives from the fact that greenhouse gas emissions elsewhere among the top ten have virtually stopped increasing. More precisely, for the period 1979–89, commercial energy consumption grew 14 per cent in Canada, 12 per cent in Japan, 3 per cent in the USA (but this overstates the carbon dioxide emission situation slightly, since in all three countries the amount of energy generated from nuclear sources increased by over 100 per cent in the same period). In the EC 12 (including former East Germany), there was a drop in commercial energy consumption of 2 per cent.[23] This is a direct consequence of the reducing energy intensities of the economies of industrialised states, which is a trend likely to continue. It is a trend, moreover, which has been somewhat assisted by arrangements to curb regional pollution from energy-related sources. The nett effect of the LRTAP Protocols has indirectly been to curb carbon dioxide emissions amongst the parties even though they were aimed at other pollutants.[24] The continuation of the downward trend is made even more likely as a result of the collapse of the economies of the constituent parts of the former USSR. Even here, when these transitional economies recover, the recovery is unlikely to see the very high energy intensities of former years reached again.

The exposed five, by contrast, increased energy consumption by 59 per cent in the same period. Were the five to slacken the rate at which they contributed to global warming (in 1990 accounting for about 20 per cent of the global total), they could at least be confident that the benefit of so

---

22 Rowlands, *The Politics of Global Atmospheric Change*, p. 198.

23 *World Resources 1992–93*, pp. 316, 317.

24 This should not be exaggerated – it is true that the replacement of coal by natural gas as fuel for power stations is encouraged by the Protocols and reduces carbon dioxide emissions automatically, but fitting catalytic convertors to motor vehicles increases fuel consumption and hence carbon dioxide emissions.

doing would not be swamped by the actions of others.

The exposed five less developed states

Of course there is no reason to expect the five to take the lead in slackening their emissions of greenhouse gases unless they expect a return. Their costs – through, for instance, increasing domestic reliance on nuclear power – will be large. On the other hand, just as the innovation of the ODP assisted in the securing of the Montreal Protocol, the Greenhouse Index would allow each of the big five to make their contribution to easing the greenhouse effect in their own way (as the USA with its not quite wholly legitimate reference to the Montreal Protocol has already discovered).

The obvious return is a lower ceiling on the possible extent of disruption to their large agriculture sectors, and savings on sea defences. The return is however doubly provisional. First there is no guarantee that even if they did nothing, every member of the group would be hurt. All, it is true, would see rises in sea levels requiring more or less expensive attention. But for some, depending how the dice fell, the agricultural sector might benefit more than enough to offset the costs of sea defences as the climate instead of deteriorating in their corner of the world became more benign.   Secondly, whilst scientific investigations into global warming have probably taken enough care to avoid Vickers's charge of amounting to 'Western science'[25] (see the IPCC's Special Committee on the Participation of Developing Countries) it cannot be said that the sort of convergence in scientific opinion that occurred over the ozone layer in 1985 has yet happened over global warming. Without such a convergence, it is difficult to see the exposed five moving.

Another difficulty stems from the consideration that the exposed five have very little history of being able to act as a group. In spite of the fact that three of the five (India, China and Brazil) were able to make common cause at the Berlin Climate Summit, China and India are more normally viewed as regional rivals, as are, pitched some decibels lower in intensity perhaps, Brazil and Mexico. Brazil's situation in the Southern Hemisphere adds a further complication.   The IPCC model predicts smaller temperature rises for the Southern Hemisphere than for the Northern and

---

25 Rowlands, *The Politics of Global Atmospheric Change*, p. 75.

Brazil may feel as a result that it would be running smaller risks than the rest if it did nothing.

Should they be able to act as a group, the five are not lacking in collective bargaining power. Their combined population is about 46 per cent of the global total, representing amongst other things a formidable export market for the OECD states.

But the chief obstacle to the five doing anything is the rest of the top ten, which for practical purposes may be taken as comprising the USA, the EC and Japan (all OECD states). The transitional economies of the former Soviet Union fall into a problematic category since data are not always reliable. Appendix I sidesteps the data problem by pretending that the former USSR continues to exist, although as can be seen from data for the carbon dioxide emissions of constituent states of the former USSR, this pretence is not seriously misleading.

OECD and global warming

In order to stabilise the equivalent amount of carbon dioxide in the atmosphere at the 1995 level, it would not be enough to freeze emissions at current levels. Obviously this continues to add carbon dioxide to the atmosphere by the same amount annually. To bring down atmospheric concentrations there will have to be actual reductions in emissions. But a freeze would be worthwhile first step. But to achieve even a freeze, there will have to be substantial contributions in the form of actual reductions in emissions from other than the five exposed states. Why should the OECD states oblige?

A minor reason, but one which should not be overlooked, is that as Table 8A.1 shows, some small OECD states are exceptions to the general rule and could themselves easily be directly hurt by climate change. Of the top twenty emitters, Australia, with its long coastline relative to its GNP and high proportion of population living in coastal zones, is the second most exposed to climate change (according to our Exposure Index); Canada, with its enormous coastline, is eighth most exposed, ranking alongside China. Outside the top twenty emitters but still within the OECD, New Zealand has twice the coastline relative to GNP that Canada has and an even greater concentration of its population in coastal zones than Australia.

The major reason why the OECD states should contribute to controlling emissions of greenhouse gases is simply that it would amount to a rather subtle form of international aid on the part of the developed world. It would defend against a change of a kind that was predictable only on a statistical basis which would correspondingly devalue foresight and render moot assumptions upon which many foreign policy decisions, including decisions about trade and aid, are currently made. It is a form of corrective feedback done in the interests of stability since stability is a precondition for foresight to operate,[26] and done with the benefit of scientific modelling so as to minimise lags. The politics involved, then, is rather high, in two senses. If nothing were done the relative power of leading states could alter unpredictably, since the changes in the international political environment will confer gains and create losses unequally. But for something to be done, the same states will need to allow their energy policies, something states are normally quite sensitive about, to come under a degree of international control. And it is precisely the intimate link between energy use and size of GNP in the first place that involves the rich states centrally in the global warming issue.

An international arrangement to curb emissions of greenhouse gases then would be an interesting kind of collective undertaking. The OECD states would, through accepting limits on how much fossil fuel they burned (or the equivalent according to the Greenhouse Index of the activity in question), purchase stability – not for its own sake, but for the scope it permits for the exercise of foresight. This is a collective good and attempts at free-riding might be anticipated by the smaller members of this grouping. These attempts will be least marked, perhaps, by those for whom the arrangement also promises safety. A central fund to discourage free-riding promising technology transfers to parties to the arrangement in good standing, along the lines of the LRTAP Nitrogen Protocol, ideally including assistance with the substitution of fossil by nuclear energy, would be necessary.

In parallel, the exposed five and the remainder of the less developed countries would also accept limits on the Greenhouse Index of their emissions. The object here would not be stability so much as safety. But here again free-riding would be a potential difficulty. Whilst it could be tackled using the same central fund approach, there would be a difference in that gauging compliance with the arrangement – verification – would be harder than in the OECD case. The Greenhouse Index of a non-

---

26 See A. N. Whitehead, *Adventures of Ideas*, (Harmondsworth, Pelican Books, 1942), p. 91.

industrialised state would typically include methane emissions from agriculture or carbon dioxide emissions from deforestation. Neither of these is as easy to measure as the fossil fuel consumption of an industrialised state. In addition, the big five could hardly limit their own emissions without at least a benign indifference in the OECD states towards the five's substituting nuclear for fossil fuel.

End note

None of this suggests grounds for optimism. Indeed, none of the above theorising will be worth very much unless the USA were to become more actively engaged in the global warming question. Whilst it remains on the sidelines, the whole affair has a look of shadow-boxing. It is easy to see why the USA is lukewarm (the fact that it is lukewarm is another reason, of course, for not likening the climate change issue to the protection of the ozone layer). Certainly we can point to the relatively high energy intensity of the US economy. We can also point to the long-standing restrictive policies adopted by the USA towards the international spread of nuclear energy. We can even note (Table 8A.1) that its own degree of national exposure to the consequences of global warming is very small, even for an OECD state. But the fundamental reason for US aloofness is to be found in our earlier analysis via the Olson Themes of the nature of collective action. As the weightiest participant in a genuine collective attack on the question of climate change, the USA would find itself on the receiving end of the free-riding tendencies of other, by definition less weighty, parties to the arrangement. Unless there were guarantees that these tendencies could be nipped in the bud, which seems rather improbable given the necessarily global span of the arrangement and hence the large number of participants, the USA will be reluctant to stick its head in this particular noose. After all, free-riding means that costs and benefits are being shared unevenly and in matters of relatively high politics such as this one, where national control of energy policies would in some degree have to be surrendered, the relative power position of the USA is seen as being at stake.

This is not altogether a unique circumstance. Something of the same risk-avoiding nervousness was even encountered over the Montreal Protocol, where the USA, not surprisingly, found itself being asked to make the biggest financial contribution to the central fund (for the discouraging of free-riders) and jibbed at the request. The Law of the Sea conference ran into last minute but profound US objections. The updating of the Antarctic Treaty took place against a background of US misgivings, although these were eventually swallowed.

Complete pessimism would therefore be inappropriate. As we have seen, US nervousness about being free-ridden upon has made it cautious about subscribing to collective environmental arrangements before. But where these arrangements have nonetheless gone forward, probably more hesitantly and after more delay than would otherwise have been the case, the USA has eventually fallen more or less into line (even over the Law of the Sea, at least in part). As risk-avoiders, US administrations have had to keep in mind the possibility that the generally more welcoming attitude to an arrangement to guard against climate change shown by most of the other OECD states may be a mirage, since the brake on proceedings currently being applied by the USA relieves them of any need to be too outspoken concerning any reservations they too might harbour. US procrastination puts this sort of possibility to the test.

From a matter where power considerations and national rivalries are an obstacle to solving one kind of environmental problem, we now move to consider a different sort of problem, that allegedly posed by global overpopulation, where national rivalries have altogether a more benign effect.

Appendix 1: Global Warming Audit

The main table below contains eight columns. Seven of these columns report or slightly manipulate data that have already been collected and published. They are based on data in *World Resources 1992-93* and refer to the situation in 1989, except where otherwise stated (e.g. the entry for the GNP of Burma/Myanmar is an estimate for 1992 reported in *The Economist*, March 9, 1996). The data are not therefore always the most up to date available, but the break up of the USSR creates statistical problems. Data sufficient to create a more up to date version of column D, listing percentage contributions to global emissions of greenhouse gases using the IPCC Greenhouse Index, but explicitly taking into account contributions from the successor states to the Soviet Union, are not available. That this is probably not too much of a drawback can be seen by comparing column E with a 1992 update that ranks the top ten emitters of CO_2 from industrial sources as follows: USA, China, Russia, Japan, Germany, India, Ukraine, Britain, Canada, Italy (*World Resources 1996-97*, p. 318).

The eighth column, column A, puts some of these data to work in order to construct a composite index ranking states according to their vulnerability to the effects of global warming.

States are taken to be vulnerable to global warming either if the percentage of their GNP due to agriculture is high, or if their coastline is long relative to the size of their total GNP, or if they have a large percentage of their population living in coastal regions. Each of these indices of vulnerability is treated with equal importance when it comes to compiling the composite index.

So, to give an example, column H refers to the percentage of GNP due to agricultural production. The USA, with 2 per cent in 1989, gets an index here of 17 (it is the seventeenth biggest in the column). The second index comes from column G – the length of coastline, in thousands of kilometres relative to the size of GNP in thousands of billions $ (US). Here again the USA scores low down, once more 17th on the list and an index therefore of 17. The final index comes from column C, the percentage of the state's population living in coastal zones. In this instance the USA stands quite high, at 6th place, and with an index therefore of 6. The composite US exposure index is then $17 + 17 + 6 = 40$.

By contrast, Indonesia's composite index is 11. This is the smallest total in the table and accordingly gives Indonesia an overall ranking of 1 in column A. The USA comes in at 17 in this column for overall exposure (only France and Germany have higher composite indexes). The lower the ranking, of course, the greater the exposure to the damaging effects of global warming.

Table 8A.1 Global warming audit

	A	B	C	D	E	F	G	H
USA	17	258	29	17.8	22.4	5.24	3.8	2.0
USSR	14	299	8	13.6	17.4	2.66	17.6	15.0
China	8	1223	5	9.1	11.0	0.39	37.2	32.4
Japan	13	126	71	4.7	4.8	2.92	4.7	2.6
India	5	947	8	4.1	3.0	0.29	43.8	31.7
Brazil	5	165	30	3.9	1.0	0.37	20.3	8.6
Germany	19	77	5	3.4	4.4	1.43	1.8	2.0
Britain	14	58	48	2.2	2.6	0.83	14.9	1.8
Mexico	11	98	10	2.0	1.5	0.17	54.7	8.0
Indonesia	1	202	29	1.7	0.6	0.09	607.8	24.1
Canada	8	28	14	1.7	2.1	0.50	181.8	3.3
Italy	12	57	42	1.6	1.8	0.87	5.7	3.7
France	18	57	19	1.5	1.6	1.00	3.4	3.3
Thailand	3	60	23	1.5	0.4	0.06	53.3	16.9
Poland	16	39	8	1.5	2.0	0.07	7.1	15.0
Colombia	4	36	11	1.4	0.2	0.04	60.0	16.8
Burma		46	17	1.1		0.03	103.3	
Nigeria	7	128	11	1.1	0.4	0.03	28.3	30.7
Australia	2	18	78	1.1	1.2	0.24	107.5	4.2
S. Africa	8	39	21	1.1	1.3	0.09	32.2	5.8
KEY	A	B	C	D	E	F	G	H

A   Exposure Index

B   Population (millions) 1995

C   % population in coastal zones

D   % contribution to global emissions of greenhouse gases, by IPCC GH index

E   % contribution to global industrial emissions of carbon dioxide

F   GNP (US$ thousand billion) 1989

G   Coastline/GNP (thousands of km/thousands of billions US$)

H   Value of agricultural production as percentage of GNP.

Appendix 2: Metaphorical Greenhouse

The metaphor that the earth is like a large greenhouse with a comfortable surface temperature only because some minor natural constituents of the atmosphere – water vapour, carbon dioxide and ozone – act to absorb heat radiated from the surface that would otherwise be lost to space is too well established to quibble over. Real greenhouses in fact are warmer than otherwise only partly because glass is transparent to daylight but opaque to the infra-red wavelengths which would otherwise carry off the heat from the plants and soil within. Their chief warming effect comes from the fact that the roof prevents warmed air from escaping.

We can extend the metaphor slightly to liken the earth's atmosphere to a greenhouse of post-modern design where the panes of glass are set in frames of different shapes (some triangular, some rectangular, some pentagonal, some circular, some oblate). Moreover some of the panes of glass are intentionally missing. Adding carbon dioxide (which we can think of as corresponding to triangularly shaped panes of glass) to the atmosphere initially stops up those relatively few triangular panes that were missing but has progressively less efficient a warming effect after all the triangular spaces have been filled. But any warming at all means more water vapour in the atmosphere (as in any well watered greenhouse) which can be thought of as stopping up some of the relatively few rectangular panes that are missing.

Adding methane is the equivalent of glassing over the pentagonal panes which were previously virtually all unglazed, and nitrous oxide, from industrial and agricultural sources, glazes the largely unglazed oblate panes. Adding CFCs does the same for the previously entirely unglazed circular panes. Naturally, volume for volume, these pollutants have a more dramatic effect on global warming than carbon dioxide, because their shape, in our metaphor, more precisely matches the shape of the bulk of the missing panes in the roof.

Finally, it should be pointed out that the differently shaped panes of glass involved are also different in another property; they deteriorate and drop out of their frames at different rates. Thus some greenhouse gases stay in the atmosphere a long time before being chemically broken up – carbon dioxide and most CFCs fall into this category. Others, such as methane, will have a much briefer stay. So it can be seen that greenhouse gases that match the shape of empty panes exactly have a powerful effect, but only for as long as they reside in the atmosphere.

9 Population

In previous chapters population has been referred to as a classic instance where market forces acting by themselves will tend to produce a stable outcome – so that there is balance between the demand of population for sustenance and the capacity of the earth to supply it – but not one that is desirable. That is to say, the tendency of market forces alone is not to produce, in our definition, a sustainable outcome.

This is essentially the Malthusian position.

Malthus

Arithmetical and geometrical growth

Malthus states that:[1]

---

1 Thomas Malthus, *An Essay on the Principle of Population*, Antony Flew, (ed.), (London, Penguin Books, 1988), p. 71.

> Population, when unchecked, increases in a geometrical ratio. Subsistence increases only in an arithmetical ratio. [Because] food is necessary to the life of man, the effects of these two unequal powers must be kept equal. This implies a strong and constantly operating check on population from the difficulty of subsistence. This difficulty must fall somewhere and must necessarily be felt by a large portion of mankind.

He adds that 'population does invariably increase when the means of subsistence increase'.[2]

The stable balance point between population and resources to sustain the population is then reached when resources are sufficient to meet the needs of the population at the time so as to allow the population just to reproduce itself. Were the population to grow beyond that level, the amount of resources per head would drop and the population would in time decrease. Were on the other hand resources to grow beyond the equilibrium level this would encourage the population to grow, over time, until a new equilibrium was reached, with the population again receiving just enough sustenance to allow it to reproduce itself. Note, the equilibrium point would itself imply premature deaths. Children born in excess of the two (or slightly more, to allow for infant mortality) per family needed for exact reproduction would in one way or another die before adulthood. Parents who produced only two children would not survive beyond the addition of these children to the workforce.

Malthus is clear that the equilibrium point (not, as we can see, itself particularly desirable) may not even be reached smoothly. He imagines a case where for some reason the population was smaller than could be supported. Sustenance per head is for the time being more than adequate and the population multiplies. But sustenance overall has not increased and soon the population has exceeded what can normally be carried, with consequent 'severe distress' for the poor.[3] At this point the population ceases growing. But it is in excess and accordingly leads to a drop in the price of labour. This in turn encourages employers to employ more labour to 'turn up fresh soil, to manure' and generally improve the land already under cultivation. Eventually this makes sustenance per head plentiful again, and the whole cycle repeats itself.

Malthus describes the process as one of oscillation.[4] The world

---

2 Malthus, *An Essay on the Principle of Population*, p. 119.

3 Ibid., p. 77.

4 Ibid., p. 77.

dynamics school, referred to in Chapter 1, aggregating matters to global scale, and using explicit systems language, speak of overshoot.   The undesirable consequences are the same in both cases.

In describing the overshoot, Malthus remarks that making an estimate of the periodicity of the swing to overshoot then to correction is difficult. Essentially this is the same difficulty that properly attaches to the calculations made by the world dynamics school of the point in time when demand on the resources of the globe as a whole (unless something is done) will exceed capacity to supply.

Moral restraint

As we saw in Chapter 1, in his later writings on the subject,[5] Malthus recognised the potential of his model to be self-defeating, in that an awareness on the part of labour of the tendency to an unsatisfactory equilibrium in the wages paid to it could in theory lead labour consciously to restrict its own supply.   He was doubtful if this could be done by political action in the form of labour collectively combining to form a quasi-monopoly (as with, for example, trade unions).   He felt (anticipating Olson) that labour was too numerous compared to the owners of capital (whose correspondingly greater facility in forming collectives or 'combinations' Malthus held responsible for worsening the condition of labour by periodically underpaying it).[6]   Instead, he suggested a more satisfactory equilibrium – a sustainable one, in our definition – could be reached if population essentially kept itself low through what he calls 'moral restraint'.[7]   If everyone or almost everyone postponed the production of children, through delayed marriage or in some other way, the naturally limited number of years in which females are fertile would ensure that relatively few children could be born.   This would be collectively prudent.   A smaller population than otherwise would be able to command higher wages for its labour and these wages would permit better living standards and mean fewer premature deaths.

Malthus indirectly recognises the tenuousness of an arrangement of this

---

5   His original essay went into a number of expanded editions. A convenient summary of Malthus's later thinking comes in his *A Summary View of the Principle of Population*, first published in 1830, 32 years after the *Essay*. It is reprinted in the Flew edition of the *Essay*, pp. 218, 272.

6   *An Essay on the Principle of Population*, p. 79.

7   *A Summary View*, p. 250.

kind through the vehemence of his notorious condemnation of 'poor laws' – public support for families whose poverty-stricken breadwinners have not the means to do so. Part of the impulse to the moral restraint he was later to advocate was meant to come from the individual calculating that he or she should have no more children than they could afford to keep. The safety net of poor law simply weakened the incentive so to calculate. Of course part of the tenuousness of the moral restraint arrangement derives from its public good character. Free-riders who accepted no restraints on their own fertility would still benefit from the restraint shown by others. Eventually the whole would collapse.

Aggregated to a global level, this tendency towards an unsatisfactory equilibrium between population and its means of sustenance which seems inherent in the Malthusian analysis has by the end of the 20th century yet to emerge unequivocally. The world dynamics school claim that it is just round the corner. But as Hirsch says, the 'four-fold increase in world population since Malthus wrote has gone along with a rise rather than a fall in food consumption per head [which amounts to] a verdict of not proven on the analysis founded solely on physical limits to growth'.[8]

Return to first principles

One way in which to make progress from this point requires a return to first principles. The weakest part of the Malthus position is not his claim that population grows geometrically (or as we would say today exponentially), although this too needs further discussion, but that the means for its sustenance grow arithmetically.

The case for exponential growth is very simple. In the absence of checks, the number of offspring in any one year from a population of any living thing, from corn (as seeds) or from sheep (as lambs) or from human populations is simply proportional to the size of the population already present. This new, larger population then becomes the base for a new, larger increase and so on. At the end of the 18th century Malthus saw the human population of the newly independent USA as corresponding

---

8 Fred Hirsch, *Social Limits to Growth*, (London, Routledge and Kegan Paul, 1978), p. 19. Malthus (*Essay*, p. 75) seems to have thought one thousand million a plausible figure for the world population at the end of the 18th century – modern observers do not disagree. The figure for 1995 is 5.8 thousand million.

perfectly to the theoretical case of a population growing without checks, and he took its then rate of increase – a doubling in size every 25 years – as what all human populations were capable of if placed in similarly ideal circumstances. Interestingly, Hardin claims that this figure can no longer be seen as a maximum. He cites the case of the inhabitants of the Bikini atoll in the Pacific who were resettled by the US government on other South Pacific islands prior to the use of Bikini for nuclear bomb tests. The resettled population has since the move doubled its size every 13 years.[9]

The precise figure for the minimum doubling time for human populations is not actually a problem in principle for Malthus, although a good knowledge of it (something which even today it cannot be said that we have) is essential for calculating for instance the length of the oscillation cycle or overshoot referred to above.

But the proposition of arithmetical growth in the means of sustenance, because of its seeming antithesis to exponential growth, is more fundamental to his model.

Microbe model

An example of the contrast between the two comes from a fictitious train journey by bacteria travelling from London to Aberdeen and taking 10 hours. They travel in a wagon in the form of a tank containing a large amount of nutritious broth, within which 10 bacteria are placed at the start of the journey. The bacteria need a minimum of one cubic centimetre each of broth in order that they may barely survive. But given the scope to do so, they increase in numbers exponentially at such a rate as to double their numbers every 20 minutes. The tanker starts off with a generous 1000 litres of broth, or 100,000 cubic centimetres per bacterium.

As time elapses, the distance of the bacteria from London grows arithmetically, given the train moves at a reasonably steady speed. Sustenance for the bacteria is also increased arithmetically. Every 50 miles the train stops briefly and a further 1000 litres of broth are added to the tanker wagon. However, the number of bacteria in the tanker grows exponentially. After one hour, they are 50 miles from London and have grown in number to 80 (recalling that their doubling time is 20 minutes).

---

9 Garrett Hardin, *Living Within Limits: Ecology, Economics and Population Taboos*, (New York, Oxford University Press, 1993), pp. 88, 89.

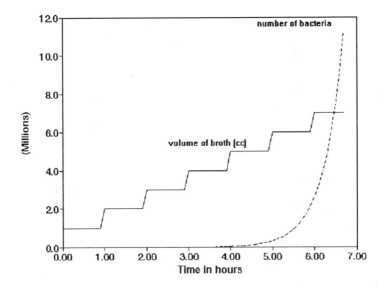

Figure 9.1 Arithmetical vs geometrical

The tanker is topped up to 2000 litres, so the bacteria now have 25000 cubic centimetres each. After 2 hours they are 100 miles from London and 640 in number. The tanker has another 1000 litres added, so the bacteria now have 4690 cubic centimetres each.

If the multiplication of the bacteria received no checks at all, by the time they reached Aberdeen, 500 miles from London, their number would have grown exponentially to ten thousand million. This would imply ten million litres of broth in the tanker wagon. This volume of broth would weigh some ten thousand tonnes, a quantity that would normally need at least ten whole trains to accommodate.

In practice, as we saw, sustenance for the bacteria grew only arithmetically and the graph shows the point at which the supply of sustenance and the demand for it coalesce. The graph shows that this happens about 6 hours and 40 minutes after leaving London, with 7000 litres of broth in the tanker, which supports 7 million bacteria.

The arithmetical increase in sustenance in this case creates no difficulties of principle: the increase in sustenance was simply defined so as to be arithmetical. But sustenance for human populations only in part comes from without: part comes from the expenditure of human effort. Even that part that comes from without is not obviously limited to an arithmetical rate of increase.

Malthus's later writings on population include points made in reaction to contemporary critics of the arithmetical growth section of his model.[10] Malthus acknowledges of course that human populations live on foodstuffs such as corn or mutton. And he accepts that like other living things, corn and sheep can increase in number exponentially – indeed much more rapidly than human populations. A sheep population in the absence of checks (but after allowing for death from old age) seems to be capable of doubling in two years.

At first sight, then, here we have sustenance growing exponentially, just like the human population it is meant to support. But Malthus insists that this kind of food and its increased availability is tied to the availability of suitable soils and pastures. These in turn are ultimately limited (i.e. are a given and do not actually increase at all) simply by geography. While he accepts that less fertile areas can be made more fertile by human intervention (as in the above discussion of population overshoot when cheap labour was used to improve land), progressively worse land will need progressively greater efforts (and diversion of labour) made to improve it.

This is certainly a strong defence, but it is still hard to see how all these various factors affecting the availability of sustenance neatly combine to produce the nett result of arithmetical growth over time.

In order to clarify the situation, we return briefly to our travelling bacteria. The illustration is misleading in an important sense. As the bacteria in the tanker reach the point where their number is exactly that which the nutrients available can support, they do not reach this point of saturation without breaking step in their breeding process. Rather, as the critical minimum amount of sustenance per head is reached it is a matter of experimental observation that the rate of increase in the population of the colony of bacteria itself starts to slow down. Moreover, this is a general phenomenon. Indeed it is reasonable to regard the exponential increase model for populations only as a first approximation. A second and better approximation to what seems to determine the size of natural populations of living things over time is the so-called logistic equation.

---

10 *Summary View*, pp. 223, 225.

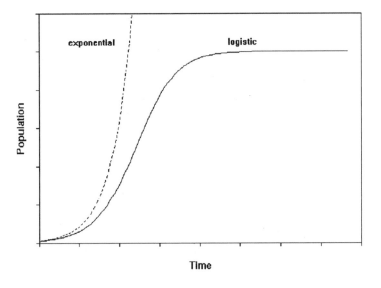

Figure 9.2 Logistic curve

When populations are small, exponential increase still applies. But no population can increase indefinitely since there is always an upper limit set by the population's environment (we postpone discussion of whether or how this limit is itself 'fixed'). The trend of increase of a natural population over time is then as seen in the graph – a logistic curve in the typical shape of an elongated 'S'. It illustrates a rate of population growth that is now dependent on two things. It depends as before on the exponential growth rate (e.g. the 20 minutes doubling time for our bacteria colony). It also depends on how near the population is to its upper limit or carrying capacity.

The exponential growth rate remains important, but it is the growth rate that is observed only in the absence of environmental constraints and, therefore, when the population is small compared to carrying capacity. It is the growth rate of human populations that Malthus was looking for when he cited the rate of population increase in the USA. Recorded growth rates elsewhere may have been lower because human populations elsewhere were nearer to the carrying capacity provided by their environment. Carrying capacity, according to May, 'is determined by food, space, predators and other things'.[11]

Mutualism

Among the 'other things' mentioned by May, where humans and one or two other species are concerned, is intervention by the population in question in order to increase its own carrying capacity. May suggests that certain species of bees are a case in point. The bees' environment at any one time can be thought of as consisting of a population of flowers. But the number of these flowers is partly determined by the number of bees exploiting them for nectar, since in so doing they fertilise flowers rather efficiently. This increases the population of flowers over what it otherwise might have been, which in turn can support an increased number of bees. This process of 'mutualism' must itself have inbuilt checks, since the planet as we know does not solely comprise bees and flowers.

It is not very difficult to extend the mutualism model to human populations and, say, sheep. The carrying capacity of a human population living on sheep will depend on the number of sheep. In the steady state, when both populations are stable, milk and meat from the sheep will be sufficient to allow the human population just to reproduce itself. But this equilibrium is probably only temporary. The carrying capacity of the sheep's environment is dependent on the number of humans. Progressively more intelligent husbandry by the human population can increase the upper limit to the number of sheep that can be sustained on a fixed amount of land. Preparation of the soil and application of fertiliser can increase the proportion of the land that is suitable pasture for sheep. Shepherds can tackle predators and arrange for the provision of shelter and food for the animals over the winter months. Skilful breeding can select for sheep with just those characteristics that put the least demands on the carrying capacity of their environment (e.g. greatest resistance to disease), and so on. The more sheep there are, the greater in turn the human population that can be supported.

Writing fifty five years before May, Whitehead also has mutualism in mind, when in discussing Malthus he stresses the importance of not paying too much attention to the fixed side of the environment. Successful

---

11 Robert M. May, 'Models for Single Populations', in Robert M. May (ed.), *Theoretical Ecology: Principles and Applications*, (Oxford, Blackwells Scientific, 1981), p. 7.

organisms, he says, modify their environment (in our example, domesticated sheep must be considered successful). Whitehead compares the situation in North America after the arrival of European settlers with the situation before. The native tribes of North America 'accepted' their environment which meant it could support only a rather small population. The Europeans pursued a different policy, more mutualistic in our terms, which permitted the same land to support a human population twenty times or more larger than before.[12]

Where does this leave Malthus and his arithmetical increase in carrying capacity versus exponential increase in population? Whitehead seems to be saying that more may depend on how humans organise their demands on their environment than Malthus seemed to be suggesting. Systematic farming, as opposed to more haphazard methods backed up by hunting, increased the carrying capacity of North America by more than an order of magnitude. Hardin broadens what is essentially the same point to recognise in the agricultural revolution (i.e. the very early discovery by mankind that growing crops and husbanding animals had certain advantages over the 'hunter-gatherer' lifestyle) and later in the Industrial Revolution very large steps towards progressively more efficient mutualism.[13] The reason arithmetical growth is left behind is that mutualism has about it something of the properties of a nuclear chain reaction. More sheep mean more men which mean more sheep. The onus almost shifts to explaining why there has not been an even more explosive growth in both populations than that which has already occurred.

Malthus confounded?

So there is no difficulty in seeing why Hirsch admits to doubts about the accuracy of what Malthus was claiming. World population by the end of the 1990s has grown to 5 or 6 times what it was in Malthus's day. Hirsch's observation in 1978 that this increase in population had been accompanied by an increase in the amount of food per head remains true. Between his own time of writing and 1990 world food production per head had increased by a further 4 percent.[14] But why does Hirsch prefer a

---

12 A. N. Whitehead, *Science and the Modern World*, (Cambridge, Cambridge University Press, 1926), pp. 256, 259.

13 *Living Within Limits*, p. 116.

14 *World Resources 1992–93*, (New York, Oxford University Press, 1992), p. 272.

Scottish not proven verdict on Malthus rather than condemning him outright? Why Hardin's pessimism that the huge improvements in mutualism of the agricultural and industrial revolutions may not be repeatable (the problem, he believes, being energy supplies)?[15] Why the pessimistic tone of the world dynamics school about overpopulation and their Malthusian plea for moral restraint? Why does Peacock's old claim remain valid that 'the Malthusian doctrine has never been entirely removed from textbooks on economics'?[16]

The reason, essentially, is that the facts are as consistent with a pessimistic as with an optimistic interpretation. If the great surges in the efficiency of mutualism are over, world population will continue to increase until food production per head peaks and then starts to fall. At some point not much later, world population will start to stabilise at the Malthusian value where food per head is just sufficient to allow the population to reproduce itself. May's deliberately highly simplified model of mutualism between two populations (see the appendix to this chapter) is wholly consistent with such an outcome.

Levels of analysis

However, it will have been noticed that discussion in this chapter so far has drawn no distinction in principle between population questions as they may affect a state – as with Malthus's Britain and the USA at the end of the 18th century; or the world as a whole – as with Hirsch's verdict on Malthus at the global level. Many analysts, not least the world dynamics school, are naturally drawn to make their analyses of population at the global level. This is not only because of an ideological predisposition to imagine that the world 'ought' in some way to be a whole, but also because it neatly sidesteps questions of immigration and emigration which were apt to plague Malthus's own attempts to verify his model.

But the core point of the present chapter is that the convenience of the global analysis may have led some observers to miss an important clue in the form of a further check to population growth deriving from international rivalries between states.

---

15 *Living Within Limits*, pp. 147, 159.

16 A. T. Peacock, 'Theory of Population and Modern Economic Analysis II', *Population Studies*, 7, 3, 1954, p. 228.

Strategic importance of population

Malthus and Hardin are correct in having little faith in the capacity of populations to limit themselves even when presented with advance warning of what overpopulation will mean. However, in a world where significant rivalries exist between states engaged in the pursuit of power, if they wish to survive, let alone prosper, states may have an incentive to control their population growth. Why should this be so?

Consider a state with no migration of population and very little international trade whose population has stabilised at the highest possible level, where any further increase would lower sustenance per head below the level needed for the population to reproduce itself. Such a state would be vulnerable to external danger because it would have few unalloyed resources with which to defend itself from predatory neighbours. Government could still exact taxes in order to equip an army or to compensate possible allies, but it could only do so by causing the deaths of a large number of its own population. The remedy could be as bad as the danger it was meant to grapple with.

Consider on the other hand a state which followed domestic policies which kept population significantly below the maximum that resources could support, but not so far below as to reduce the size of the tax base excessively. A population somewhere near this optimum would be better safeguarded from external threats. Taxation of an optimum population could raise resources for foreign policy purposes without creating mass starvation. States with a large tax base of this kind will prosper in their dealings with other states, states without will become the targets for those that are better placed.

Optimum population

The concept of optimum population as outlined above is only as secure as the assumptions that lie behind it, even if some of these assumptions are less crucial than others.

Firstly, the assumption of no international migration of population is not exact. But what can be said is that states tend not to allow 'free trade' in persons and closely control international movement of peoples (or strive to do so). Population is treated in practice very much like a 'strategic commodity', exactly as our model would lead us to expect. On the other hand, international trade in the ordinary sense of the term does take place and to an increasing extent, although within limits set by strategic considerations (that is to say, considerations arising from an awareness that states do not always harbour benign intentions towards other states). Our model simply suggests that just as intelligent restrictions on international trade can provide buffers against contrived shortages of commodities and therefore enhance system stability, these same considerations may also help provide buffers against excess population growth. We return to this question below.

Secondly, narrowing what is to be understood as the international power of a state to the size of its mobilisable tax base is most easily justified in circumstances where the economic dimension of power is dominant. In the post Cold War era, it can at least be said that the relative importance of this dimension of power is on the increase.

Thirdly, along the economic dimension, there remains some uncertainty as to which economic indicator should be maximised. The optimum population could either be the population that corresponded to maximum income per head or the population that corresponded to maximum total national income, or some population intermediate between the two if these were different. As can be seen in the appendix to this chapter, both May's ecological model and the detailed economic model due to Meek (after Peacock) show that maximising either can correspond to a population below the Malthusian limit.

Finally, in order to be effective, domestic population policies would in one way or another need to create practical incentives (or remove practical disincentives) on the part of individuals to exercise the equivalent of Malthus's moral restraint.

As will have been gathered, the concept of an optimum population is not an easy one to pin down. So there is no intention here of going beyond Boulding's cautious endorsement: 'The power-population function [for a state] may well be parabolic, with a maximum power at some point'.[17]

It will be recalled that in Chapter 1 we described strategic calculation on the part of states as introducing an element of slack into the system, and compared it to the other buffers provided by the untapped natural resources of the sea bed and Antarctica. The main virtue of slack, it was said, was to promote stability. The above argument illustrates how stability in terms of population may also be enhanced by strategic calculation.

---

17 *Three Faces of Power*, (Newbury Park, Sage, 1989), p. 192.

Consensus on 'disconnectedness'?

This position or a position close to it is already occupied by modern commentators on international environmental politics who have already arrived there by their own routes.

Herman Kahn and colleagues take up a position they believe to be the opposite of the world dynamics school. Kahn takes the view that it is possible to go too far in insisting on seeing environmental problems in a global context:[18]

> the organic interdependence [between states] it suggests would ensure that a dislocation anywhere would be a dislocation everywhere. We prefer redundancy, flexibility and a degree of 'disconnectedness'. If India, for example, goes under, we want to be able to help save her, not go down with her.

In asking for redundancy, Kahn is aligning himself with Vickers and his approval of the stabilising effect of unexploited areas of natural resources as buffers against strains on the international economic system. On disconnectedness, Kahn focusses on the international trade in energy resources. Greater national self-sufficiency here, involving among other things greater emphasis on nuclear power (which without breeder reactors – which he considers unproven – he correctly sees only as a temporary stop-gap) increases disconnectedness at the very point where the usual virtues of connectedness, in the form of the international energy market, are least marked, as a result of the near monopoly position of the OPEC powers.[19]

Hardin's discussion of population and the dangers of overpopulation, which is very much in the world dynamics vein, leaves him extraordinarily close to Kahn.[20] Together, they share Boulding's worries about 'the globalisation of the world. If you have only one system, then if anything goes wrong, everything goes wrong'.[21] Hardin therefore also wants more disconnectedness and his direct concern, like that of the present chapter,

---

18 Herman Kahn, William Brown and Leon Martel, *The Next 200 Years*, (London, Associated Business Programmes, 1977), p. 216 fn.

19 Ibid., pp. 65, 67 and p. 215.

20 Hardin's hostile attitude to Kahn seems to be based on Kahn's later work, *The Resourceful Earth*, (Oxford, Basil Blackwell, 1984), where Kahn (pp. 1, 45) does take a strident anti-world dynamics school tone. Kahn died in 1983.

21 *Living Within Limits*, p. 295.

is overpopulation.

But he appears to be unusually gnomic in terms of prescriptions (which include recommendations concerning the abolition of interest rates, which aims to overcome a well-known market imperfection by abolishing the market for capital altogether). He advocates a bar by rich countries on immigration from poor countries. This in one way is simply a sharper sort of disconnection than ours, which merely noted that governments took a restrictive attitude to population movements anyway since they treat population as a strategic resource. In another way it is incompatible.

Recognising that there may indeed be an optimum population for states to aim for, his faith in the guidance obtainable from models in this respect is so low that he prefers experiment. Various states pursuing different population policies under zero international migration will throw up winners and losers. The example of the winners, Hardin says, then provides the necessary model and signpost for action.

Of course the trouble with this is that it is a call for moral restraint (not that it sounds much like one) and surely encounters the problem of free-riding. The thrust of the present chapter is far more in the Vickers' vein of valuing model-building. Populations are strategic commodities of a peculiar kind in that states can have too much as well as too little. Strategic, i.e. selfish, calculations will propel states towards controlling their populations the better to exert influence over their neighbours. These controls on population at the level of states provide control on population for the globe as a whole.

Summary

Our population model starts with Malthus and the tendency for populations to grow to the stable limit of providing only enough sustenance per head to allow the population to reproduce itself. This stable outcome falls outside our definition of sustainability on the grounds of its undesirability. Inevitable temporary overshoots of population above this carrying capacity will lead to an accelerated number of premature deaths, otherwise they would not be temporary. Even at carrying capacity, the average condition of the populace is not to be envied – since resources beyond the minimum necessary for the populace to reproduce itself do not exist, the average share of these is zero.

But the mutualistic relationship between human populations and their means of sustenance magnifies human carrying capacity. Taking the globe as a whole, both population and food per head have increased since Malthus's time. If human ingenuity can find scope for continued steps upwards in mutualism, human carrying capacity will be reached, if ever, only at a distant date when scope for further increases in mutualism runs out. If, on the other hand, this is too optimistic a view, and all the great upward steps in mutualism have already been taken, the nature of international politics can virtually be relied on to intervene to prevent population growth getting out of hand.

This is because successful states are able to survive in the sometimes turbulent waters of international politics only if they have deployable resources to put at the service of an active foreign policy. States with populations at carrying capacity have few such resources, so successful states will not include those that have populations at carrying capacity. Returning to Hardin by the back door, these successful states will become models for others, not because of altruism but because of selfishness.

Appendix: Malthus, May and Meek: Ecology and Economics and Optimum Population

May's model, which he stresses is simplified to the point, or even beyond it, of oversimplification, begins with the logistic curve.

Two populations, that of man and sheep, with virtually no interaction between them at this stage, can each be considered as having reached the carrying capacity of their environments. Their populations are accordingly static.   There is just enough food per head for each to allow the populations to make good their losses due to deaths.

We now imagine the discovery of mutualism in the form of systematic sheep farming. May models this simply by allowing the carrying capacity of the sheep's environment now to depend on the number of men, who are now in a position to domesticate and shepherd the sheep, and the carrying capacity of man's environment to depend on the number of domesticated sheep, which provide additional food. May, for simplicity, assumes that the carrying capacity of each species, in an echo of Malthus, increases arithmetically with increases in the number of the species opposite in the mutual relationship.[22]

One man acting as a shepherd can increase the population of sheep by 30 (say).   Suppose 30 domesticated sheep could increase the population of humans by two. The two new humans, put to shepherding, could increase the sheep population by 60. This in turn could support four new humans, and so on. Since this arithmetic leads to infinite increases in sheep and people, it is obviously unrealistic.

May's method of injecting more realism is simply to insist that if one man can increase the sheep population by 30 (on our count), something more than thirty new sheep are needed to support, in turn, one additional

---

22 Suppose N_p is the number of people and N_s the number of sheep. Prior to mutualism, the growth of each population can be represented by two logistic curves: $dN_p/dt = hN_p(1 - N_p/K_p)$ and $dN_s/dt = sN_s(1 - N_s/K_s)$. K_p and K_s are the carrying capacities of the non-interacting human and sheep populations, respectively, and h and s their respective percentage growth rates in the absence of checks. May then assumes that with mutualism, human carryimg capacity is no longer fixed at K_p but can increase to $K_p + aN_s$, i.e., arithmetically with increases in the numbers of sheep. Similarly, K_s can increase to $K_s + bN_p$. He makes the proviso that $a \times b$ must be less than 1. The graph plots the mutualistic dN_s/dt against N_p. The straight line is $dN_s/dt = 1 \times N_s$ (1 refers to the 1 sheep per year assumed to be minimally required for the human population just to reproduce itself). See Robert M. May, 'Models for Two Interacting Populations', in Robert M. May (ed.), *Theoretical Ecology: Principles and Applications*, pp. 94, 100.

man.

This still produces a rise in the populations of both, but one that is now held within limits.

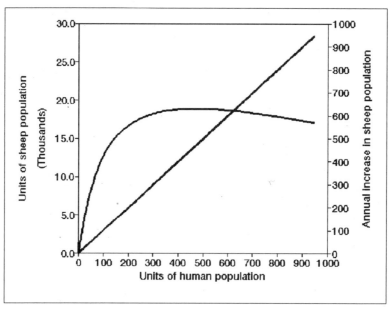

Figure 9A.1 Mutualism in action

The more human ingenuity can narrow the gap between the number of sheep a man can add to the sheep population and the number of sheep needed to support a single man, the higher these limits to the population growth of each can become.

Malthus, in modern parlance, was both an economist and an ecologist. In order to make a bridge between the ideas of May, a theoretical ecologist, and those of economists who have also interested themselves in the population question, we make a small modification to May's original model.

The populations of men and sheep are assumed to be mutualistically entwined, with the conditions required by May in place to allow enlarged but not infinite new carrying capacities. A small additional provision is made that man requires from the sheep occasional mutton, as well as milk and wool.

Bearing in mind that the figures employed are purely illustrative, the graph shows two things. The curve represents the annual increase (right y-axis) in the sheep population. The straight line shows the human subsistence level of one sheep per head per year (minimum necessary for human population just to reproduce itself). The shape of the curve near the point where it is cut by the straight line is nearly parabolic. Where the two intersect we get the equilibrium population of people (x-axis) and the equilibrium population of sheep (left y-axis).

The equilibrium point is stable. However, a new burst of human ingenuity (in the form of applied science) is capable of increasing both the number of sheep and the number of people that can be supported, 'moving' the curve rightwards and upwards.

The equilibrium point as shown corresponds to a human population of 625 units and a sheep population of 19,000 units. The human population, without checks, is taken to have a doubling time of 25 years. The sheep population, without checks, is assumed to double in two years. Mutualism is assumed to take the form of one extra man being able to add 30 to the sheep population, with 31 additional sheep being needed to provide for one extra man. The pre-mutualism starting point was a population of each of only 100 units. So mutualism has produced a 2 orders of magnitude increase in the sheep population and almost an order of magnitude increase in the human population.

In spite of its simplicity, May's model is richer than has so far been indicated. It is not purely a static model. The stable equilibrium point described by May is stable because an excess of population above the stable point will not persist, but will return to the stable point usually after oscillating about it. This is the equivalent of Malthus's oscillations or the overshoot feared by the world dynamics school. May's point is the more effective the mutualism, and the greater the multiplication it creates in the carrying capacity of each of the populations, the longer will be the period of overshoot if it were to occur. This is also equivalent to saying that were a smooth approach of population to carrying capacity that had exhausted scope for further upward movement (or to a smaller figure to permit a better standard of living) desired, curbs on population growth need to be put in place a rather long time before: a generation ahead of time is probably insufficient.

In terms of optimum population, the May curve is rather straightforward, at least at sizeable levels of population. The annual output of sheep per head of human population starts off rather high and does not alter much until population reaches around 100 units. It then progressively reduces. Total output of sheep per annum does however reach a peak at a human population of about 450 units. Output per head of population is also higher at this point than at the intersection point, so the population of 450 has a claim to be considered optimum.

Meek

Meek approaches the concept of optimum population from the perspective of economics.[23]

He considers a state with a fixed amount of land and capital and isolated from the rest of the world engaged in the production of corn. Corn he takes to be symbolic and the amount of it available per head to be representative of living standards.

When population is low, he reasons that there will be relatively few workers to exploit the amount of capital and land so that output (of corn) will also be low. As population grows, however, output will also grow. But this process cannot go on indefinitely. The law of diminishing returns in economics says that the application of increasing amounts of labour to a fixed amount of capital eventually leads to a saturation in the total amount of output obtainable, when additional amounts of labour add virtually nothing to total output.[24]   Meek's version goes further and considers that beyond a certain point additional labour actually can detract from the total output. That is to say, saturation gives way to reduction. Peacock (whom Meek cites as the inspiration for his own analysis), in a more formal discussion, shows that an eventual fall in total output with increasing amounts of labour is what Malthus implies in his discussion of oscillation (the consequences of labour overshooting carrying capacity).[25]

In graphical form, as Meek shows, output of corn per year rises as population increases until it reaches a maximum after which it declines. There is an obvious similarity with May's treatment with the difference that Meek has human output per head rising from a small value as human

23 R. L. Meek, *Figuring Out Society*, (London, Fontana, 1971), pp. 26, 37.

24 See, for example, R. G. Lipsey, *An Introduction to Positive Economics*, (London, Weidenfeld and Nicolson, 1983), pp. 213, 214.

25 A. T. Peacock, 'Theory of Population and Modern Economic Analysis, I', *Population Studies*, 6, 2, 1952, pp. 119, 120.

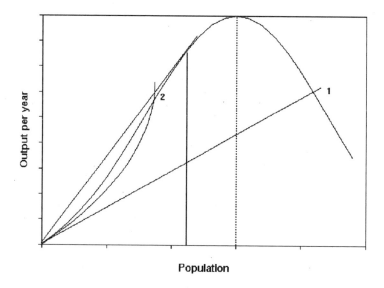

Figure 9A.2 Population and diminishing returns

numbers increase, reaching a maximum and then falling back again. On the same graph Meek plots the minimum output needed to sustain a population at a given size. Plotted against population this takes the form of a straight line. This straight line intersects the total output curve at a point where total output per head (or average output) is just sufficient to allow the population to reproduce itself ('1'). This corresponds to a population larger than the one that corresponds to the maximum output obtainable (light vertical line) and larger still than the one that corresponds to maximum output per head (maximum living standard).

This is not the end of the story. In reality capital is not fixed in quantity or quality. First, it can be accumulated over time: second, its productivity can be increased by the application of scientific knowledge. So the peak of the curve of output against population can move both upwards and rightwards, accommodating progressively further increases in population. Qualitatively, at least, May's mutualism model says much the same thing. The equivalent of capital accumulation and scientific progress for May's ecological model are increases in the degree to which humans and sheep may be mutually beneficial.

Peacock draws attention to the difficulty of generalising Meek's analysis to states which are not isolated from the rest of the world but engaged in international trade.[26] He is willing to see the Meek model applied more or less as it stands to the global level of aggregation but dislikes its consequent lack of utility for guidance of policy. He concludes only with the advice that the Meek model may be more applicable to states with relatively low participation in international trade than to those more intensively involved.

Returning to Meek, the condition of the maximum population that can be supported at a given level of capital and scientific knowledge is Malthusian and unenviable. As he rightly points out, this need not be so provided an increase in population were accompanied by a progressively upward definition of what constituted a minimum standard of living. In such a case, the equilibrium population can be lower than before (at the point of intersection '2'). Here Meek collides with Malthus in seeing fewer difficulties than his more pessimistic predecessor in labour's managing to ration itself and hence bid up its value to the owners of land and capital.

However this may be, the exigencies of international politics will have the effect of encouraging states to pursue domestic policies which will create a tax base larger than that associated with the Malthusian equilibrium. Creation of an optimum population can only be done by government creating incentives for restraint in the production of children. That these incentives need not be a burden on the population is of course strongly implied by Meek's talk of redefining upwards what corresponds to a minimum standard of living.

---

26 'Theory of Population and Modern Economic Analysis II', pp. 228, 230.

10 Conclusion

Summary

Our starting point was a modified version of Checkland's original systemic representation of economic activity and the pollution it generates expanded to the global level and enlarged in scope to accommodate flows of waste and goods connected with the exploitation of global commons, as sinks for pollution and sources of supply, respectively.

Sustainable development was taken as a goal commanding wide assent. It was taken to mean that the above system should be stable, i.e. tending to persist over time, and that the norms, from which departures from the equilibrium point are to be measured, should be desirable. Departures from these norms are signals which should stimulate the making of corrections, via political intervention, if necessary.

Prompt rather than delayed correction of departures from set norms is itself normally desirable. As Vickers says, 'the more sluggish the response to [the departure from the norm] the more violent the ultimate adjustment and the greater the chance the system will have passed some

215

point of no return'.[1]

For this reason, scientific understanding of the effects of pollutants on the natural environment is a boon. Without it, evidence of harm to the physical environment as the result of discharge of particular categories of waste can inevitably come only after the event, often a long time afterwards. Thus a scientific contribution to the monitoring of pollution norms is seen as wholly consistent with the application of the precautionary principle, if this in turn is taken to mean a bias towards acting politically to attend to norms sooner rather than later or 'giving the benefit of the doubt' to the case for action as opposed to that for delay.

Many kinds of market-based flows of commodities within and between states are taken to have strong self-regulating tendencies, simply because they are market-based. Accordingly, no specific 'monitoring' of fluctuations in supply and demand is identified as necessary. One important exception is world trade in energy, where near-monopolistic control of oil supplies seriously hampers the operation of market forces. Essentially, shortages of oil, as experience shows, can be contrived. But the trouble with a contrived shortage of anything is that costly responses in the form of developing full-fledged substitutes, say, will be shrunk from because everyone knows the contrived shortage could vanish tomorrow, leaving the investment in substitutes high and dry.

Nonetheless, political action by larger consumers of energy to acquire a greater degree of independence from oil exporters would dilute this monopoly and therefore restore balance to the market in energy. The nearest and soonest available (because proven – researched and developed) substitute energy source, coal excepted, is nuclear fission. In turn, difficulty has been experienced in setting norms for the permissible level of discharge (the sanctioned level) into the physical environment of the radioactive waste products associated with this energy source. Detailed consideration of this question leads to the surprising discovery that in Britain at least norms for the permissible harmfulness of released waste have historically failed to gain acceptance for the very simple reason that they have been set unreasonably high. That is, the risks to life the releases represent are high comparable to other risks deemed acceptable by citizens of modern states. Why this instance of norm setting has gone wrong in this way is itself an interesting question. The solution, either reducing

---

1 Geoffrey Vickers, *Freedom in a Rocking Boat*, (London, Allen Lane The Penguin Press, 1970), p. 130.

releases or compensating the minority of the population that are exposed to these risks would seem obvious, but it is possibly now too late.

Where something goes wrong with norm setting, as in the nuclear power case in Britain (and, of course, elsewhere), there is a tendency for the vacuum left by political failure to be filled by political innovation. The rise of Green politics may be seen as a 'market-driven' (demand evoking supply) response to a demand for improvement to the political machinery of norm setting in environmental matters.

If greater national self-sufficiency in energy, via nuclear or some alternative, means a reduction in international interdependence, something less than complete interdependence is in any case probably desirable from the point of view of the stability of the whole. A completely rigid system with no slack would render the whole vulnerable to a failure of a part.

A very simple example of what is meant is the desirable slack in the international trading system in fuel and minerals created and maintained by the as yet untapped natural resources on and under the bed of the oceans, and in the Antarctic land mass. The existence of these buffer reserves cannot really be said to have been engineered, but it is easily seen how they put a safety net under how far future or current groupings of supplier states may go in putting monopolistic pressure on importing states.

The impulse on the part of states not to become wholly interdependent where so-called strategic commodities are concerned, provided it is not taken too far, is another desirable buffer.

This comes over most strikingly, at least in principle, in matters of population.

If labour can be treated as a commodity, then the market-based norms for the remuneration of labour are in the long run stable enough, but are far too Malthusian for them normally to be considered desirable. Incomes per head in such a world would be sufficient only to allow the population to reproduce itself. In this sense it is agreed that if the world were a single state or comprised of states that did not mutually interact, there would be a tendency to over-population in that the default stable point would mean a population so large that incomes would be at bare subsistence levels. The use of the word 'tendency' is deliberate in that the reaching of the default state is delayed by the accumulation of capital and by improvements in its productivity through scientific innovation. In default of the latter two phenomena, the tendency manifests itself.

But a degree of inter-state competitiveness encourages governments to aim for populations with incomes per head sufficiently far above the

Malthusian level of bare subsistence in order to provide a worthwhile tax base to fund the conduct of active external policies. Such populations are described as optimum. This is because they are smaller than the maximum population national resources could support, for that population being at the Malthusian limit would have no spare resources at all: equally they cannot be very close to zero since a zero population would provide no tax base either.

Accordingly, competitiveness between states encourages national governments to devise incentives to keep their populations at or near optimum levels which are below the maximum size they are capable of reaching. In classical 'market-forces' style, the private national incentives of states to act to keep their populations limited, simultaneously means that global population, by the same token, is also kept limited.

The advantages of market-based norms are usually great enough to make it sensible when setting norms elsewhere to work with the grain of the market rather than against it. In any case, norm setting in one part of the system that shares a theme with norm setting in another part reduces the chances of collision.

The market has a part to play in regulating the pollution of the physical environment and in the exploitation of commons resources: but it is not in the forefront. In each case a system of political monitoring is necessary to set norms, police norms and to act to correct departures from norms. The problem is national competitiveness and, to a lesser degree, market failure.

In matters to do with the pollution of a physical environmental space, common to at least two states, arising as a result of emissions to the air or water of waste from some economic activity, to do with the production of energy, say, the selfish motivation of the states involved is normally not to desist. To desist will cost money (assuming that economic activity is governed by market forces or a very close facsimile, current economic activity will contain no obvious scope for further savings through greater efficiency). But the gains from desisting will be shared with neighbouring states, who cannot normally be excluded from benefiting from the somewhat cleaner waters or atmosphere the desisting state has created. Matters become particularly difficult where the number of interacting states is large. An agreement amongst them not to pollute becomes very vulnerable to cheating, because a single cheat will reason that it can derive virtually all the benefits of pollution control whether it individually contributes or not to the cost of doing things more cleanly.

Even when numbers are small, particular difficulties in arriving at an agreement that benefits all parties can be expected when some parties are seen as benefiting relatively more than others. Amongst rivalrous states, where the pollution control proposals are seen to touch upon components of national power directly, relative gains matter most. The further the pollution question finds itself removed from such 'high' political or strategic issues, and the smaller the number of participants in the agreement to set and police the norm, the more easily achieved and more stable the agreement will be.

The nearest to generally applicable advice in the matter of international pollution control is that attempting too much at once by too many participants is wrong. The reverse of attempting a little, as a first step, with a minimum of participants that can later be expanded to include others seems to have most chance of success. It means that a start can be made sooner rather than later, ahead of full scientific understanding of the problem, if needs be. Such scientific understanding as there may be is valuable in that it allows action, at least in principle, to be taken ahead of actual experience of the damage caused by pollution. This of course assumes general agreement as to the political disinterestedness of science. This cannot always be taken for granted.

Importantly too, small steps are more reversible than large ones should science change its mind. Small steps are also easier to learn from – as a source of negative feedback – than large ones (because 'other things' are more likely to have remained equal). This includes learning about fellow participants. Small steps mean that risk-averse states, anxious about being taken advantage of by cheats, can learn whether or not their fellow participants are trustworthy for only a small stake.

As the number of participants grows, protection against unravelling and encouragement for remaining stragglers to join can be got by the larger participants creating a central fund. This is then used to reward smaller members if and only if they become and remain parties to the arrangement in good standing. This method of countering free-riders will only work if the arrangement includes a scheme for verifying whether members are indeed in good standing.

The step-by-step counsel needs to be interpreted intelligently. The least promising situation in some ways for the setting of all sorts of environmental protection norms is the naturally asymmetric one. States sharing a river will take a very different attitude to the regulation either of extraction from or pollution of the river waters depending upon whether they are upstream of their neighbours or downstream. If the upstream states were at the same time *downwind* of their neighbours, the advantage of coupling right from the start an international arrangement to curb acid rain, say, with a clean river arrangement would seem obvious. Step-by-step, which would have the issues taken separately, would seem ill-advised in this case.

Poor progress in tackling the question of global warming is partly for asymmetry reasons. Unlike, say, controlling the release of gases damaging to the ozone layer, where the big emitters were OECD states mainly fouling their own nests, the chief emitters of greenhouse gases are causing only slight, or at any rate indirect, problems for themselves but potentially much more serious and immediate problems for the more agriculturally-dependent economies of the world.

A better analogue for the control of global warming than the oft-cited Montreal Protocol on protection of the ozone layer may be the less glamorous series of intra-European (essentially) agreements on controlling the release of regional atmospheric pollutants. Here, upwind states were eventually brought within the scope of the arrangements.

What is true for norm-setting for controlling pollution of a common space can, as we have seen, also be true for norm-setting in the matter of extraction from a common source. A group of states faced with a falling trend in catches of fish would be better off setting, with scientific advice, a quota for the group below the current total catch to allow the fish stock to recover. But the larger the group the easier it is for one member to reason that its own adhesion to the quota or not could scarcely be decisive for the future of the fish stock. The temptation is then to cheat. If one could reason this way, so could others, and the arrangement would collapse. The parallel with the temptation to cheat within an international agreement to limit discharges of pollutants into a common space is clear.

The evolving convention that states with coastlines should have exclusive economic control over waters out to 200 nautical miles from their shores is a part solution to the fisheries problem. What was a common is now partitioned into nationally owned sections of ocean and it seems reasonable to assume that no owner of fishing grounds would allow its grounds to be overfished. At a minimum, where fish straddle adjacent zones, the required collective response would normally involve only an encouragingly small number of states.

But 'overfishing', if this means failing to make the best of one's fishing grounds, or even second best, out of fear that a unilateral attempt to act responsibly would be punished by the selfishness of other states with whom the grounds are shared, is not the same as saying that the owner (singly or a small collective fishing zone-straddling species) has no incentive to fish the grounds to exhaustion. Living resources can be tapped indefinitely if the extraction rate is below the natural replacement rate. If the maximum natural replacement rate were 10 per cent, say, and the fishers extracted 10 per cent of the population of fish annually, this would be a conservationist policy. But if circumstances were such that the rate of interest obtainable by the exploiter were 11 per cent, it would seem to pay the exploiter to catch all the fish as soon as possible and bank the proceeds. Very similar calculations apply even when commons questions do not arise. National owners of slow-growing forests who face high interest rates will feel a pressure to cut them down as soon as possible. Owners of elephants in a similar position will feel a pressure to cull herds to extinction and bank the proceeds from the sale of ivory.

Comprehensively felling forests or culling elephants may thus in certain circumstances make complete sense to their owners but create alarm and puzzlement elsewhere. It is this apparent market failure for interest rates properly to reflect preferences that gives a twist to the problem of setting international norms for the exploitation of living resources. This applies even when commons issues are absent. When they are present, as with whales or even, to a degree, elephants, they add to the difficulty. One way in which international agreements to control the pollution of common spaces can arise is as outgrowths from a unilateral initiative. In fact, partly because it is hard to see how there ever could be an incentive for a unilateral (even conditional) initiative to exploit a common source sustainably, arriving at a stable collective solution for the exploitation of a common source seems to be intrinsically harder to achieve than for the equivalent commons problem where pollution is the issue.

Again, when there is a particular difficulty in setting norms, political innovation is apt to fill the vacuum. The analogue of the part played by Green politics in the setting of norms for, e.g., the national exploitation of civil nuclear power, is the emergence of the preservationist movement (e.g. 'save the whale'), within states and internationally, in the matter of setting norms for the exploitation of living resources. Preservationism contends that there is no sustainable rate of exploitation greater than zero. Conservationism is seen to have failed as a result of excessive faith in market forces to provide for sustainable exploitation even once commons matters have been resolved, itself no easy thing.

Whilst it is not hard to see what stokes the fires of the preservationist case, it is too soon to be sure that the failure to set conservationist norms does not owe something to the simple coincidence that ownership of a wide range of living resources is concentrated in the hands of poor states who are particularly short of capital. Remedying the shortage of capital through international aid could contribute to a non-preservationist, i.e. conservationist solution. A reasonable preservationist retort would perhaps quote Vickers about sluggish responses to departures from norms. Waiting for capital-starved states to be bailed out may mean considerable delay and a correspondingly greater risk that the system will have in the meanwhile passed the point of no return – no more elephants, no more whales.

Another solution available at least in principle stems from the correspondence with the exploitation of mineral resources. Owners of mines are also under temptation from high interest rates to work out their mineral deposits as rapidly as possible. This creates little alarm partly because whereas there are often substitutes for minerals, it scarcely makes sense to speak of substitutes for elephants. The other reason is that the problem is largely academic because of the formation of quasi-monopolistic groupings in the mineral extraction business, which encourages conservation. Monopolistic groupings made up of states with large numbers of wild elephants for the marketing of ivory should also encourage conservation.

Questions answered

The above gives summary answers to a series of questions. The questions fall into three categories. There are those that were specifically posed, e.g. concerning the future of nuclear energy. There were those that emerged, e.g. concerning the probability that the collective action problem for restricting discharges of pollutants into a common sink may be somewhat easier solved in principle than the analogous problem where extraction from a common source is concerned.

Thirdly, answers have been provided to questions that were not specifically posed, but fell into the category of 'questions in the air'. Two of these perhaps merit special recapitulation: what is the precautionary principle; and what is the part played by natural science in creating and coping with environmental threats?

The interpretation of the precautionary principle given here is intimately bound up with the systems approach taken. Indeed, the holist quality of the approach means that the question about science is linked to the question about the precautionary principle.

Sustainability means stability plus desirability. Preserving stability means correcting any tendencies for the system to deviate from selected norms. Delay in correcting such tendencies can simply be dangerous, but delay is inherent in such matters. Data are nearly always out of date, so deviations from the norm may have occurred long before they are brought to notice. The problem of delay does not end there, for, as Vickers observes, further time is then invariably needed to arrive at a politically agreed view of the situation. It follows quite simply that almost anything whose effect is to work in the opposite direction and to speed up the feedback process is to be welcomed. To err, or rather to appear to err, on the side of acting too soon, i.e. to follow the precautionary principle, normally ensures not that action is precipitate but merely that it is less delayed than otherwise would have been the case.

Whilst this may make sense of the precautionary principle, it could be said that it does not appear to do much more than that. It could be asked what there is in this interpretation in the way of actual guidance to policy makers or advisers to policy makers so that they might act differently in practice. The answer is that simply being given a good reason for thinking that there may be something in the precautionary principle will by itself help alter attitudes and tilt action in a desirable direction.

Natural science, to the extent that it provides good models of the external world, is allied to the precautionary principle, since at least in theory it permits corrective action to be taken ahead of actual experience of the consequences of a departure from the norm. Global warming is an anticipated problem and the anticipation is made possible only because there are serviceable scientific models of the physics and chemistry of the atmosphere. Again from our systems perspective, whilst time is always going to be needed to arrive at an internationally agreed view of the situation concerning a particular environmental problem, science helps here too to the extent that the underlying assumptions of Western science are now globally accepted.

However, science is also that which scientists do. Their models of the natural order are usually of interest to them for their own sakes, not for any utility of the kind discussed above. Just as science it not automatically a useful adjunct to economic betterment it is not automatically a useful adjunct to the precautionary principle. Bridges have first to be built between the preoccupations of scientists and the preoccupations of the concerned public, spanning the territory of 'trans-science'.

End point

Finally, just as scientists provide models of the real world, in most cases of extraordinary power and elegance, so do social scientists. Of course the models provided by the latter are more tentative and provisional. Indeed we pointed out in Chapter 1 that in Boulding's terminology of systems complexity, if the real world as the subject matter of social science is of complexity Level 8, then the cybernetic model we have used throughout this book is of Level 3. But even necessarily somewhat crude social science models that attempt to simulate the real world provide a kind of information about that world that is instantly available and, at least in theory, widely accessible (the very sophistication of natural science models of course reduces their accessibility in comparison). This information is inferior to actual experience in terms of its certainty, but a good model strives to be as truthful as possible. It is superior to actual experience in its timeliness. Experience teaches only after the fact, a good model teaches sooner than that, creating the opportunity in principle for corrective negative feedback to be applied early. And, of course, our cybernetic model in its support for the precautionary principle insists that corrective negative feedback can normally do most good when it is least delayed.

So this summary is also a conclusion, the first draft of that more portable and accessible version of the whole, without which the chances of the whole joining the negative feedback queue for quick insertion into the system which it has purported to describe must inevitably be reduced.

Index